The Art of Decoding Microservices

An In-Depth Exploration of Modern Software Architecture

Sumit Bhatnagar
Roshan Mahant

Apress®

The Art of Decoding Microservices: An In-Depth Exploration of Modern Software Architecture

Sumit Bhatnagar
Edison, NJ, USA

Roshan Mahant
Richardson, TX, USA

ISBN-13 (pbk): 979-8-8688-1266-8
https://doi.org/10.1007/979-8-8688-1267-5

ISBN-13 (electronic): 979-8-8688-1267-5

Managing Director, Apress Media LLC: Welmoed Spahr
Acquisitions Editor: Melissa Duffy
Development Editor: Laura Berendson
Coordinating Editor: Gryffin Winkler

Cover designed by eStudioCalamar

Distributed to the book trade worldwide by Apress Media, LLC, 1 New York Plaza, New York, NY 10004, U.S.A. Phone 1-800-SPRINGER, fax (201) 348-4505, e-mail orders-ny@springer-sbm.com, or visit www.springeronline.com. Apress Media, LLC is a California LLC and the sole member (owner) is Springer Science + Business Media Finance Inc (SSBM Finance Inc). SSBM Finance Inc is a **Delaware** corporation.

For information on translations, please e-mail booktranslations@springernature.com; for reprint, paperback, or audio rights, please e-mail bookpermissions@springernature.com.

Apress titles may be purchased in bulk for academic, corporate, or promotional use. eBook versions and licenses are also available for most titles. For more information, reference our Print and eBook Bulk Sales web page at http://www.apress.com/bulk-sales.

Any source code or other supplementary material referenced by the author in this book is available to readers on GitHub (https://github.com/Apress). For more detailed information, please visit https://www.apress.com/gp/services/source-code.

If disposing of this product, please recycle the paper

Table of Contents

About the Authors

Sumit Bhatnagar has nearly two decades of hands-on experience in the IT industry, serving as a visionary leader and a respected authority in the realm of modern software architecture. Specializing in J2EE, microservices, and cloud-based applications, Sumit has a proven track record of delivering cutting-edge solutions in the financial domain.

An accomplished project leader, Sumit combines deep technical expertise with strategic insight, seamlessly bridging the gap between innovation and implementation. His contributions to the industry have earned him prestigious accolades at a global platform. As a distinguished member of the Forbes Technology Council and IEEE, Sumit is at the forefront of technological advancement, continually shaping the future of software development. His extensive portfolio of published research papers and thought leadership in renowned journals underscores his commitment to pushing the boundaries of what's possible.

In *The Art of Decoding Microservices: An In-Depth Exploration of Modern Software Architecture*, Sumit leverages his vast experience and deep understanding to provide readers with a comprehensive guide to mastering microservices. Whether you're a seasoned developer or an aspiring architect, this book is your gateway to understanding and implementing robust, scalable, and resilient software solutions.

Roshan Mahant is a seasoned expert in strategizing and designing IT solutions, with a strong emphasis on successful execution. As a Senior Technical Consultant at Launch IT Corp, he specializes in e-governance platform enhancements, particularly in public sector IT modernization using the microservices architecture, and the Amanda e-governance licensing platform. Over his 15-year career, Roshan has mastered holistic analysis, systems integration, architecture design, and strategic consulting, enabling the transformation of critical governance functions across various state agencies. His work has significantly impacted several government boards, including the Iowa Board of Nursing and the Michigan Gaming Control Board.

Before joining Launch IT Corp, Roshan served as the Director of Access Technologies, where he developed innovative mentoring techniques and software products. With a master's degree in CAD/CAM from Nagpur University, Roshan continues to contribute to the field through research papers, conference reviews, and technical book critiques, earning him various esteemed memberships and awards.

About the Technical Reviewer

 **Andres Sacco** has been working as a developer since 2007 in different languages, including Java, PHP, Node.js, Scala, and Kotlin. His background is mostly in Java and the libraries or frameworks associated with this language. In most of the companies he worked for, he researched new technologies to improve the performance, stability, and quality of the applications of each company. Recently, he published a book on Apress about the latest version of Scala. He also published a set of theoretical-practical projects about uncommon testing methods, such as architecture tests and chaos engineering.

Acknowledgments

Writing this book has been a journey filled with hard work, learning, and inspiration, and it wouldn't have been possible without the incredible support and encouragement I've received along the way from my family and friends.

To my son, **Aaren**—this book is dedicated to you. Your curiosity, resilience, and boundless enthusiasm are my greatest motivation. May you always explore the world with a sense of wonder and creativity, finding your own path just as I have found mine.

Finally, to every reader of this book: may it serve as a stepping stone in your journey through the world of microservices. Here's to the continuous pursuit of knowledge and growth.

—Sumit

This book is a culmination of countless hours of dedication, exploration, and passion for the world of microservices. I am deeply grateful to all those who have contributed to my journey and to the development of this work.

This book is dedicated to my beloved son, **Ved**. Your bright spirit, determination, and joyful energy inspire me every day. May you follow your dreams with the same passion and commitment that brought this book to life.

I am also immensely grateful to my family and friends whose patience and support have been unwavering throughout this journey. Thank you all for helping make this book a reality.

—Roshan

Introduction

Purpose of the Book

Are you getting started with software development and architecture and feeling overwhelmed by the microservices landscape—or maybe you have been developing software for years and want to improve your understanding of the world of microservices? This book is for you. Whether you are looking for an introduction or are already knee-deep in this landscape, *The Art of Decoding Microservices: An In-Depth Exploration of Modern Software Architecture* cuts through the jargon and complexity to provide a comprehensive introduction to microservices that you can understand and apply.

The aim is to educate developers, architects, DevOps engineers, and IT leaders about how to develop and build microservices—whether it's a greenfield project or a renovation of an existing system. We'll teach you the basics, dive into advanced patterns, and point out common failures so you can avoid the headaches. Underpinning the book is the belief that microservices are more than a mere technical wave: they are business enablers, allowing you to be more agile, more scalable, and better equipped for digital transformation. You'll certainly come away with insight into best practice, but also confidence in your ability to make better decisions, to innovate, and to manage in this ever-changing world of software.

Designed to be your trusted companion, this book is theory-rich and chock-full of hands-on examples of how to design and build systems. Whether you're a novice microservices player looking to learn the ropes or an experienced systems professional seeking to tune your systems, you'll find a host of tools and practical guidance to help you achieve your architectural goals... and maybe even have some fun along the way.

Who Should Read This Book?

If you're involved in software development and architecture and need to cut through the buzz, *The Art of Decoding Microservices: An In-Depth Exploration of Modern Software Architecture* is the book you've been looking for. It's both a beginner's guide and a Swiss Army knife, a handy reference for those making their first foray into microservices as well as a refreshing and clear text for those who have been around the block a couple of times already.

From novice to microservices seasoned veteran, there is something for everyone in this book. Newcomers will benefit from an accessible, jargon-free introduction to microservices, while seasoned practitioners will find advanced patterns and tools that take their systems to the next level. You'll learn how to build scalable, resilient, and maintainable systems, based on real-world examples and case studies. You'll learn the nitty-gritty of CI/CD pipelines, container orchestration, and service monitoring, so you have a playbook for keeping microservices running. You'll also receive both strategic advice and practical tips for going from monolith to microservices, so you'll be better prepared to tackle your own migration. This book bridges the gap between theory and practice, providing a wealth of information for study and innovation. You will be equipped to assess the technical and business pros and cons of adopting microservices so you can make the right decisions for your organization and its future.

Whether you're in the trenches of code, leading a team, or making strategic decisions about your company's tech stack, *The Art of Decoding Microservices* will help you gain the knowledge you need to succeed in this fast-paced world of software development. It's helpful to have a basic understanding of software development and architecture before jumping into the deep end—but don't worry; we'll take you from novice to ninja in no time. Enjoy!

What You Will Learn

In this book, you will learn:

What are microservices? And why should you care? The first few chapters of this book answer those questions and more, explaining what exactly a microservice is, how it differs from a monolithic architecture, and why adopting this style of software design can bring tremendous value to your organization.

Designing Microservices: You'll learn important design principles for microservices, including how to decompose a monolith into microservices and how to design for failure.

Microservices Communication: Learn about the various "speaking styles" of a microservices architecture, such as the difference between synchronous and asynchronous communication and when to use each.

Deployment and Scaling: What is containerization? How can we orchestrate applications with packages such as Kubernetes? How can we scale microservices for more load?

Security and Monitoring: How to secure your microservices in a distributed system, and how to monitor the health of your system and the performance of your services.

Case Studies: Real-world examples of businesses that made the move to a microservices architecture, what the problems were, and how they dealt with them.

Best Practices and Antipatterns: The book ends with a chapter on best practices and antipatterns you should have in mind when working with microservices.

By the end of the book, the reader will have a solid understanding of microservices architecture and will be ready to apply these ideas to design, build, and run highly scalable, resilient, and efficient microservices-based systems.

How to Use This Book

Following along with the text, this book will take you on a tour of microservices, from the foundations of the architecture to its most complex twists and turns. Whether you're getting started with microservices or are already a veteran, here's how to get the most out of this book.

Start at the Beginning for a Complete Understanding: If you're just beginning with microservices, please start at Chapter 1. No skipping ahead. Each chapter follows on from the previous one, in a natural progression that will ease your way into the more difficult material later on.

But Don't Miss the Big Picture: The book is designed to walk you through from basics to more advanced topics. You don't build a house by starting with the roof. As you progress through the logical flow, you'll build the foundation before you venture into the deep waters of microservices.

Use It As a Handy Reference: Have been working with microservices for a while but need a refresher on a particular topic? You can start wherever you need. The table of contents and index will help you rapidly jump to the topic you are looking for—perhaps you need to brush up on scaling strategies, or learn to manage APIs, or how fault isolation works, or other topics.

Quick Reference Tools: Summaries, diagrams, and checklists are interspersed throughout the book as a way to provide quick snippets of information to refresh your memory, without having to reread entire chapters.

Get Your Hands Dirty with Exercises and Examples: This isn't a book to read. It's a book to do. The hands-on activities and examples guide you through the process of putting theory into practice. Here's where the rubber hits the road.

Play with Code Samples: Each of the samples in the book exists in a playpen. This means that you can run it, break it, tweak it, rework it, and generally have some fun. Try modifying and extending these examples to increase your learning process.

Learn from Real-World Case Studies: Winning with Case Studies: Pay particular attention to the real-world case studies. These aren't just success stories; they're packed with useful and actionable insights you can steal, um, I mean, apply to your projects.

Reflect on the Challenges and Solutions: While it's a great feeling to breeze through a case study, the real benefit of reading these books is in the reflection. The challenges and solutions presented here will make you a better problem-solver and give context for applying best practices in the real world.

Stay Updated with Online Resources: Supplementary Materials: Check the online book for any additional materials—code repositories, further reading, or updates. These are a great way to stay in touch with the latest tools and techniques.

Get Involved in the Community: Join an online discussion forum or community for microservices. You can share what you have learned or pose questions or even help others as you are able to do so.

Gradually Apply Concepts: Keep It Simple: Once you've worked through what you've learned into a pattern of service, it's time to deliver it. But start simple, with just the basic service, and work out the finer structure, those service machines, as you gain confidence. You have to crawl before you run.

Continuing to Learn: Microservices, like all technology, is continually evolving. This book will give you a great foundation, but always be curious and keep learning. New tools, techniques, and best practices come out all the time.

Final Thought: It's a Marathon, Not a Sprint: Learning to master microservices isn't something you sprint through. It's about the journey. Go slow, absorb, and have fun. Each chapter gets you a little closer to understanding how you can make microservices work for you, and before you know it, you'll begin building systems that are scalable, resilient, and, yes, damn cool!

Happy learning!

CHAPTER 1

Evolution of Software Architecture

In the past few decades, software architecture has been on a wild roller coaster ride, morphing and twisting to accommodate the ever-expanding needs of businesses, the relentless march of technology, and the unpredictability of project management whims. Let's dive into this chapter and discover the exciting history of software architecture. It has been a journey from procedural code's early days to today's cloud-powered wonders. It's like watching an old, reliable bicycle transform into a self-driving, cloud-powered electric vehicle—while still expecting it to be just as simple to ride. What began as the humble art of structuring code has evolved into today's cloud-native labyrinths, where even the most complex software systems are designed to make life, ideally, less of a digital headache. But, of course, every now and then, they do throw in a few migraines just to keep things interesting. Since software architecture is the core of technical business, this roller-coaster ride shows little sign of slowing down into the future. It's safe to assume that there will be more automation—with more AI being leveraged in the system optimizers and actuators to help us make the best decisions. There will be even more serverless architectures, where instead of worrying about underlying infrastructure, developers will be fine with just programming at a higher abstraction level. Whatever the future holds, it's safe to say that we will continuously transform software architecture once again to handle the next wave of challenge.

After all, this evolution—from procedural programming to the cloud-native wonders of today—is part of a larger story about how technology starts to be seen: not just as tooling for solving a particular problem, but as an environment in which entire businesses, industries, and innovations can be constructed. The ride has been a little bumpy at times, but software architecture has made it all possible, one paradigm shift at a time. Let's discuss more about this evolution in detail.

The Early Epoch: Structured Programming

The journey began with structured programming, where simplicity ruled the day, and the goal was just to keep your code from looking like a tangled bowl of spaghetti. Back in the 1960s and 1970s, software was pretty straightforward—or as straightforward as anything involving early computers could be. Programs were written in procedural chunks, where developers broke down their tasks into neat little subroutines. Think of it like following a recipe: Step 1, do this. Step 2, do that. Step 3, profit. While this was great for keeping things organized, it didn't exactly lend itself to the growing complexity of the digital age.

The Golden Age: Object-Oriented Programming

By the late 1980s and into the 1990s, software had ballooned into massive beasts, and chaos was threatening to reign once more. Enter object-oriented programming (OOP), arriving like a superhero with a cape—except the cape was probably a Java or C++ manual. OOP didn't just focus on what software did, but what it was. It neatly packaged data into objects, like putting a tiger in a digital zoo enclosure where it wouldn't eat your other code. Concepts like inheritance, encapsulation, and polymorphism—words so complex they practically required their own user manuals—were introduced to tame the software wilderness. The result? Code that was modular, scalable, and didn't require you to consult a magic 8-ball every time you wanted to update a system.

Component-Based Software Engineering (CBSE)

By the start of the 1990s, the software engineers were asking: "Can't we push this just a bit further?" Enter Component-Based Software Engineering (CBSE). CBSE was a natural progression from OOP, but it took the principle of modularity to the nth degree. If OOP allowed developers to create building blocks, CBSE provided a whole catalog of those. With CBSE, software systems could be split up into reusable components that could be developed, tested, and deployed independently—just like the furniture pieces, they could be used again and again. CBSE applications developed faster and proved to be more reliable than their monolithic predecessors. No need to reinvent the wheel every time you have a new feature.

Monolithic Architecture

Meanwhile, the trusty monolithic architecture was still trucking along, especially for applications with clearly defined boundaries. With monolithic designs, you built an entire application as one gigantic, indivisible unit. Think of it like building a house, but with all the rooms sharing the same walls and plumbing. It worked—until your house got so big that renovations turned into a nightmare. While monolithic architecture made development and deployment relatively straightforward, things got messy when you tried to scale or maintain the application. If one room flooded, the whole house had issues. It was fine for smaller applications, but not ideal for complex, ever-growing systems.

Service-Oriented Architecture (SOA)

By the time we'd tottered into the early 2000s, the demand was for more flexibility and agility, like a gymnast, only with a lot fewer somersaults. Enter service-oriented architecture (SOA). The premise was to take the big, monolithic applications of the past, break them down into smaller distinct services, each one managing a specific business function but offered up for consumption over the network. SOA represented a way in which different systems could all remain independently interconnected, avoiding the descent into chaos; it was perfect for enterprise systems looking to increase scale and integrate diverse technologies and for the web services revolution and the explosion in standard protocols such as SOAP and REST. It wasn't just a technical trend. SOA represented a revolution in the way that businesses could scale. And it arrived right on time.

Microservices Architecture

By the 2010s, people were starting to realize that monolithic designs couldn't cope with the requirements imposed by modern applications—especially those with ambitions to conquer the cloud. Microservices architecture was the finely tuned, more evolved cousin of SOA. Instead of a handful, a microservices architecture breaks up an application into potentially hundreds or thousands of loosely coupled services. Each service may be coded, deployed, and scaled independently. It's like gluing together a piece of furniture from individual jigsaw puzzles. Each piece snaps together but doesn't weigh the other pieces down; the result is a flexible architecture that's perfectly suited to maps of a cloud. It thrives in situations where continuous delivery and aplomb are essential.

Cloud-Native Architectures

Side by side, the rise of microservices paralleled another emerging trend in the software world. If microservices made applications more agile, it turned out the real cherry on top was cloud-native, born specifically for platforms in the cloud. By combining the flexibility of microservices with the cloud's scalability and resilience, these modern architectures leveraged the latest technologies—containers (think Docker) and orchestration (Kubernetes, anyone?)—in order to do the following in one go: (1) break down apps in smaller services, (2) run all of those application services everywhere, (3) have them scale automatically on demand, and (4) recover from failure without anyone feeling it. Cloud-native is all about moving fast in dynamic environments, making it MVP for any large enterprise with multiple moving pieces.

Looking Forward: Serverless and Beyond

And now we're in an era of serverless computing—I'm beginning to feel like we've reached the "final boss" of complexity. With serverless, you as a developer can build and run applications without ever having to deal with the servers underpinning this infrastructure. Imagine you're cooking dinner and, instead of having to wash up, the kitchen magic-resets itself. Serverless is kind of like that: you're able to focus solely on the code, and the server infrastructure takes care of itself. I reckon this marks the next development frontier in reducing operational complexity and increasing deployment cycles: it feels like we've hit our stride with serverless, and anywhere else to go, at least not until we're all soon-to-be-redundant automatons trapped in some pixelated utopia… But we're the tech industry, so you know we'll find a way.

In general, each generation of software architecture diagram somewhat resembles the process of your favorite game character leveling up—with each successive generation, more powers are acquired, more restrictions are removed, and—especially—the potential is far greater. Structured programming, mainframe, distributed computing, client-server, and many of the other driving forces I've covered up to this point, such as monolithic and service-oriented architecture, are all ancient history; the world we (and developers) live in looks different now with the possibilities of serverless computing. It's hard not to imagine that the future of the field will look even different as artificial intelligence, machine learning, and automation continue to reshape the landscape of how software is built and orchestrated.

But since I still have plenty of work to do before my soul is harvested by our machine overlords, I'll walk you through each of these architectures in the next few sections. So, without further ado, grab your field plow and join me.

Monolithic Architecture

Monolithic architecture is like that sweater that fits everyone—except, unlike that sweater, it is never comfy, but instead tries to hold every component of your app together in one big, tightly woven ball. The user interface, the business logic, the data access, and every other part of the app are all squished together into one giant, monolithic codebase. You tweak that one part, and you are touching the whole thing, as shown in Figure 1-1. It's like moving the furniture around in a house where every single piece is bolted to the floor. And when deployment time comes? The entire app has to go out, packaged together as one indivisible blob. Yay!

This diagram illustrates a *monolithic architecture* for a shopping application. In this setup, all components of the application—UI Code, Catalog Service, Discount Service, Order Service, and ORM (Object-Relational Mapping)—are tightly integrated into a single, large application. Both desktop and mobile clients interact with the monolithic system, which handles everything in one big package. All services within the shopping app share the same codebase and connect to a single database. While simple to develop and deploy initially, this architecture can become a challenge as the app scales, as changes to one part of the system often require redeploying the entire application.

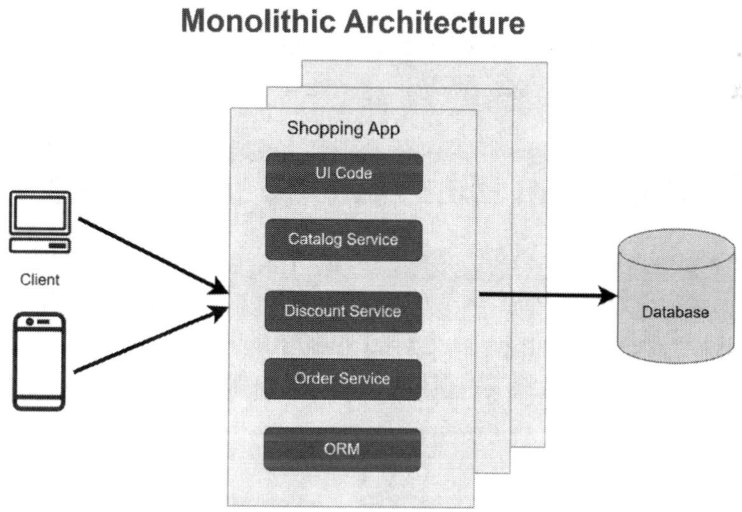

Figure 1-1. *A typical monolithic architecture*

Key Characteristics

Single Codebase and Deployment Unit: All your code—frontend is contained in one place, backend, everything at one place. If you change a line of code in one part of the application, you have to rebuild and redeploy the entire application. Really, the entire application. Remember that WordPress bug? You also had to repaint your house because you wanted to change the color of one door. Single Codebase, Single Deployment Unit: Yes, that's what this is.

Tightly Coupled Components: Everything is so interdependent; it's like conjoined twins of the digital world. Make a change somewhere; usually, you'll need to make a change somewhere else too. And you get to do lots of unexpected tweaking too, just when you least feel like it.

Simpler Development and Deployment: On the surface, monolithic architectures feel incredibly convenient. You've got fewer moving parts, so development, testing, and deployment might seem more straightforward. There's just one app to think about, one app to deploy, and one app to rule them all. So why bother with anything else? Well, because, eventually, things get complicated. Fast.

The Trouble with Monolithic Architectures

Maintenance Mayhem: Your app gets so large that your codebase turns into a sprawling mess. Even when you're adding new features, it starts to feel like you're defusing a bomb—something little can go wrong, and it blows up in your face. They didn't just fix code, they explored it, like traversing a jungle with only a flashlight and the dim hope of finding an exit somewhere.

Scaling Bottlenecks: When you want to scale a monolithic app, you have to scale the whole thing—warts, boils, and all. Even if there's only one part of the app under pressure—let's say the checkout page is getting slammed during a closeout sale—you have to scale the whole app, from its UI all the way down to the database and everything in between. It's the mechanic approach to a broken windshield wiper—take the whole car to the garage. This "all-or-nothing" scaling approach comes with significant costs. Scaling up a large, single-block application demands considerable infrastructure resources, which can quickly translate into hefty bills for server space, memory, and CPU usage. Moreover, the downtime or slowdowns involved in scaling a monolith can indirectly impact revenue, as users may experience lag or downtime. In contrast, a microservices architecture would allow only the checkout service to scale, optimizing resource allocation and potentially cutting costs by focusing on the specific part of the application that's in demand.

Reliability Riddle: When one component decides to throw a tantrum and crash, it's not just that part of the app that takes a nap—the whole system can go down with it. Picture your entire house losing power because your coffee maker short-circuits. That's the kind of drama you sign up for with monolithic architectures.

Obsolescence Handcuffs: Commit to monolithic architecture and you're essentially married to a certain tech stack. It's great—until it isn't. Need to modernize? Want to jump on board with the latest and greatest? Well, good luck with that! You might be looking at a full-on teardown and rebuild, since everything's so tightly intertwined. Upgrading isn't exactly a quick breakup; it's more like trying to escape a locked room without the key.

Deployment Drag: With a monolith, every tiny change means redeploying the whole app—whether you're fixing a login bug or adding a new button, the entire application has to go through the redeployment process. Got a small bug in the login form? Yep, better buckle up because the whole app's getting redeployed just for that. How did we end up here? If you pulled out the "dropped cherry" metaphor back in 1998, it wouldn't have fit. Back then, your cherry-dropping app would've been its own little piece of code, calling on the cake app when needed. You'd spin it up, drop your cherry, shut it down, and leave the cake app untouched. Simple days, huh?

When Monoliths Aren't Monsters

But don't abandon the monolith altogether. For short-run projects or ones with small scaling requirements, monolithic architecture can still be the right call. It's quick to get started up and running, and you don't have to worry about the overhead of managing many services or the orchestration of communication between them. If your app will have a simple few-function structure and you want to keep things basic, you can comfortably stick with a monolith.

Yet for larger, more complicated systems, where scaling, malleability, and continual motion might be more stricter, monoliths feel awkward—like a suit that might fit, but can't possibly be as comfortable as it should, and anyway, you're going to rip the thing by the end of the night.

Client-Server Architecture

The client-server architecture is a foundational model in the world of computing, defining the interaction between two parties: a client and a server, as shown in Figure 1-2. This architecture underpins much of modern software development, enabling scalable, efficient, and maintainable systems. In this section, we will explore the principles of client-server architecture, its components, benefits, common patterns, and examples of its application in real-world scenarios.

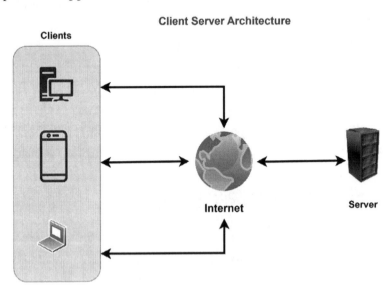

Figure 1-2. A basic client-server architecture

Principles of Client-Server Architecture

Client-server architecture operates on a simple yet powerful principle: the division of duties between service requesters (clients) and service providers (servers). This separation of concerns allows for more organized and scalable application development.

- **Client:** The client is the entity that initiates communication by sending requests to the server. It can be a web browser, a mobile app, or any software that requires data or services.

- **Server:** The server is the entity that receives and processes requests from clients, providing the necessary data or services in response. Servers can host databases, web pages, APIs, and more.

The communication between clients and servers typically happens over a network, following specific protocols such as HTTP, HTTPS, FTP, or WebSocket.

Components of Client-Server Architecture

Client-server architecture can be broken down into several key components:

- **Client**

  - **User Interface (UI):** The frontend part of the client, where users interact with the application

  - **Client Logic:** Processes user inputs, manages the user interface, and prepares data to be sent to the server

- **Server**

  - **Server Logic:** Processes client requests, executes business logic, and interacts with the database

  - **Database:** Stores and manages data, accessible by the server

  - **Middleware:** Software that connects different components or services, facilitating communication and data management

- **Network**

  - The medium through which clients and servers communicate, typically the Internet or an internal network

Benefits of Client-Server Architecture

The client-server model offers numerous advantages that have contributed to its widespread adoption:

- **Scalability:** Servers can handle multiple clients simultaneously, and additional servers can be added to manage increased load.

- **Maintainability:** Separation of client and server logic simplifies updates and maintenance, as changes can be made independently.

- **Security:** Centralized servers allow for better control over data access and security measures.

- **Flexibility:** Clients can be thin (minimal logic) or thick (extensive logic), and servers can be scaled up or out based on demand.

Common Patterns in Client-Server Architecture

Several architectural patterns have emerged within the client-server model to address specific needs and enhance performance:

- **Two-Tier Architecture**

    - Consists of a client and a server. The client directly communicates with the server, which handles both application logic and database management.

- **Three-Tier Architecture**

    - Adds a middle layer (middleware) between the client and server. The client interacts with the application server, which then communicates with the database server. This separation enhances scalability and maintainability.

- **N-Tier Architecture**

    - Extends the three-tier model by adding more layers (e.g., presentation, application, business logic, data access). Each layer has a specific responsibility, further improving modularity and scalability.

- **Microservices Architecture**

    - A variant of N-tier architecture, where the application is broken down into smaller, independent services. Each service is responsible for a specific functionality and communicates with others through APIs.

Real-World Examples

Client-server architecture is ubiquitous in modern computing. Here are some real-world examples:

- **Web Applications:** A typical web application involves a web browser (client) sending requests to a web server. The server processes these requests, interacts with a database if necessary, and returns the appropriate web pages or data.

- **Email Systems:** Email clients (e.g., Outlook, Gmail) act as clients, connecting to email servers via protocols like IMAP or SMTP to send and receive emails.

- **Online Gaming:** In online multiplayer games, the game client communicates with a game server that manages game state, player interactions, and other game logic.

- **APIs and Web Services:** Clients such as mobile apps or web applications communicate with servers hosting APIs to fetch data, authenticate users, or perform other operations.

Summary

Client-server architecture remains a cornerstone of modern software development, providing a robust framework for building scalable, maintainable, and efficient applications. By understanding its principles, components, and common patterns, developers can design and implement systems that meet the demands of today's complex computing environments.

Service-Oriented Architecture

Service-oriented architecture is the software equivalent to the Swiss Army knife; it provides you with lots of potential tools, all nicely organized in services that don't get accidentally pressed and activated while you are unwrapping them and planning where to use them. SOA is an architectural style that makes it possible for services to play together within an organization, like members of the same orchestra. Each has their own special part to play, but when the players of an SOA orchestra get together, they produce a harmonious business process or need. Each service of an SOA orchestra, like a soloist, can be created, managed, and deployed separately. Figure 1-3 illustrates service-oriented architecture (SOA) where multiple clients (desktop, mobile, and laptop) interact with services over a centralized structure.

In SOA, services are organized in various components as follows:

- **Service Locator:** It is responsible for helping clients to find available services.

- **Service Broker:** In charge of communicating between services.

- **Service Provider:** Responsible for delivering actual functionality.

Service-oriented architecture focuses on building a reusable, modular, and communication-efficient system, which helps to integrate and maintain large-scale applications in a distributed environment.

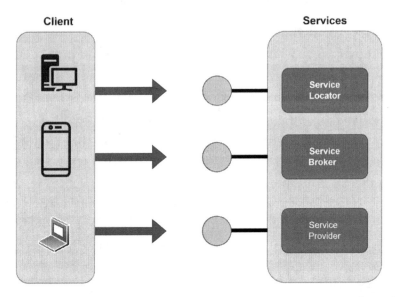

Figure 1-3. *An illustration of service-oriented architecture (SOA) showcasing how clients (web, mobile, and desktop) interact with services through key components like the Service Locator, Service Broker, and Service Provider*

Key Principles of SOA

- **Loose Coupling:** SOA services are like good neighbors. They tap on your shoulder, wave, but don't have five minutes to talk about your kids and the weather. Things can change. One service might get a facelift. It doesn't have to drag everyone else with it. You don't rebuild your kitchen so the bathroom falls in.

- **Service Abstraction:** You go to a restaurant. You order your food, but you don't have to know what is happening in the kitchen. Same goes for service-oriented architecture (SOA). The service's implementation is hidden from the consumer. You interact with a well-defined interface—not the ingredients or amount of pots on the stove.

- **Reusability:** If implemented effectively, SOA services should be used again and again—you shouldn't need to write a new box for each new feature. You can keep the power drill at your disposal for adding picture hooks wherever you want. Rather than building new functionality from scratch, you can copy an existing artifact and adapt it to your own needs.

- **Composability:** You can mix a few SOA services together to make something new. An example would be customizing a sandwich from different items at the deli. Each item is nice on its own, but mixed together they can make a complex experience that's so much more than the sum of its parts.

- **Interoperability:** SOA is a world diplomat. It ensures services can talk to each other irrespective of the programming language they are written in or the hardware or software programming platform they're running on, through standard communications protocols such as HTTPS, SOAP, and REST. There is an interpreter at an international conference who translates for people coming from every corner of the planet, and everyone can understand and be understood.

- **Discoverability:** Have you ever just been running an app, absolutely convinced there is a feature that does something, and you just can't find it? SOA avoids this problem. Services are documented and discoverable, that is, listed in a central registry, like a phone book of available services.

Core Components of SOA

- **Service Provider:** The provider is the chef in this culinary metaphor. They compose the service and cook it to eat; they write the menu (i.e., the service contract) and keep it on hand, so that when a customer orders a dish or component thereof, they make it available.

- **Service Producer:** On the other side of the slash mark, you have the service producer—the customer performing the service, whether they're in an unskilled or highly technical role—generally, the person providing the service out of their own skills. They have to follow the service contract, which is what telling people what's on the menu is all about, and they also have to accept the orders on how to make it. They don't care how fast they make what they're making, as long as it comes out the way the consumer ordered it.

- **Service Registry:** Your friendly neighborhood phone book, which can be thought of as Yelp for services provided by your SOA. Providers publish their services here, and consumers browse through it. They locate the services they need, along with detailed instructions on how to use them.

- **Service Bus (ESB):** If they are the spices of the kitchen, the Enterprise Service Bus (ESB) is the conveyor belt in the kitchen; it's the component that moves everything around; takes care of communication between services, message routing, and message transformation; and makes sure that all the different protocols are playing nicely together.

Benefits of SOA

- **Adaptability and Agility:** SOA is the kind of architecture that can roll with the punches. Businesses change track, needs evolve, and with SOA you are able to tweak and adjust on the fly—reuse and reconfigure what you've already got out there. You don't have to rebuild the factory to make a new part; you just bolt a different part onto the end.

- **Scalability:** Since each service stands on its own, you can scale individual services based on demand. It's like you can introduce more seats at your restaurant for extra service for a lunch rush without entirely expanding your building.

- **Cost Efficiency:** You're reusing services with SOA, so development costs go down. This is the software version of hand-me-downs: if it's perfectly good, why build new every time? You save time, money, and resources.

- **The Big Benefit: Better Integration:** SOA is the king of integration, regardless of whether there are many moving parts. It ensures that your systems can talk to one another easily, with ease of data and process flow.

- **Better Coordination:** Because each service is independently developed, several teams can work on different parts of the system altogether, unencumbered by other teams. The living metaphor for this is multiple kitchens in one restaurant, each with its own head chef. Everyone doing their job without messing with anyone else.

Challenges of SOA

- **Complexity:** SOA can get complicated. Managing all those independent services requires careful orchestration and governance, or things might spin out of control.

- **Performance Overhead:** All that communication between services adds some lag. It's like adding extra steps to a process—useful but not always fast.

- **Security:** Ensuring secure communication between services can be tricky, especially when dealing with sensitive data.

- **Governance:** Managing the life cycle of services, keeping everything compliant with standards, and maintaining quality require strict oversight.

Real-World Use Cases

- **Financial Services:** SOA allows banks to break up services such as customer management, transaction processing, and fraud detection and make each service work as an individual task while allowing the bank to run without having everything stuffed into a single bulky system.

- **Business:** SOA binds together files documenting patient history, billing and charges, medical imaging, etc., as if it were a hospital with distinct departments working together to provide the patient with the right care at the right time and a safe employee environment in the long term.

- **Retail:** Electronic marketplaces come to life thanks to SOA. Keeping track of inventory, fulfilling orders, processing payments, providing customer service— each of these tasks is done by a discrete SOA service that can stand alone but also works with all the rest to create a holistic shopping experience.

Best Practices for Implementing SOA

- **Clear Service Boundaries:** Your services shouldn't have too much overlap—each one should be responsible for something and do its job. If all your vendors were electricians, they'd be fine; if all your programming pasta cookers, you'll be okay. But no one wants their plumber to attempt electrical work.

- **Agree on Standard Communication Protocols:** Get everyone to speak the same language. Standardize how your services talk to each other. It's much easier for the services to integrate with one another, and everyone is spared those embarrassing "Wait, what?" moments.

- **Robust Security:** Secure your services as if they were a vault. Encrypt, authenticate, and control access to sensitive data.

- **Monitor Services and Availability:** Keep an eye out for your services—check how they are performing, if they are available or if they are being used. Always keep an eye on your brands—have they gone offline or is something wrong with available data?

- **Adopt SOA in Stages:** Don't try to do SOA all at once; start with the most important services and scale up over time. The analogy would be "get your feet wet" rather than "dive into the deep end."

Summary

Building a system based on service orientation is a potentially powerful way of composing modern systems, thereby equipping organizations to become more modular, more agile, and thus more scalable. To be sure, it can seem complex, messy, and difficult at times, but done properly, service orientation provides flexibility and efficiency that can dramatically change the way a business operates. If you have existing systems that you would like to integrate, if you have a need to build new apps, or if you need to build a new layer that enables you to scale apps you already have, SOA fundamental concepts will plant the seeds for the next steps of your innovation and growth. And we will discuss these concepts later in this chapter. Strap yourself in; we are going for a ride!

Microservices Architecture

Microservices architecture is like breaking your big, clunky app into a series of smaller, bite-sized pieces—each piece doing its own job, yet all working together to make the whole thing run smoothly. Every service corresponds to a specific business function, and they communicate with each other through well-defined APIs as represented in Figure 1-4. It's become a hit because of how scalable, flexible, and perfect it is for teams embracing DevOps and continuous delivery.

Figure 1-4 shows the architecture of microservices, where multiple independent services work together through an API Gateway. The client communicates with various services through the API Gateway, which acts as a mediator. Key components include the Identity Provider for authentication, CDN for delivering static content, and microservices that handle distinct functionalities, managed by the Config Server and Admin Server. Services use message queues (Kafka) for asynchronous communication, while tools like Sleuth + Zipkin provide tracing. The system also includes service discovery to locate services and management tools to monitor and control them. The backend interacts with a remote service and a database, with data being pulled from a repository to complete requests. This architecture supports scalability, flexibility, and efficient service management.

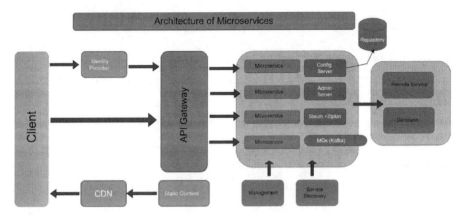

Figure 1-4. *A typical microservice-based application*

Key Principles of Microservices

- **Single Responsibility:** Every service has one job and only one job. It keeps to its lane its mind around a single business function. No multitasking here.

- **Loose Coupling:** Microservices don't share joint bank accounts. They hang solo, each one going about their business and leaving their neighbors alone. That way, if they decide to dye their hair blue, the people next door don't have to dye theirs too.

- **Independent Deployment:** Want to update or patch one service? Go ahead. Play by play, one microservice at a time, means that changes can be made without a big drama and can roll out much more quickly. Picture a team fixing just one room in your house while you're able to keep the rest of it open for business.

- **Decentralized Data Management** (having a database for each microservice): If each microservice has its own database, it avoids a single point of failure, reducing the risk of bringing down the entire system if one database goes down.

- **Automated Infrastructure:** When a lot of microservices are running around, automated infrastructure is your best friend. From building through deployment to monitoring, automated infrastructure does the heavy lifting without your human oversight.

- **Resilience:** Microservices know how to roll with the punches. When one fails, built-in safeguards like circuit breakers and retries jump into action, keeping things moving forward. It's like having a bad day but still powering through—these services are pros at bouncing back and carrying on.

Core Components of Microservices

- **Service Discovery:** Microservices feature a component that dynamically finds either via components such as Eureka or by other means. It's like the GPS of your car.

- **API Gateway:** The bouncer at the door, checking their credentials, handling all the client requests, and making sure they get to the right microservice. It also takes care of things like authentication, rate limiting, and logging—all the behind-the-scenes work. By using tools like Kong, Tyk, Apigee, etc., organizations can easily manage complex traffic flows and secure their microservices with minimal overhead.

- **Service Mesh:** Think of it as the traffic cop managing the flow of data between services. It handles communication, load balancing, and even security for service-to-service interactions.

- **CI/CD:** Continuous integration and continuous deployment are the secret sauce for getting changes live quickly and efficiently. They automate the testing and deployment processes, so you can push updates without fear of everything falling apart.

- **Containerization:** Microservices are often deployed in containers (hello, Docker!) to keep them lightweight, portable, and consistent across different environments. Orchestrators like Kubernetes step in to make sure everything is balanced and scalable. Even if these terms are new to you, don't worry; we will explain these in detail later in the book.

Benefits of Microservices

- **Scalable:** You can scale individual services in response to demand instead of scaling the whole app. You turn up the heat on one burner, instead of cranking up the whole stove.

- **Adaptable and Agility:** Each team can innovate and deploy their service independently, with faster innovation times and quicker time to market. Less waiting and more doing.

- **Resilience and Fault Isolation:** When one service fails, the whole app doesn't have to go down in flames. Each microservice failure is contained, so the rest can keep running smoothly.

- **Technology Diversity:** Different services can be built using different languages or frameworks, which means teams can choose the best tool for each job. One microservice might love Python, while another prefers Java—and that's perfectly fine. This flexibility also extends to different versions within each technology stack, enabling teams to upgrade or maintain specific versions as needed without impacting the entire system. For example, one service might be running the latest version of Node.js, while another sticks with an older, stable release of Java. This approach allows teams to optimize each service independently, balancing innovation and stability across the system.

- **Improved Collaboration:** Small teams can own their own microservices and be more productive. Break down your orchestra into specific sections. You get exactly what they're good at and everybody blows together.

Challenges of Microservices

- **Complexity:** The more microservices you have, the more moving parts there are. Orchestration, monitoring, and management get tricky, and good tools and practices are called for to keep things ticking over.

- **Data Consistency:** Keeping data consistent across multiple services is like herding cats, either adopt an event-driven architecture or settle for eventual consistency.

- **Network Latency:** More services talking to each other means more chances for delays. Optimizing with caching or load balancing helps, but network hiccups are always lurking.

- **Security:** Securing communication between microservices and managing authentication can get complicated, especially when you have a lot of services running around doing their thing.

- **Operational Overhead:** You're going to need strong CI/CD pipelines, monitoring, and infrastructure management, which can increase the operational workload.

Microservices vs. Monolithic Architecture

In the monolithic one, everything is put into one big, fat application. It is initially easy to build, but hard to maintain, scale, and update as it gets large. In the microservices architecture, however, the app is divided into smaller independent services, and that makes it easier to maintain, scale, and even deploy each service separately. The difference is like the one between building one giant jack-of-all-trades machine and one with a collection of gadgets that are more specialized.

Microservices vs. SOA

While on the surface there are some similarities, such as the focusability and loose coupling, microservices and SOA are not the same. SOA is all about big, enterprise-wide service concepts that cut across a whole range of business functions. In contrast, microservices are much smaller in scope, often focusing on individual functionalities, and emphasize DevOps practices with continuous deployment.

Summary

The move to microservices is a profound shift in application design and development, but by breaking applications down into small, independently deployable services, it offers flexibility, scalability, resilience, and data isolation that monolithic systems could never compete with. Of course, microservices come with their own set of challenges, which can be managed with the right tools and best practices to keep your applications lean, mean, and fit for purpose. But while microservices let us break up large applications into more manageable pieces, they are not the only architectural style that allow us to create systems that are more dynamic and responsive. In the next section, we will introduce a complementary approach that embraces events as a way to make systems more reactive and scalable. Let's enter the realm of Event-Driven Architecture (EDA). You are going to find out how event-based systems can decouple systems, improve resilience and scalability, and accommodate real-time data flow. Get ready to see how events can turn your applications into dynamic, high-performance machines!

Event-Driven Architecture (EDA)

Event-Driven Architecture (EDA) is the cool kid on the block when it comes to software: it's all about reacting to things while they're happening. Event-driven design, as an architectural style, is based on the fundamentals of event generation, detection, and consumption. An event might be a data change, a user action, a system state update, or anything else that a service or a component wants to communicate about without interfering with another service or component. The event mechanism connects decoupled services or components, glues together distributed services, and increases the throughput and responsiveness of the system by sending small payloads and avoiding shared state while also enabling vertical and horizontal scalability as represented in Figure 1-5.

This diagram depicts Event-Driven Architecture, in which an Event Producer generates events and sends them to an Event Broker. The broker receives the events and sorts them in different topics (Topic 1, Topic 2, Topic 3), making it easier to route the event to the correct Event Consumer. Each event will be published in the corresponding topic, and only the Event Consumer subscribed to that topic will receive and process the event asynchronously. Event-Driven Architecture promotes loose coupling, allowing systems to respond in real time to change in a system without being directly coupled to each other, making it suitable for creating scalable and flexible applications.

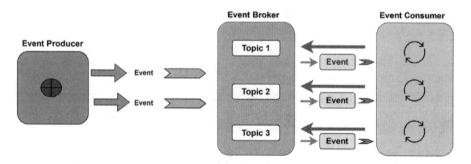

Figure 1-5. *Typical representation of how event-driven architecture works*

Key Concepts of Event-Driven Architecture

- **Events:** An event is, more or less, a headline: "Something happened!" It might be a user pressing a button, an inventory update, or a system error. An event is immutable—it tells you about a change that occurred, and that's it.

- **Event Brokers:** Gossips who publish events—an app, a service, a device, whatever. These are the ones that tell everyone that something has changed.

- **Event Producers:** On the other side stand the producers which are the events itself. Pro of the occurrence of an event and what denotes the occurrence of that certain event.

- **Event Consumers:** Listeners of that event subscribe and react to these events, such as running a processing or workflow.

Events don't just float around aimlessly—they travel through event channels, like message queues or platforms such as Kafka or RabbitMQ, to reach their destination. But the magic happens when we act on these events, not just process them. Once an event arrives, it's time to parse, filter, and separate the signal from the noise. Sometimes, we enrich or transform the data before taking action, ensuring the event is not only processed but also leveraged to drive meaningful outcomes.

Types of Event-Driven Architectures

- **Simple Event Processing:** One typical use case is of the form "when X happens then do Y"—for example, when a sale is made, send a notification. Simple event processing is exactly what it sounds like: it is about processing a single event to produce a single, immediate result.

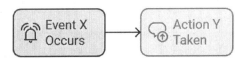

Figure 1-6. *Typical representation of how simple event processing is done*

- **Complex Event Processing (CEP):** Where the magic happens. Here's where you have multiple events come in, infer things along the way, and infer some kind of conclusion. This would be like a fraud detective— taking all these different elements, deduce different things, watching a system for real-time analytics.

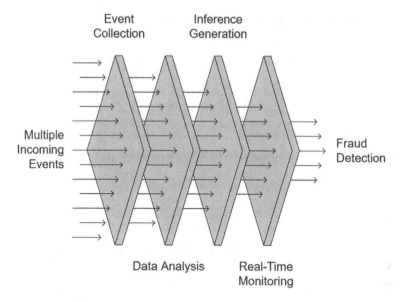

Figure 1-7. *Typical representation of how a complex event processing is done*

Benefits of Event-Driven Architecture

- **Decoupling:** EDA is the architectural equivalent of a party animal—it allows components to "do their own thing" without tight binding between them. Everyone can party on, with less dependency drama.

- **Scalability:** Since event producers and consumers are decoupled, each can scale up or down independently, as needed by demand. No need to scale up all, for example, because one part needs more attention than usual.

- **Responsiveness:** Systems respond in real time in an event-driven world, which leads to better overall experience in the way a system is used. It's like having a system that stays on the lookout, ready to jump into action the moment something happens.

- **Flexibility:** EDA makes it easy to add new event producers or consumers without changing the system's other elements. This is the kind of architecture that punches back.

- **Fault Tolerance:** One component fails, but it doesn't pull everything else down with it. EDA isolates failure, allowing the rest of the system to continue operating as if nothing had happened.

Challenges of Event-Driven Architecture

- **Complexity:** Building and managing an event-driven system isn't always a walk in the park. Handling events reliably, ensuring they're processed in the right order, and managing idempotency can feel like juggling chainsaws.

- **Data Consistency:** Events are flying between components which makes keeping data consistent across a distributed system challenging. You might have to settle for eventual consistency and use compensating transactions.

- **Monitoring and Troubleshooting:** When your system is spewing events every which way, finding out where something went wrong can be like finding a needle in a haystack. Strong logging and monitoring tools will need to be in place to keep things in check.

- **Latency:** Events don't always arrive instantly. There could be some time gap depending on the mechanism of event delivery, so performance needs to be optimized.

- In an event-driven architecture, flow is hard to organize since you have to choose between "choreography" where services respond to events without any central coordination and "orchestration" where a central coordinator directs the flow of events and controls the order of events (all options have pros and cons, depending on your system complexity and desired degree of control).

Real-World Use Cases

- **Ecommerce:** Retail platforms love EDA for handling real-time inventory updates, order processing, and user actions. It ensures customers always get up-to-date info and that the system scales during those Black Friday rushes.

- **IoT:** The Internet of Things thrives on event-driven architecture. Whether it's reacting to sensor data, device alerts, or user interactions, EDA ensures IoT systems respond in real time.

- **Financial Services:** Banks use EDA for high-speed fraud detection, transaction processing, and analyzing market trends. Real-time event handling means no delays in catching suspicious activity.

- **Gaming:** Online gaming platforms rely on EDA to manage player actions, update game states, and send notifications in real time. No one likes lag in their game, and EDA helps keep things moving smoothly.

Implementing Event-Driven Architecture

- **Use a Good Event Broker:** A good event broker, like Apache Kafka, Apache Pulsar, RabbitMQ, or AWS SNS/SQS, for distribution is the foundation of your system.

- **Define Event Schemas:** Ensure everyone has the same understanding of what constitutes an event and what shape or format it should take.

- **Build Producers and Consumers:** Extract the pieces that produce and process the events, keeping them loosely coupled and independent.

- **Make Idempotent:** Make sure the event handlers are idempotent so that the event handler can repeat the event (if it is retriggered) without any problem.

- **Monitor and Log Events:** You will also want to monitor and log the events, to ensure that everything is running smoothly. You can use tools such as ELK (E - Elasticsearch, L - Logstash, and K - Kibana) stack or Prometheus and Grafana to make sense of the flood of information. If you're hearing Prometheus and Grafana for the first time, don't be afraid. We got you covered. Stay tuned.

- **Robust Error Handling with Retries:** In the event of a glitch, your system needs to be capable of gracefully righting itself so it doesn't come to a dead stop.

Best Practices for Event-Driven Architecture

Start small—don't try to boil the ocean. Begin with a few key events, then scale up as you grow more confident in your system. As your event model evolves, keep things consistent across versions by using versioning and schema validation.

Optimize event processing by batching, filtering, and aggregating events whenever possible.

Maintain loose coupling between producers and consumers by introducing intermediaries like event brokers, which keeps your system flexible and adaptable.

Lastly, always plan for scalability by designing the system to scale horizontally, allowing you to add more producers and consumers as demand increases.

Summary

In many respects, EDA is a true disruptor: a way to come up with responsive, scalable, and elastic systems that change at the speed of their users. By decoupling each component, EDA economizes the work required to develop new features, increase scalability, or implement new functionality into a system. It also relies on events as the main communication mechanism between these components, a choice that enables systems to react in real time and adapt to a changing landscape. Nothing comes without a cost, of course. According to systems developers, the major drawbacks might include a steep learning curve, a more complex architecture, and the introduction of an additional consistency layer that might otherwise be unnecessary. Nonetheless, when executed properly, EDA can dramatically improve how modern, distributed applications operate.

However, we're also going to look at serverless architecture, another way to create modern applications with a whole new set of benefits. What if you never have to manage servers again? Seems too good to be true? You will want to stick around to learn how serverless elevates cloud-based computing to an entirely new level of simplicity and scalability.

Serverless Architecture

A magic trick for developers: all of a sudden, you can build and deploy whole apps without having to think about servers. The way serverless works is that, on the cloud, the provisioning, patching, and scaling of servers are handled by the cloud provider, off-stage. You are able to focus purely on writing your code. In a way, it's like driving a car: you don't have to know about the engine. This is cost-effective, scales great, and it enables a blazing speed of development—the most important aspect of anything from simple APIs to heavy data processing.

Figure 1-8 showcases a serverless architecture utilizing various services. Clients (such as desktop, mobile, and laptop users) interact with the system. CloudFront and S3 serve static content, ensuring quick delivery of assets like images or HTML. For dynamic processing, requests are routed through the API Gateway, which directs them to AWS Lambda functions, where the core application logic is executed without managing any underlying servers. Data is stored in DynamoDB, an AWS-managed NoSQL database. This architecture allows for scalable, cost-efficient applications that run on demand, eliminating the need for server maintenance or provisioning.

Serverless Architecture

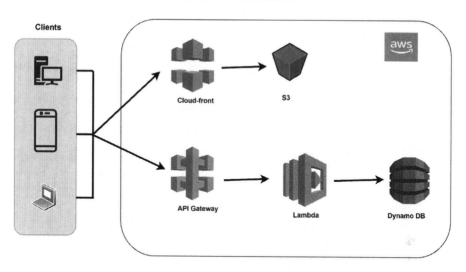

Figure 1-8. *A serverless architecture design*

Key Concepts of Serverless Architecture

- **Functions as a Service (FaaS):** This is the core of serverless. Think of bite-size chunks of logic that run only in response to an event, and each of which does one thing (if that). They scale independently and vanish when they're not needed.

- **Backend as a Service (or BaaS):** The backend is what makes your app go, and it is easy to build—but it is also the most repetitive part of development, since every app requires this. The concept of BaaS was an eye-opener for me. It's like "I don't want to cook, I just want to order Chinese": let the database, authentication, and storage of your app be handled by a third party.

- **Event-Driven Everything:** Serverless is event-driven, meaning that everything happens because of events—an HTTP request, a file upload, a job scheduled by a cron-like service, and so on. The system does nothing unless you snap your fingers.

- **Auto-scaling:** A serverless architecture will scale up or down depending on the amount of demand. Need more resources? You don't even have to think about it; it'll manage it for you. A quiet period? It'll scale down. No lifting of fingers required.

- **Pay-As-You-Go:** The best thing about serverless is that you only pay for the time your code runs. No idle servers or resources, so super cost-effective.

Benefits of Serverless Architecture

- **Cost-Effectiveness:** No more paying for unused server time. With serverless, you pay only for the actual compute time your functions demand—nothing more, nothing less.

- **Scalability:** A serverless app scales with ease. If you're dealing with 10 users or 10,000, the system will scale up automatically, and you don't have to babysit anything.

- **Reduced Operational Overhead:** Developers can finally just focus on building stuff. No more patching servers or worrying about capacity planning. Just code, deploy, and you're done.

- **Faster Time to Market:** Less infrastructure to manage means quicker development cycles. You can deploy updates or new features rapidly, which is great when you're racing to beat deadlines.

- **Resilience:** Since your cloud provider handles most of the backend heavy lifting, serverless systems come with built-in resilience. They've got the redundancy and fault tolerance covered.

Challenges of Serverless Architecture

- **Cold Start Latency:** The first time you call a function, there's a delay while a new instance is spun up by the cloud provider. Before you can pour your tea, you must wait for the kettle to boil.

- **Limited Execution Time:** There's usually a limit to how long a serverless function can run, so they aren't great for tasks that take a long time. You wouldn't want them running a marathon—they're sprinters.

- **Debugging Complexity:** When you don't have access to the underlying infrastructure, debugging feels like you have a murder on your hands, and they've stolen half the evidence.

- **Vendor Lock-In:** If you start using serverless services with a particular cloud provider, it's difficult to switch to someone else. It's like picking a favorite coffee shop. You find your groove, and waiting online feels like a hassle.

- **Security Concerns:** While the cloud provider handles infrastructure security, developers still need to make sure their application is secure, from permissions to proper coding practices.

Serverless vs. Traditional Architectures

In more traditional architectures, you're responsible for the server, the storage, and the network—you're basically steering a massive ship. You need to provision resources, plan capacity ahead of time, and handle everything that goes on behind the scenes. In serverless, all of that is abstracted away from the logic side of things, infrastructure, but if you're trying to avoid and enjoy the benefits of workloads that can scale up and down dynamically, serverless is the way to go.

Real-World Use Cases

- **Web Apps:** Serverless is great for building web applications that scale. You can use AWS Lambda, Azure Functions, and Google Cloud Functions to handle all the backend logic, while you take care of the user experience.

- **Data Processing:** Serverless functions are useful for processing real-time data streams or performing ETL (Extract, Transform, Load) operations. Just point them at the data and let them do the job.

- **Microservices:** Serverless fits beautifully into a microservices architecture. Each function can be responsible for one task, making it easier to build, scale, and maintain.

- **IoT Applications:** With countless devices generating data, serverless architecture can handle the real-time processing and reactions that IoT solutions need.

- **Chatbots and Voice Assistants:** Whether it's a chatbot answering queries or a voice assistant giving you the weather, serverless functions can handle the logic and responses with ease.

Implementing Serverless Architecture

- **Choose a Cloud Provider:** Pick your provider—AWS Lambda, Azure Functions, or Google Cloud Functions are the top choices.

- **Define Functions:** Break your application logic into small, independent functions. Each one should handle a specific task and be deployable on its own.

- **Set Up Event Sources:** Define the triggers that will call your functions—whether it's an HTTP request, a database change, or a scheduled event.

- **Manage State:** Since serverless functions are stateless, use managed services like DynamoDB, Cosmos DB, or Firestore to store persistent data.

- **Implement Security:** Ensure that your functions are locked down with proper identity and access management (IAM) configurations and secure communication channels.

- **Monitor and Optimize:** Keep an eye on your functions using cloud monitoring tools. Track performance, identify bottlenecks, and tweak for faster execution.

Best Practices for Serverless Architecture

Minimize cold starts by optimizing your function code or using techniques to keep functions "warm" with scheduled invocations. Keep your functions small and efficient, with minimal dependencies, as faster functions are also more cost-effective. Leverage managed services for tasks like databases and authentication to reduce your operational load—no need to reinvent the wheel. Always have visibility into your system with proper logging and monitoring to catch performance issues or errors early. And remember, design for failure—implement retries, fallbacks, and error handling to keep your system resilient when things inevitably go wrong.

Summary

Serverless architecture is a revolution in how we build and run modern applications. Freed from having to deploy and manage servers, and able to program applications as a series of events and steps handled by functions, developers can deliver applications that are scalable, cost-effective, and resilient—in a matter of weeks, rather than months. Serverless is hard, but it's worth it. It's a no-brainer for many use cases and can help organizations achieve scalability, cost efficiency, and faster time to market using best practices and the right tools.

Microservices Comparison with Monolithic and SOA Architectures

So, let's start at the beginning and work our way through three fundamental architectural styles: monolithic, service-oriented architecture (SOA), and microservices, because no two applications are alike, and, like tools, some approaches fit a workstyle better than others.

Table 1-1. *Differences between Monolithic, SOA, and Microservices Architectures*

	Monolithic Architecture	SOA (Service-Oriented Architecture)	Microservices Architecture
Architecture Overview	When you go monolithic, you're building one big, happy family— everything lives together in a single codebase. **Single Codebase:** Everything's in one place, which is neat… until it gets messy. **Tight Coupling:** Components are interconnected like a set of conjoined twins— you can't mess with one without affecting the others.	SOA simply takes this monolith, breaks it up, and packages it as free-standing services, except with a little more corporate polish than the term "architecture" might suggest. **Service Composition:** Applications are composed of loosely coupled services, each of which provides a distinct functional capability. **Middleware Dependency:** The ESB handles the messaging between services. Sounds great— until it becomes a performance bottleneck.	Microservices is the cool, modern architecture that splits your application into a collection of small, independently deployable services. **Independent Services:** Your app is made up of tiny, independent services, each with its own job. No more "one size fits all." **Decentralized Communication:** Communication happens through lightweight protocols like REST or gRPC, and services often talk to each other via messaging queues. No heavyweight ESB slowing you down.

(*continued*)

Table 1-1. (*continued*)

	Monolithic Architecture	SOA (Service-Oriented Architecture)	Microservices Architecture
	Single Deployment: Want to fix a tiny bug? Guess what—you're redeploying the whole app. Hope you're not in a rush.	**Standardized Protocols:** SOA loves SOAP and XML. Sure, it's structured and powerful. But it gets a little... old school.	**Service Autonomy:** Each service manages its own data and logic. This is like giving each team member their own toolbox, and they don't have to share (which is always better, right?).
Scalability	Eh, not great. Scaling means adding more horsepower to a single server, and that gets expensive fast. This approach is like trying to fit more people into a crowded elevator— eventually, you run out of room.	Better than monolithic, but the ESB can get overwhelmed if too many services are pinging it at once. It's like having a really efficient assistant— until you bury them in too much paperwork.	This is where microservices shine. Each service can scale independently, which means you only throw resources at what needs it. It's like adding more tables to a crowded restaurant—no need to expand the whole building.

(*continued*)

Table 1-1. (*continued*)

	Monolithic Architecture	SOA (Service-Oriented Architecture)	Microservices Architecture
Development and Deployment	Any small change requires redeploying the entire application, which can slow down development. Picture yourself trying to redecorate your living room but having to rebuild the whole house each time.	Services can be reused, which helps speed things up a bit, but deployment can get complicated with all that middleware to manage.	Supports continuous deployment, and because each service is small and independent, you can move fast. Think of it like running a race with a team—you don't all have to cross the finish line at once.
Data Management	The whole app usually leans on a single database, which can become a bottleneck. It's like having one giant pot of soup for everyone—it works, but it's not ideal if someone needs a custom dish.	Services tend to share a data model, so you get more flexibility than monolithic but still run into limitations.	Each service has its own database, allowing for "polyglot persistence." One service might use SQL, another NoSQL— whatever works best for that specific job. Now everyone gets their own bowl of soup, custom-made.

(*continued*)

Table 1-1. (*continued*)

	Monolithic Architecture	SOA (Service-Oriented Architecture)	Microservices Architecture
Fault Isolation	If one piece fails, the whole ship sinks. It's a house of cards—one wrong step, and the whole thing goes down.	Better fault isolation, but because services rely on the ESB, a single snag can still take down the whole thing.	If one service fails, the others can keep on trucking. It's resilient by design, and it employs patterns like circuit breakers to gracefully handle issues.
Communication and Integration	All communication happens internally within the application. It's like a family dinner where everyone's at the same table. Simple, but there's not much privacy.	Services talk to each other through the ESB, using protocols like SOAP. It's powerful, but a bit slow and clunky.	Communication is lightweight and decentralized. REST, gRPC, and messaging queues get the job done efficiently. Bonus points for often being event-driven, making everything even more flexible.

(*continued*)

Table 1-1. (*continued*)

	Monolithic Architecture	SOA (Service-Oriented Architecture)	Microservices Architecture
Technology Stack	You're stuck with one tech stack for the entire app. Want to try something new? Be prepared for a major refactor.	Mixed technologies are allowed, but the ESB can limit your choices. Think of it as working within a corporate dress code—there's flexibility, but only to a point.	Total freedom! Each service can use a different language, framework, or database. You can work in whatever you want to work in— jeans and hoodie or suit and tie—it doesn't matter.
Governance and Management	**Centralized Governance:** Governance is straightforward but can become a bottleneck as the application grows. **Unified Management:** Easier to manage as a single entity but less flexible.	**Centralized Governance with Flexibility:** Requires governance for service contracts and ESB but allows some service autonomy. **Service Management:** More complex due to the involvement of ESB and multiple services.	**Decentralized Governance:** Encourages decentralized decision-making, leading to innovation and agility. **Service Autonomy:** Each service is managed independently, requiring sophisticated tools for orchestration and monitoring.

(*continued*)

Table 1-1. (*continued*)

	Monolithic Architecture	SOA (Service-Oriented Architecture)	Microservices Architecture
Security	**Unified Security:** Easier to implement and manage security policies centrally. **Single Attack Surface:** A breach can potentially compromise the entire application.	**Service-Level Security:** Security is handled at the service level but can be complex due to multiple services. **Middleware Security:** ESB provides centralized security controls.	**Service-Level Security:** Each service must implement its own security, increasing complexity. **Zero-Trust Model:** Often adopts a zero-trust security model, ensuring secure service-to-service communication.

Conclusion

Microservices architecture offers significant advantages over monolithic and SOA architectures, particularly in terms of scalability, flexibility, and resilience. While monolithic architecture is simpler and easier to manage for small applications, it struggles with scalability and maintainability as the application grows.

SOA improves on monolithic by promoting service reusability and loose coupling but often involves complex middleware and centralized governance. Microservices take these concepts further, emphasizing small, independently deployable services, decentralized data management, and polyglot programming. This approach provides greater agility, scalability, and fault isolation but requires sophisticated tools and practices to manage the increased complexity. Understanding these differences helps organizations choose the right architecture based on their specific needs and context.

Having grasped the basics of why microservices are different from other architectures, it's time to get beneath the surface and look at what really makes them tick. We'll start with the core concepts in the next chapter. You'll learn about the Single Responsibility Principle (because, hey, nobody likes code that tries to do too much), then move into why independence and autonomy are nonnegotiable in this world, and why decentralized data management is central to the architecture. We'll cover the basics of APIs and communication, the principles behind scalability and fault isolation, and the importance of continuous delivery and DevOps. You'll see what polyglot programming means and how it's done, as well as learning about service discovery and load balancing. We'll round off the journey with a look at some key topics, such as logging and monitoring and security.

It's time to roll up your sleeves and see how all these parts fit together to create a powerful, flexible architecture that is revolutionizing how we build applications. In the next chapter, we will explore the core concepts of microservices.

CHAPTER 2

Overview of Microservices

Definition and Core Concepts

Let's dive into this chapter and explore the magic of microservices—what we like to call "breaking up with your monolith." It's an architectural style that splits a big, fat, entangled application into a bunch of small, autonomous services, each one built around a single business function. It's like splitting up a giant, blobby machine into a bunch of small gadgets, each of which does its part but is free to work on its own agenda. No more would every tiny tweak require a full redeployment of the whole app. Each microservice can be developed, deployed, and scaled independently; you can update the whole thing piecemeal, without throwing the entire machine into disarray. These independent modules can be developed, deployed, and scaled separately, making life a lot easier when you need to update or replace something. And instead of heavy, complicated communication methods, they typically talk to each other through lightweight protocols—think HTTP-based APIs.

By doing this, you are potentially setting yourself up for continuous delivery and deployment, faster time-to-market, better scalability, and easier maintenance. If you can change a service or add a new one without redeploying the whole system, you have a much more flexible, future-proof architecture on your hands.

© Sumit Bhatnagar and Roshan Mahant 2025
S. Bhatnagar and R. Mahant, *The Art of Decoding Microservices*,
https://doi.org/10.1007/979-8-8688-1267-5_2

Key Characteristics of Microservices

- **Loosely Coupled and Independently Deployable:**
  Each microservice operates as an island, focusing on
  one piece of business functionality. Imagine every
  microservice as its own house on the same block—
  independent, autonomous, with the ability to grow or
  shrink without impacting its neighbors. If you need to
  renovate one house, you don't have to tear down the
  whole neighborhood. Each service is wrapped around
  a single business function, and each can be scaled or
  upgraded without requiring that others come along for
  the ride.

- **Communication:** Microservices aren't just isolated
  islands—they still need to chat with each other. But
  instead of shouting across the room, they communicate
  over networks using lightweight protocols like
  HTTP. They interact through REST APIs, event streams,
  or message brokers. So, while they're decoupled,
  they're not silent—they just keep the chatter efficient
  and nonintrusive.

- **Technology Stack:** One of the coolest things about
  microservices is the freedom to mix and match tech
  stacks. Each microservice can use whatever language,
  database, or technology works best for that particular
  service. It's like being able to use a different tool for
  each job—Java for one service, Python for another, and
  maybe even some fancy NoSQL database thrown into
  the mix. No need to lock yourself into a single stack.

- **Business Capability:** Microservices are structured around business needs, which makes perfect sense if you're in the trenches managing complex systems. Each service focuses on a specific business function, like payment processing, customer management, or inventory tracking. This focus keeps everything aligned with real-world business operations—what I'd call building tech that actually serves the business, not the other way around.

- **Size:** Microservices are intentionally small. Each one is laser-focused on doing one thing really well. They're not out to handle everything under the sun, and that's the point. The smaller, the better. But don't let that fool you—they can handle heavy lifting when needed, thanks to messaging and smart scaling.

- **Why Microservices Love Continuous Delivery:** Microservices fit perfectly with continuous delivery. Since you're only updating one small piece at a time, you don't need to redeploy the whole app just because you added a feature or fixed a bug. It's like being able to swap out a flat tire without having to rebuild the whole car. This makes microservices especially useful for cloud-native applications, serverless computing, and any setup where deploying small containers is the name of the game.

But, Here's the Trade-Off...

Of course, most things worth doing are not without their downsides, and as you decouple everything you add more moving parts to your infrastructure. It's kind of like taking your one-stop shop and swapping it for a fleet of specialist delivery vehicles. Microservices can help with the big, hairy management problems of large complex systems, but you shouldn't be using them for everything. If your app is still tiny and manageable as a monolith, then perhaps microservices would be a bit of an overkill, and you might end up drowning in the management overhead of many services, when an ordinary monolith would have sufficed.

Core Concepts of Microservices

1. Single Responsibility Principle

Over the past few years, the concept of microservices architecture has encouraged a whole new way of thinking about software systems, encouraging us to move away from traditional monolithic application designs and toward a more distributed approach to application design. The cornerstone of this transition lies within a simple concept called the Single Responsibility Principle (SRP). SRP is a fundamental tenet of object-oriented programming, but it is at least as important in microservices.

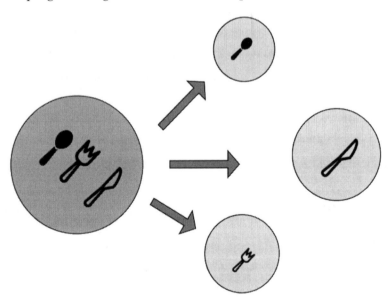

Figure 2-1. *Representing single responsibility*

Figure 2-1 visually represents the Single Responsibility Principle (SRP) within microservices architecture. The large circle with multiple utensils (spoon, fork, knife) symbolizes a service that handles multiple responsibilities, which can lead to complexity and difficulty in managing. The arrows pointing to smaller circles, each containing a single utensil, illustrate breaking down that monolithic service into smaller, more focused microservices. Each of these smaller circles represents a microservice with a single responsibility, like handling one specific function (spoon, fork, knife), adhering to SRP. By doing so, each service becomes easier to develop, maintain, and scale independently, without overlapping concerns.

The Single Responsibility Principle states that "Every software module, class, or function should have a single responsibility, and that responsibility should be entirely encapsulated by that class." Applied to microservices, this means that each one should change only for a single reason; that is, each service should perform a single role or handle a single piece of the application's functionality. This logic can help you make your services small enough to be manageable, understandable, debuggable, and scalable independently of one another.

Take an ecommerce application, for example. Instead of cramming everything from inventory management to user authentication and order processing into one massive codebase, SRP encourages breaking these into separate services. So, you'd have one microservice managing user accounts, another handling inventory, and yet another processing payments. The beauty here? If the payment processing service hits a snag, the rest of the system keeps humming along. This division makes things much easier to develop, maintain, and—most importantly—debug when something inevitably goes wrong.

One of the real game-changers with SRP is how it enables scalability. Each microservice is its own island, focused on a specific function, which means you can scale them independently. For example, during peak shopping times, your payment service might get slammed with traffic, but your inventory service is just chilling. With microservices, you can scale up just the payment service without touching the others. It's like upgrading just the drive-thru window at a busy fast-food joint without having to expand the whole restaurant. It's efficient and cost-effective, and it keeps your system agile.

SRP also simplifies the interfaces between services. Since each microservice is focused on doing one thing, it communicates with others through clear, well-defined APIs. This minimizes the tangled mess of dependencies you often see in tightly coupled systems. Unlike a tangled spaghetti bowl of dependencies, they provide clean, manageable lines between services, reducing complexity and making your codebase a lot easier to deal with in the long term.

In short, SRP is the foundation of microservices architecture. Splitting services into smaller pieces does not only lead to smaller or easier-to-manage services—it usually also results in more resilient, scalable, and maintainable systems. SRP makes microservices architecture possible by enabling you to design and build microservices in a modular way: each microservice can be built and tested, deployed, and scaled independently.

Understanding the Single Responsibility Principle

Definition and Rationale

The Single Responsibility Principle (SRP) is like the golden rule of clean design: "A class should have only one reason to change." In plain speak, it means a class should do just one thing, but do it really well—like a barista who perfects the art of coffee instead of trying to whip up a mediocre soufflé on the side. Imagine bundling user authentication, payment processing, and report generation in one service—it's not just asking for trouble; it's practically RSVPing to chaos. By sticking to SRP, you gain maintainability, testability, and that sweet sense of modular zen, all while avoiding the tech equivalent of juggling flaming swords.

Of course, SRP isn't without its quirks. Defining a "single responsibility" can sometimes feel like deciphering a riddle wrapped in a mystery inside a conundrum. Too broad, and you're flirting with spaghetti code. Too narrow, and you might end up with so many micro-classes that your codebase resembles a hoarder's garage. The trick? Balance. And here's where your microservices expertise shines. In microservices, SRP mirrors service granularity—a Notification Service handles alerts; a Payment Service handles payments. Simple, clean, and purpose-driven.

Application to Microservices

SRP in the context of microservices means that each service should be designed to perform only a single business function. For example, an ecommerce microservices platform might have microservices for order processing, inventory management, payment processing, and customer management. Each of these should have all of the functionality necessary to perform its own domain encapsulated in it and operate independently of each other. Table 2-1 represents the importance of this principle. Table 2-2 explains how to implement this principle.

Table 2-1. *Importance of Single Responsibility Principle in Microservices*

Enhancing Modularity and Cohesion	Keeping SRP helps you make your microservices more modular and cohesive. Modularity means that each service is self-contained, so you can develop, deploy, or even scale that service independently of the others. Cohesion means that every part of the service is contributing to one, and only one, purpose. You're building a collection of specialists, not jacks-of-all-trades; and even though they're all working together, the whole thing will be easier to manage and understand.
Simplifying Development and Maintenance	Say you've written a microservice to handle a single business function. It's like breaking open a book where each chapter makes sense. As a developer, you don't need to balance a dozen unrelated functions at once. You won't need to stash a pile of information into global variables, and it's much simpler to test. You don't have to battle your way through half a dozen layers of obfuscation before you can get to the one thing you care about. You get to dive deep into one thing.
Facilitating Independent Deployment and Scaling	Thanks to SRP, microservices can be deployed without dragging the whole system along with them. Need to make a change? You only need to redeploy that one service. Plus, since services are built for single functions, you can scale them individually. If your order processing service is under heavy load, you can scale just that service, leaving others untouched. It's like upgrading just your car's tires for off-road driving without having to replace the whole engine.
Reducing Risk and Enhancing Stability	One of the big wins with SRP is reducing the ripple effect of changes. When functionality is isolated in its own service, tweaking one doesn't risk breaking everything else. This isolation helps protect the overall system, keeping it more stable and resilient. Less risk, fewer bugs, and no system-wide meltdowns when a small change goes sideways—who doesn't want that?

Table 2-2. *Implementing Single Responsibility Principle in Microservices*

Identifying Business Capabilities	The first step in getting this right in your microservices architecture is to identify your business capabilities. That means figuring out what core functions your business needs to do and breaking down your application into logical chunks that fit together in meaningful ways. Tools such as Domain-Driven Design (DDD) are a great help here, allowing you to model what are known as "bounded contexts" that make sense to both the business and the technical side of your organization.
Designing Self-Contained Services	Each microservice should be a little fortress—self-sufficient, containing all the logic, data, and dependencies it needs. This means every service should have its own database, and it should avoid sharing data models with others. You want your services to be able to stand on their own without constantly needing to ask their neighbors for help.
Ensuring Loose Coupling	While SRP makes each service cohesive internally, you also want to keep services loosely coupled with each other. This can be done through well-defined APIs and asynchronous communication methods like messaging or event-driven systems. Keeping services loosely coupled means they can evolve and adapt independently, without being held back by the internal changes of others. It's like neighbors who stay friendly but don't snoop into each other's business.

(*continued*)

Table 2-2. (*continued*)

Practicing Continuous Refactoring	SRP isn't a "set it and forget it" kind of deal. As your application grows and business needs shift, you'll need to keep an eye on your services to make sure they're sticking to their single responsibility. Continuous refactoring is key—regular code reviews and architectural check-ins will help keep everything streamlined and focused.
Leveraging Automation and CI/CD	Automation is your best friend when applying SRP to microservices. Continuous integration and continuous deployment (CI/CD) pipelines allow each microservice to be developed, tested, and deployed on its own. This ensures that changes in one service don't spill over and affect the others, aligning perfectly with SRP's core goal of independent, cohesive services. Automation tools take the heavy lifting off your shoulders, keeping everything in sync without the usual headaches.

Challenges and Considerations

- **Balancing Granularity:** One of the most challenging aspects of applying the Single Responsibility Principle (SRP) to microservices is getting the right level of granularity. Go too broad, and you're back to square one, with services so chunky they start feeling like mini-monoliths. Go too fine, and suddenly you've got a tangled web of tiny services, each one doing the digital equivalent of "holding a door open," and you're drowning in interservice communication overhead. The key here? Balance. You've got to factor in the business context and technical constraints to find that sweet spot where services are small enough to be manageable but not so tiny that they trip over each other.

- **The Data Juggling Act: Managing Data Consistency:** Each of your microservices is its own kingdom, with its own data to rule over. That much decentralization makes it hard to keep your data consistent across all those little kingdoms. In microservices, each service is like its own kingdom—self-governed, with its own data to rule. While this decentralized data management gives you flexibility, it also brings a whole new set of challenges when it comes to keeping your data consistent across all those little kingdoms. Enter eventual consistency, distributed transactions, and sagas—techniques designed to keep your services in sync without breaking SRP.

- **Taming the Wild: Handling Cross-Cutting Concerns:** Security, logging, monitoring—these are the things that don't care about SRP. They creep into every corner of your microservices architecture, and they demand attention. But how do you handle these cross-cutting concerns without violating SRP? That's where strategies like sidecar patterns, service meshes, and centralized logging step in. Think of them as the glue that holds your services together, managing security, observability, and more, without compromising the single responsibility focus of each individual service.

Summary

The Single Responsibility Principle is like the MVP of microservices design. By keeping each service laser-focused on a single business capability, SRP makes your architecture more modular, less of a headache to develop, and a breeze to scale and deploy independently. It reduces risk because when you make changes, you're not tugging on a thread that unravels the whole system. Sure, there are challenges—finding the right granularity, managing data consistency, and handling cross-cutting concerns—but with smart design, continuous refactoring, and a little help from automation tools, these obstacles become manageable. In the end, embracing SRP in your microservices setup leads to a system that's not just resilient and scalable but also adaptable, ready to grow and evolve with your business needs.

2. Independence and Autonomy

Independence and autonomy are not just buzzwords in the world of microservices architecture. They're the pillars that support the entire approach. These principles are what make microservices so effective: they enable you to build systems where each component can function on its own, but also work together to create a robust, scalable application.

Let's start with independence. This means that each microservice is like its own little island—it can function perfectly well without having to rely on other parts of the application. Thanks to well-defined interfaces and APIs, every microservice can do its job and communicate with others without needing to poke around in someone else's code. Think of it like a group of coworkers who can get their tasks done without constantly asking each other for help. This separation makes it so much easier to update and maintain individual services. As long as the interfaces remain the same, you can tweak one service without worrying about breaking the rest of the app. Take a social media platform, for example—if the team working on the user profile service needs to push an update, they can do so without disturbing the services handling messaging or the news feed. No need for mass coordination, just a clean, independent update.

Then there's autonomy, which goes hand in hand with independence. Where independence is about services doing their own thing, autonomy is about them being the boss of their own domain. Each microservice controls its own data, its own logic, and makes its own decisions based on what it knows. This level of self-governance is what makes microservices so resilient. If something goes wrong with one service, its failure is isolated— it won't take down the whole system with it. Autonomy is like having a self-contained emergency backup for each microservice. If one part of your application hits a snag, the rest keep chugging along, unaffected. No domino effect of failures here!

Another beautiful side effect of autonomy? Teams can work on their microservices without getting bogged down in delays that typically plague monolithic architectures. No more waiting for everyone else to finish their work before you can deploy your updates. In a microservices setup, each team can develop, test, and deploy on their own schedule. Imagine a retail application where the checkout service team can implement user feedback and optimize the purchase flow without having to check in with the team managing the product catalog. They can move fast, push updates, and keep the checkout process running smoothly—all without stepping on anyone else's toes.

Furthermore, autonomy also allows you to mix and match your technology stacks across your services. You're not forced to use the same framework or language throughout. If your microservice is tasked with crunching lots of data, then you might pick a tech stack that's best at fast and efficient processing of large data sets, whereas another service that's dealing more with user interactions might opt for a completely different tech stack that's optimized for web performance. It's a "right tool for the right job" philosophy that allows teams to pick the technology best suited for the task at hand.

In the end, it isn't just about the technical principles of independence and autonomy. It flows from the organizational culture of agility, flexibility, and resilience that microservices encourage. A modular, scaled, and resilient architecture allows teams to move fast, deploy often, and iterate quickly to respond to business needs of the day—because, of course, the business needs of tomorrow will be different. For any company that wants to evolve into a nimble digital organization in terms of its approach and its products and services, microservices isn't just a tech strategy. It's a mindset shift, and you should make the leap as soon as you can.

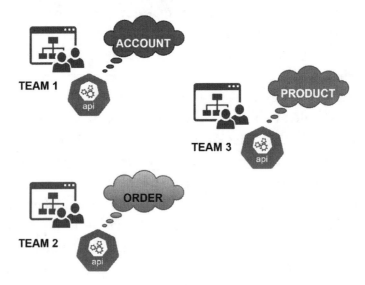

Figure 2-2. *Representing the concept of independence and autonomy*

Figure 2-2 illustrates the concept of **independence and autonomy** within a microservices architecture. Each team (Team 1, Team 2, and Team 3) is responsible for a distinct business function—Account, Order, and Product, respectively. Each team operates its own **independent microservice**, signified by the API icons, allowing them to develop, deploy, and scale their services autonomously without needing to coordinate changes with other teams. The separation of responsibilities fosters independence, where each service can function and evolve independently, while the autonomy ensures that each service controls its own data, logic, and functionality, minimizing the impact of changes across the system.

Understanding Independence and Autonomy

Definition and Rationale

Let's talk about independence and autonomy, two concepts that are like the backbone of microservices architecture. These principles give microservices their power, allowing each service to stand on its own two feet without needing to constantly lean on others. Microservices independence is rather straightforward: you don't need to know what's going on inside any other service to execute your piece of the puzzle. Autonomy, in contrast, is independence on steroids. It's not just the ability to do what you do, it's the ability to own the whole process all the way through. Each service is in total control of its data, logic, and deployment.

But why does this matter? For starters, when one microservice goes down or needs an update, it doesn't pull the rest of the system down with it. Rather, you get a more resilient system that can keep humming even when one part encounters a pothole. Table 2-3 represents the importance of this principle. Table 2-4 explains how to implement this principle.

Key Characteristics

- **Self-Containment:** Each microservice is like its own mini fortress—it encapsulates all the logic, data, and dependencies it needs to do its job. It doesn't need to run across the street borrowing tools from another service.

- **Independent Deployment:** Want to update one service? No problem. You can deploy it without having to touch the rest of the system. This makes frequent updates a breeze without the fear of breaking everything else.

- **Autonomous Teams:** Here's where the autonomy really shines. Each team has full ownership of its service. It's like giving every team their own project car to build, maintain, and race, which makes development faster and gives everyone a sense of ownership and responsibility.

- **Decentralized Data Management:** Every service takes care of its own data. There's no need for sharing a communal data pool, which avoids potential conflicts and keeps things clean. Each microservice is in charge of managing its own little world of information.

Table 2-3. *Importance of Independence and Autonomy in Microservices*

Enhancing Agility and Speed	With asynchronous, autonomous microservices, your individual development groups don't need to twiddle their thumbs and wait for someone else to finish their piece of the puzzle somewhere: they can run their piece of the race at the same time, and the whole thing speeds up. It's like a relay race where everyone runs their piece at the same time: you're shipping features and updates faster than your competition's eyes can even blink.

(continued)

Table 2-3. (*continued*)

Improving Resilience and Fault Isolation	One of the biggest perks of autonomy? If one service goes down, the others don't come crashing down like a house of cards. You get fault isolation, meaning your app doesn't go into full meltdown just because the payment service decided to take a nap. The order management and inventory services? They're still alive and kicking. This kind of resilience makes handling errors way easier and helps your system recover like a champ.
Facilitating Independent Scaling	Not every microservice needs to be a "Superhero"—some need to handle high traffic, while others can kick back with a beer. Some microservices, like the user authentication service, will be scaled up to deal with heavy traffic, while others, like the user profile service, may never need to be scaled up at all and can happily tick along at their normal, steady pace. With autonomous microservices, it's the latter for efficiency, and it's the former for cost optimization.
Enabling Continuous Delivery and Deployment	Because each microservice is its own little world, you can set up separate continuous integration and deployment (CI/CD) pipelines for each one. This means you can deploy updates whenever you need, without worrying about breaking everything else. Want to push out an update for the checkout service without touching the product catalog? No problem. You'll get more frequent and reliable deployments and, honestly, less deployment stress.
Promoting Technological Diversity	Here's where autonomy really gets fun. Every microservice can use the tools and technologies best suited for its specific needs. You're not tied to a single tech stack across the board. Want to use Python for one service and Node.js for another? Go for it. Each team can pick the best language, framework, and database for their job, which optimizes both performance and developer happiness. After all, a happy dev team builds better systems!

Table 2-4. *Implementing Independence and Autonomy in Microservices*

Designing Self-Contained Services	First things first: make sure each microservice is its own little universe. It should have its own logic, its own data, and all the dependencies it needs to function. Think of each service as being fully responsible for everything in its domain. No running to the neighbors for a cup of sugar—each microservice handles its own data storage, business logic, and even any weird quirks without leaning on others.
Decentralized Data Management	Here's where autonomy gets real: every microservice should have its own database. No sharing, no communal data pool to dip into. Why? Because that would tie your services together, and suddenly they're not so independent anymore. Instead, let each microservice rule over its own data and communicate with others through APIs or asynchronous messaging. It's like giving each service its own kingdom, and they talk to each other through diplomats, not backdoors.
Independent Deployment Pipelines	Autonomy isn't just about running solo, it's also about flying solo. Set up independent CI/CD pipelines for each microservice so they can deploy updates on their own schedule. This way, when you need to roll out an update to one service, you don't have to worry about touching anything else. Automate the build, test, and deployment for each service so you can push changes safely without everything grinding to a halt.

(continued)

Table 2-4. (*continued*)

Embracing Asynchronous Communication	If services don't have to wait for each other to do their part, they can move faster—and that's where asynchronous communication can help. Use message queues or event streams so that services can communicate without having to wait for each other or even if each other is even online. It's the difference between sending a text and waiting on a phone call to come through. Messages get delivered, but no one is standing by, waiting for the phone to ring. You reduce bottlenecks, and you make the system as a whole more resilient.
Implementing API Gateways and Service Meshes	Think of an API gateway as the doorman at your building of microservices. It's the one and only place where all requests from clients can come in, and it then routes them where they need to go—it keeps things neat and tidy and prevents confusion. Service meshes take things a step further. Instead of having to manage things such as load balancing, service discovery, and security at the application layer, you can now handle them all at the network layer. You've gone from a doorman to a full concierge service behind the scenes.
Adopting DevOps Practices	However, that is not where your journey toward independence and autonomy ends. Your teams themselves need to be autonomous. Here is where DevOps comes in. When you move to a microservices architecture that is based on DevOps methodologies, you enable teams to take full ownership over the entire life cycle of their microservices, from development to deployment and monitoring. This includes not only a technical shift but a cultural one. Teams now have the ability to iterate at a much faster pace and even fine-tune their microservices in small increments, without the constant need to coordinate with other teams.

Challenges and Considerations

Balancing Independence and Consistency: Here's the rub: independence is great for agility, but when you've got services working in their own bubbles, maintaining data consistency can feel like juggling flaming swords. Strategies like eventual consistency, distributed transactions, and the saga pattern come into play here. They help you manage the chaos without breaking the autonomy of your services. It's not perfect, but it's better than forcing every service to constantly be in sync, which would kill the whole point of independence, right?

Managing Cross-Cutting Concerns: Security, logging, monitoring—those pesky things that refuse to stay neatly confined to a single service. They creep across the whole system, demanding attention. You can't just slap them onto each service and call it a day. This is where strategies like sidecar patterns, service meshes, and centralized logging shine. These tools help you manage these concerns without undermining the independence of your services, acting like the glue that keeps things running smoothly behind the scenes.

Avoiding Overhead and Complexity: Autonomy is fantastic until you've got a zillion microservices buzzing around, and suddenly it feels like you're trying to manage a hive full of bees—each one doing its own thing. While independence brings flexibility, it also introduces overhead and complexity that can spiral out of control. This is where effective orchestration, monitoring, and governance come into play. You need to have solid systems in place to make sure your collection of services doesn't turn into a chaotic mess.

Ensuring Team Collaboration: Autonomous teams are great, but they can't operate in silos. Services still need to work together, and that requires teams to collaborate—despite their autonomy. Regular communication, shared documentation, and standardized API contracts are key to making sure everyone's building toward the same goal. It's like having different chefs working on the same meal—everyone needs to know what the other is cooking up to make sure it all comes together on the plate.

Summary

Independence and autonomy form the bedrock of microservices architecture, giving you the agility, resilience, and scalability that monolithic systems simply can't match. But designing autonomous, self-contained services requires careful planning—decentralized data management, independent deployment pipelines, and asynchronous communication all need to work in harmony. Sure, there are challenges— maintaining consistency, managing cross-cutting concerns, and avoiding overhead—but the benefits far outweigh the hiccups.

3. Decentralized Data Management

Decentralized data management is like the secret sauce of microservices architecture—it completely flips the traditional approach to handling data in distributed systems. A monolithic application might have had one fairly large database that handled most of the application's data, but with microservices, every service gets its own database or storage system. And this is really the key to how microservices can deliver on their promise of flexibility, scalability, and resilience.

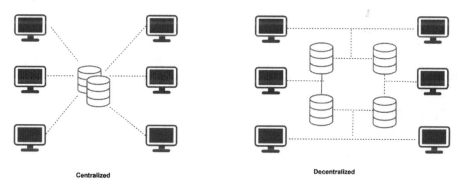

Centralized   Decentralized

Figure 2-3. *Centralized vs. decentralized databases*

With decentralized data, each microservice is an island unto itself, working with the data that belongs to its domain of responsibility as represented in Figure 2-3. This means that each service has autonomy and sovereignty over the data that is contained within it, data encapsulation is guaranteed, with the advantages that we have already listed. It is a bit like giving each service its own toolbox and making sure it never steps on another one's toes! This helps keep the messiness of the data away from each microservice, unlike a monolith, where the data management becomes a messy tangle across different business functions.

For instance, consider a healthcare app that contains services such as patient management, appointment scheduling, and billing. In the centralized model, the whole system is linked to a single database, where patient data would be stored. The patient management service would access data from that shared database, as would the appointment scheduling service. However, in the decentralized model, the patient management service has its own database, optimized for storing patient data, while the appointment scheduling service has its own database, optimized for faster reads and writes to appointment data. Billing? You guessed it—its own database too. This separation is key because it means you can update or change one service's database without having to worry about breaking things in the others. Everyone minds their own business, and the app runs smoother for it.

Breaking Down Decentralized Data Management

Definition and Rationale

Decentralized data management in microservices architecture means each service is the boss of its own database. That means the service takes full responsibility for data storage, retrieval, and integrity, without directly sharing that database with any other service. This separation keeps the boundaries around each service's data nice and clear.

The whole point of this approach? Loosely coupled services. By keeping each service's data encapsulated, you ensure that any changes in one service's data model don't ripple across the system and cause havoc in others. This independence is what makes microservices so powerful— it's what gives them the agility, scalability, and resilience that modern applications need. You can evolve one part of the system without dragging the rest of it along for the ride.

Decentralized data management isn't just a technical choice; it's a mindset shift that unlocks the full potential of microservices. Each service becomes truly autonomous, able to adapt, grow, and scale without being tied down by the rest of the system. It's cleaner, more efficient, and way less stressful to manage in the long run. Table 2-5 represents the importance of this principle. Table 2-6 explains how to implement this principle, and the best practices are there in Table 2-7.

Table 2-5. *Importance of Decentralized Data Management*

Enhancing Service Independence	When every service is independent of the others by maintaining its own data, it can remain autonomous. That is, a service can be developed, tested, deployed, and scaled without the need for coordination with other services; it can also let teams work independently of one another, with shorter development cycles and lower dependencies.
Improving Scalability	Decentralized data management allows each service to be scaled independently based on its specific load and performance requirements. For instance, a high-traffic service like user authentication can be scaled without affecting other services like order processing or inventory management. This granular scalability leads to more efficient resource utilization and cost savings.

(continued)

Table 2-5. (*continued*)

Increasing Resilience	By isolating data within individual services, the architecture enhances the system's resilience. Failures in one service or its database do not directly impact other services. This isolation helps contain and manage failures more effectively, preventing cascading failures that could bring down the entire system.
Facilitating Technological Diversity	Decentralized data management enables each service to choose the most appropriate data storage technology for its needs. Services can use relational databases, NoSQL databases, or specialized data stores like time-series databases, depending on their specific requirements. This polyglot persistence approach allows for optimizing performance and storage.

Table 2-6. *Implementing Decentralized Data Management*

Designing Self-Contained Services	Each microservice should be designed to encapsulate all the data it needs to perform its function. This encapsulation includes defining a clear data model, managing data access, and ensuring data integrity within the service's boundaries.
Decoupling Data Access	Services should communicate with each other via well-defined APIs or message queues instead of direct database access. This way, no service directly touches the database of another service. This guarantees that a service can evolve its data model without impacting other services.

(*continued*)

Table 2-6. (*continued*)

Managing Data Consistency	In a decentralized data architecture, maintaining data consistency across services can be challenging. Various strategies can help manage these challenges:

Eventual Consistency: Accepting that data will become consistent over time. This approach is often sufficient for many use cases where real-time consistency is not critical.

Distributed Transactions: Using techniques like the two-phase commit protocol to ensure atomicity across services, though this can introduce complexity and performance overhead.

Saga Pattern: Implementing a sequence of local transactions, where each step is a local transaction within a service, and compensating transactions handle rollbacks if something goes wrong.

Asynchronous Communication: Adopting asynchronous communication mechanisms such as message queues or event streams can help manage data consistency and reduce coupling between services. Events can be published whenever data changes, and other services can even "subscribe" to these events so that their data is updated when it changes.

Ensuring Data Integrity	Each service must ensure the integrity of its own data. This includes enforcing constraints, validating inputs, and handling errors within the service. Robust data integrity practices help maintain consistency and reliability within the service's data.

***Table 2-7.** Best Practices for Decentralized Data Management*

Use APIs for Data Access	Services should expose APIs for data access rather than allowing direct database access by other services. This practice ensures that services interact in a controlled manner, preserving the integrity and autonomy of each service's data.
Implement Data Backups and Recovery	Each service should implement its own data backup and recovery procedures. This autonomy ensures that services can recover independently in case of data loss or corruption, enhancing the overall resilience of the system.
Monitor and Audit Data Access	Implement monitoring and auditing mechanisms to track data access and modifications within each service. This practice helps detect and address potential issues promptly, ensuring data security and integrity.
Embrace Polyglot Persistence	If decentralized by design, you can now use the best-suited data storage technology for each service. Ask yourself what each service needs: ACID transactions or CAP, scale or ease of schema variation, and pick the appropriate data store.
Regularly Review and Refactor Data Models	With changing requirements in each service, you will have to regularly and continuously refactor the data models of each service so that they can support their responsibilities. Continuously refactoring will allow you to keep the concerns decoupled and adapt the system to change.
Handle Cross-Service Queries	For queries that require data from multiple services, consider implementing composite services or data aggregation layers. These layers can gather and merge data from various services, providing a unified view without violating the principle of decentralized data management.

Challenges and Considerations

Managing Distributed Data: Let's just be frank—it can get messy. Pretty quick. Data scattered across services. You want to keep it in sync? Data consistency? Distributed transactions? Coordination of updates across services? It's not easy. This stuff takes some thought. You're going to need to break some sweat, lose some sleep, to keep things from devolving to anarchy.

Addressing Data Security: When all your services are running their own show on their own database, security is like herding cats. By that I mean you have to make sure each service is acting with consistent, secure policies. If not, anyone can access your data at any time and expose your company to potential breaches. If a bank has lots of vaults, all those vaults must be locked down, but at the same time your broader strategy for security should still make sense.

Balancing Consistency and Availability: And here is where CAP (Consistency, Availability, Partition Tolerance) gets tricky: the existence of that trade-off between consistency, availability, and partition tolerance. When working with decentralized data, you have to make choices between remembering to update all your data so that it is always instantly consistent and accepting that there will be times when the system is unavailable, even if it doesn't have all its data in perfect sync. How you strike that balance depends on what matters most to your application: speed or accuracy?

Ensuring Interoperability: You've got independent services doing their own thing, but at some point, they all need to work together like a well-rehearsed band. For that, you'll need clear communication protocols, well-defined contracts, and consistent data formats. Interoperability is key to keeping the whole system cohesive while still letting each service enjoy its independence. Think of it like a group project where everyone does their own part, but it all fits together perfectly at the end.

Summary

Decentralized data management isn't just a technical decision—it's the backbone of a successful microservices architecture. By letting services manage their own data, you unlock a world of agility, scalability, and resilience. Sure, there are challenges: distributed data complexity, security concerns, and those tricky trade-offs between consistency and availability. But with the right design—self-contained services, decoupled data access, and asynchronous communication—you can keep things running smoothly. Best practices like using APIs for data access, setting up data backups, and monitoring everything carefully will help you sidestep many of these challenges. Embracing decentralized data management won't just make your system more robust and scalable; it'll give your organization the flexibility to innovate and adapt to changing business needs without breaking a sweat.

4. APIs and Communication

In the world of microservices, APIs and communication are like the lifeblood of the system—without them, you've got a bunch of disconnected services that don't play nicely together. APIs are the "official handshake" through which services expose their functionality, while communication strategies dictate how these services share data and cooperate to form a fully functioning application. It's like building a team: APIs define the rules of engagement, and communication decides how everyone's talking to each other (or sometimes, how they're not talking).

APIs are the front doors to your microservices, the neatly wrapped invitations to interact with a service's functionality. In a microservices architecture, each service has its own well-defined API—think of it as a menu of what that service can offer. Most of the time, these APIs are HTTP based because, well, that's what the Web likes. However, sometimes you'll see fancy protocols like gRPC (Google Remote Procedure Call) or AMQP (Advanced Message Queuing Protocol) thrown into the mix, depending on what the use case demands.

The point of APIs is that they make services accessible, both to other services and to the outside world, while keeping the details of how they work secret: a closely-guarded trade secret, so to speak. For many developers, RESTful APIs are the go-to because they're easy. Their HTTP methods—GET, POST, PUT, and DELETE—are fairly straightforward. Easy peasy. But what if you want more flexibility? What if you want to stop over-fetched or under-fetched data? Then clients can ask for exactly what they want with GraphQL. It's like ordering à la carte vs. a prefixed meal—one gives you precision; the other gives you simplicity. Designing an API for microservices is a delicate art. You need to make sure the API abstracts enough functionality to be useful but doesn't give away too much. The goal? Keep your service's internals hidden from the outside world while making sure API changes don't break the systems relying on them. It's like maintaining a sleek, bulletproof façade while the gears inside can shift and change as needed.

If you want microservices to talk to each other, do you want them to talk synchronously or asynchronously? It's like sending an instant message or leaving a sticky note on someone's desk. Synchronous communication is easy to understand: when Service A wants something from Service B, it asks and sits and waits for an answer, like true and proper conversation. The problem is that when one service is down or slow, the whole thing grinds to a halt. It's like calling someone and hearing the "all our operators are busy, please hold" message—awkward, not always resilient. On the other hand, asynchronous communication allows services to post a message to a queue or event bus and then go about their business, rather than waiting for a response. The receiving service can pick up the message whenever it feels like it—like checking emails when it feels like it. This makes the system more robust and scalable, but it also adds complexity—you have to start worrying about things such as order of messages and how you know they were delivered at all.

One of the hottest current trends in such decoupled, asynchronous communication is an approach in which services just throw events— kind of like throwing a flare up into the air—and anyone or anything that wants to pick up that event catches it and then acts on it. Services are blissfully ignorant of other services and of what to do with those events, but they don't need to be. They just fling flares and everyone does what they're supposed to do with what they catch. You get the ultimate in loose coupling: services don't care who's listening; they just throw events. Put another way, APIs and communication lie at the very core of microservices architecture—they ensure that your services don't merely survive together but that they can thrive in a system where flexibility, scalability, and resilience are paramount. It's a little bit like throwing a dinner party where everyone knows what dish they're contributing, but nobody needs to know what's happening in each other's kitchens. They just turn up at the right time with their dish.

Understanding APIs and Communication in Microservices

Definition and Rationale

When we talk about microservices, APIs and communication are the glue that keeps everything together—or more like the steady Wi-Fi signal that keeps a busy office running. APIs function as the formal contracts through which services can communicate, while communication refers to how actions are performed and data is exchanged—sometimes this is more like a phone conversation (synchronous), and sometimes this is more like "leave a message after the beep" (asynchronous).

The primary rationale behind using APIs and well-defined communication mechanisms in microservices is to maintain loose coupling between services. Loose coupling allows services to evolve independently, ensuring that changes in one service do not directly impact others. This autonomy is crucial for achieving the agility, scalability, and resilience that microservices architecture promises.

Importance of APIs and Communication

The Why Behind APIs and Communication: The main reason we use APIs and these well-defined communication methods in microservices is to keep services loosely coupled. Think of it like giving each service its own apartment. Sure, they all live in the same building, but what one does inside its four walls doesn't affect the others. This independence means services can evolve, grow, and change without dragging the whole system into chaos. It's a big part of why microservices are so great at handling agility, scalability, and resilience.

Why APIs and Communication Matter

Keeping It Loose (Coupling, That Is): With APIs in place, services do not need to have a deep understanding of other services' internal details—they only need to know the details of the API contract and follow it. This loose coupling is what makes microservices modular. It means you can build, scale, and deploy services independently. Want to tweak the payments service without touching the shipping module? No problem—everyone stays in their lane.

Making Sure Everyone Gets Along (Interoperability): APIs and standardized communication protocols ensure that all services, no matter what fancy technology stack they're using, can still play nice together. Whether one team's using Python and another's deep into Java, the services can still talk to each other thanks to the common API and communication rules. It's like getting two people who speak different languages to communicate via a universal translator—everyone's still on the same page.

Supercharging Scalability and Resilience: Communication patterns, when designed right, help services handle varying loads like pros. Let's say you've got a huge traffic spike—asynchronous communication helps services manage the load and stay responsive without everything crashing down like a game of Jenga. This also means services can recover from failure gracefully, because they're not relying on instant responses from one another.

Boosting Reusability and Extensibility: A well-designed API is like a Swiss Army knife—it's versatile, reusable, and ready to adapt. You can extend and reuse services across multiple parts of an application, or even across entirely different apps, without needing a massive overhaul. Other services or clients just have to follow the API's clear and consistent interface, and boom—instant integration with minimal fuss. Let's discuss the types of communication in microservices in Table 2-8.

Table 2-8. *Types of Communication in Microservices*

Synchronous Communication	Asynchronous Communication
Definition	**Definition**
Synchronous communication is more similar to a live conversation: you ask a question, then you wait for an answer. The client sends a request to the service and just hangs around until it gets one. This is what you'll typically get in old-school client-server setups; it's what you get with RESTful APIs or gRPC.	Asynchronous communication involves decoupling the request and response. Asynchronous communication is more like sending an email. You fire off a request and move on with your life.
Use Cases	**Use Cases**
Simple Queries: Where immediate responses are needed, such as fetching user details or product information.	**Event-Driven Architectures:** Where services need to react to events, such as user actions or system changes.
Transactional Operations: Where operations need to be performed in sequence and require immediate feedback, like processing a payment.	**Decoupled Processing:** Where long-running tasks can be processed in the background, such as batch processing or email notifications.
Pros and Cons	**Pros and Cons**
Pros: Simple to implement, provides immediate feedback, easy to reason about.	**Pros:** Enhances scalability, improves resilience, decouples services, and reduces latency issues.
Cons: Can lead to tight coupling, less resilient to failures, and may cause latency issues under high load.	**Cons:** More complex to implement, requires managing message queues or event streams, and can be harder to debug.

Summary

APIs and communication strategies are the backbone of any solid microservices architecture. They're like the secret sauce that keeps everything connected yet independent—allowing services to do their own thing without stepping on each other's toes. When you design smart, robust APIs and pick the right communication patterns, you're setting yourself up for success: your services stay loosely coupled, scale like a dream, and handle whatever gets thrown at them with grace. However, it's not just about choosing the right method—you have to get the entire ecosystem right. Whether it's the "sugar rush" of synchronous communication or the "chill-out" of asynchronous messaging, you need to get it right. Then there's the issue of securing your service interactions and monitoring the health of the system: and suddenly you have the makings of a robust, resilient, reliable microservices landscape. Master these core principles, and you'll unlock the true power of microservices. It's all about driving innovation, keeping things efficient, and staying ahead in a fast-moving world—because who doesn't want to build systems that just work, no matter how complex things get? Next, we dive into scalability, where we'll explore how to build systems that can grow effortlessly to meet increasing demand without breaking a sweat. Get ready to scale up!

5. Scalability

It's the thing that makes microservices tick, the secret sauce behind allowing your application to meet increasing workloads without breaking a sweat, letting you embrace increasing numbers of users, without the underlying technology throwing up its hands in despair (and believe me, the user demands and data volumes only ever increase). In the modern digital world, scalability is not a luxury—it's essential. Now let's take a closer look at scalability for microservices. Let's dissect just why it's important, what types there are, and how you can implement it like a pro! Figure 2-4 represents the difference between vertical and horizontal scaling in microservices.

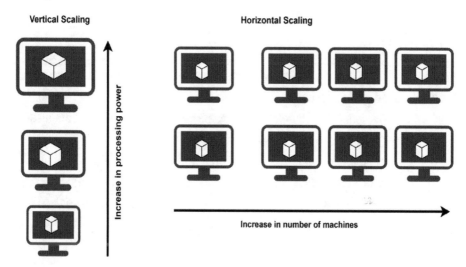

Figure 2-4. *Difference between vertical and horizontal scaling*

Understanding Scalability

Definition and Rationale

Scalability is basically your system's superpower—the ability to grow and stretch to accommodate increasing amounts of work without falling apart. In the world of microservices, it means you can scale individual services on their own terms, without having to beef up the entire application. Need more power for your order processing service but not for the user profiles? No problem. That's scalability in action.

This is why scalability is such a big deal: you can allow for unpredictable (and dramatic) spikes in load and scale the whole application in a modular manner rather than having to scale at the infrastructure or OS level. When each service scales independently, you can fine-tune resource usage, avoid blowing up costs, and keep things resilient. It's like giving each service its own power-up button for when things get crazy, ensuring optimal performance and availability even when traffic skyrockets. Let's discuss the importance of scalability in Table 2-9, followed by the types of scaling in Table 2-10.

Table 2-9. *Importance of Scalability in Microservices*

Handling Increased Load	When your user base increases and more requests are fired at your application, you'll want to be sure it can keep up. The more requests you get, the more data you need to move, and the less you can afford to worry about performance. Scalability is the feature that keeps your system from getting hot under the collar. It's like giving your app the endurance of a marathon runner, trained to work at extreme levels without breaking a sweat.
Optimizing Resource Utilization	But perhaps the most aesthetically pleasing aspect of microservices is that you can scale smartly, by tailoring each service to its actual needs. You aren't upgrading the entire application in one go, but parts of it. As a result, you avoid both the hyper-scaling of the ballooning monolith and the wasted expense that comes with that. You're paying for what you need and when you need it, like an à la carte menu instead of a buffet.
Enhancing Availability and Resilience	Scaling your architectures well is the superpower that helps eliminate failure and rapidly recover from disasters. If you can spread functional components over many instances and geographical regions, not only do you increase your availability, but you also add robustness. If something goes wrong, your users won't miss a thing. Service delivered, always? Yes, please!
Supporting Business Growth	If your product catches on—if people start to use your system, if you add new features or new markets—you'll be glad that your architecture is already in place and not scrambled to piece together as you grow. This is what it means to build your system for scale—so that it grows with you. And you grow a lot.

Table 2-10. *Types of Scalability*

Vertical Scalability (Scaling Up)	Horizontal Scalability (Scaling Out)
In the case of vertical scalability, the way to deal with increased load is to add more resources (CPU, memory, storage) to a single server. The approach is simple but ultimately limited by the restrictions of hardware. **Pros:** Easier to implement, no changes to application architecture. **Cons:** Limited by hardware capacity, potential single point of failure.	If you can apply horizontal scalability—adding more instances of a service to spread the load—then you're doing well. Microservices architecture makes horizontal scalability easier to achieve because the services are more independent of each other, and you can scale specific parts without impacting the whole. With traditional monolithic architectures, when you scale the whole, you basically have to scale it all. This means you're increasing the risk as well as the cost. The advantage of horizontally scalable systems is that you can achieve more resilience. **Pros:** Better fault tolerance, unlimited scaling potential, aligns with microservices principles. **Cons:** More complex to implement, requires load balancing and distributed data management.

Challenges and Considerations

Managing State: Let's be real—stateless services are a breeze to scale, but not every app gets that luxury. Some services need to hold onto state, and that's where things can get tricky. To keep things scalable, you'll need to get creative with managing state, like using distributed caches or databases to handle session data. It's a bit like spinning plates—you've got to keep everything in balance without letting anything crash.

Ensuring Consistency: In the wild world of distributed systems, data consistency can feel like trying to herd cats. It's no easy feat, but with strategies like eventual consistency, distributed transactions, or the saga pattern, you can keep things (mostly) in order. These techniques help you balance the need for scalability with the reality that keeping everything perfectly in sync across services isn't always possible—or necessary.

Handling Network Latency: The more your services spread across different nodes or regions, the more likely you'll bump into that annoying friend we all know too well: network latency. It can slow down performance if you're not careful. The fix? Optimize your communication protocols, throw in some CDNs, and keep those cross-service calls to a minimum. Basically, less chit-chat, more action.

Balancing Costs: Scaling services is great—until you see the bill. Scaling up can lead to higher infrastructure costs, so it's all about finding that sweet spot between performance and budget. This means optimizing resource allocation, using cost-effective cloud solutions, and implementing auto-scaling policies that don't break the bank. It's like shopping for a Ferrari but sticking to a Prius budget.

Summary

Scalability is the backbone of microservices architecture—it's what makes your app capable of growing without crumbling under pressure. Designing stateless services, leveraging containerization and orchestration, implementing load balancing, and embracing distributed databases all help make scaling a reality. Throw in some asynchronous communication and you're golden. Of course, continuous monitoring and auto-scaling make sure you're ready for whatever demand comes your way, ensuring top-notch performance and availability.

Yes, there are challenges—managing state, keeping consistency, and battling latency—but tackling these head-on with the right strategies will let you build microservices that not only scale but thrive. In today's dynamic digital world, this is how you set your organization up for growth, innovation, and success. But scalability alone isn't enough—resilience and fault isolation are equally crucial. Up next, we'll dive into how microservices handle failures gracefully and keep things running smoothly even when parts of the system go awry. Get ready to learn how to build systems that bounce back from failure like pros!

6. Resilience and Fault Isolation

Resilience and fault isolation are like the unsung heroes of microservices architecture, quietly making sure your applications stay tough and responsive, even when things go wrong. These concepts are all about building systems that don't freak out when something fails. Instead, they handle errors with grace, bounce back quickly, and, most importantly, make sure those failures don't spread like wildfire across the system. If you want high availability and reliability, resilience and fault isolation are nonnegotiable—because nobody wants an app that crumbles at the first sign of trouble.

Figure 2-5 represents a microservices architecture with a Gateway that routes client requests to various backend services (represented as APIs) and includes a Fallback Service for resilience. When clients (whether desktop, mobile, or web) send requests through the gateway, it directs them to the appropriate services. If a particular service fails—like the one connected to a broken database—rather than crashing the entire system, the fallback service steps in to handle the request. This is a great example of implementing resilience and fault isolation, ensuring that even if one component fails, the user experience remains intact by providing an alternative response or service.

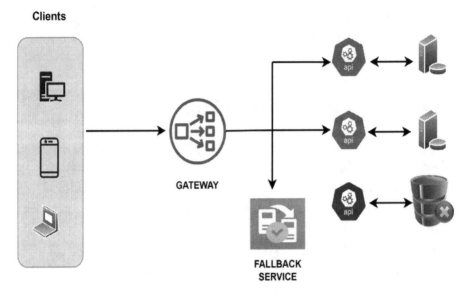

Figure 2-5. *Typical representation of microservices architecture with a fallback service*

Understanding Resilience and Fault Isolation

Definition and Rationale

Resilience is the system's ability to stay up and running when sideways happens: we tend to describe a system as being less resilient when it plays nicely with others, but goes down or reduces output if even just a few parts also go awry. Fault isolation, for instance, involves building firewalls between different parts of your system so that, if one service melts down, it doesn't bring down the whole application with it.

You may wonder: so what? In a microservices environment, you have a number of services that all work together (like a symphony: everyone plays together to create beautiful music). You don't want things to crash just because one overtired oboe player hit a sour note. The goal of resilience and fault isolation is to keep everything playing even if all hell breaks loose. By ensuring that each service handles failure gracefully and isolates faults, your application remains available and performant under chaos.

Importance of Resilience and Fault Isolation in Microservices

Maintaining High Availability: Resilient systems are like the superheroes of your architecture—they keep things running even when a few parts decide to take a nap. In a world where downtime equals lost users (and revenue), ensuring high availability is a must, especially for applications that thrive on constant uptime and reliability.

Enhancing User Experience: Nobody likes seeing error messages pop up out of nowhere. A resilient system keeps those frustrating moments to a minimum by gracefully handling failures and bouncing back quickly. It's the kind of smooth, hiccup-free user experience that keeps people coming back, boosting satisfaction and—dare I say it?—user retention. After all, a happy user is a loyal user.

Reducing Downtime and Costs: Fault isolation is like building firewalls around different parts of your system—if one service flames out, the others keep chugging along. Less downtime means fewer frantic "the system is down!" calls and lower costs for you. By containing failures and dealing with them efficiently, you avoid the dreaded system-wide meltdown and the hefty price tag that comes with it.

Supporting Scalability and Flexibility: A resilient system can scale like a pro. As traffic ramps up, it distributes loads without breaking a sweat, keeping everything stable and running smoothly. This kind of flexibility is key for growing applications or businesses navigating dynamic, ever-changing environments. After all, what's the point of scaling if your app can't handle the pressure?

Summary

Resilience and fault isolation are the backbone of any strong microservices architecture. By designing for failure—using tools like circuit breakers, timeouts, retries, and the bulkhead pattern—you create a system that can take a hit and keep on running. Don't worry about these terms as we would be discussing them in detail in the coming chapters. Add asynchronous communication, smart monitoring, regular health checks, and a bit of chaos engineering, and you're building a fortress of reliability. When you nail these practices, your application doesn't just stay online—it builds trust, delivers a smooth user experience, and ultimately drives more value for your organization. Now that we've tackled resilience, let's dive into continuous delivery and DevOps, where we'll explore how to keep that innovation flowing and ensure those microservices are always ready for the next big thing!

7. Continuous Delivery and DevOps

Continuous delivery (CD) and DevOps are the dynamic duo of microservices, helping you deliver software quickly, reliably, and, most importantly, without breaking a sweat. These practices are naturally focused on bringing development and operations closer together— think of it as getting the whole band in tune. By automating processes, encouraging closer collaboration between development and operations and ensuring that your software is always one step from being set live, CD and DevOps bring a sense of agility that every modern application craves. Suddenly, you are able to push more code, more rapidly, more reliably, less disturbingly to the rest of the system. It's the secret sauce that keeps you innovating and mutating at speed, while not blowing things up along the way. In the sections that follow, we will explore the core concepts of continuous delivery and DevOps, especially in the context of microservices. We'll dissect why these techniques are so important, how to practice them in a way that maximizes their value, and the best ways to get them to work together for maximum benefit. After all, it's all about keeping those wheels of innovation moving with minimal friction. Figure 2-6 represents how microservices are connected with DevOps and CI/CD.

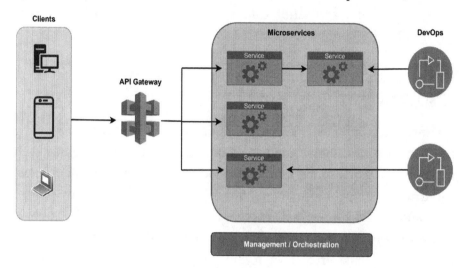

Figure 2-6. *Typical representation of microservices in conjunction with CI/CD*

Understanding Continuous Delivery and DevOps

Definition and Rationale

Continuous Delivery (CD): Continuous delivery is the software development practice whereby your code is always ready to be released to production—at any given moment, you can push changes, and those changes will automatically be built, tested, and prepared for release; it's the practice of being able to release changes at any time—drama free, no last-minute mad scramble. DevOps: The dev and ops teams finally merged into one with DevOps, and now it focuses on automating everything, making sure everyone can talk to everyone else, and making the entire process of creating software run like a well-oiled machine.

95

Why do we adopt CD and DevOps? Because it is simple: software delivery will be faster, with less work and less headache. In any case, if you have a complex microservices architecture with a lot of different services doing their own stuff, then CD and DevOps are the only friends you have to deal with this complexity and to make sure it all integrates into a coherent whole without friction.

Importance of Continuous Delivery and DevOps in Microservices

Enhancing Agility: CD and DevOps amplify your development and deployment cycles, allowing you to deploy new features and fixes faster than ever. Need to respond to user feedback or a market shift? No problem: you're nimble enough to adapt on the fly, keeping your competitive edge sharp and your customers satisfied.

Improving Quality: You avoid human error entirely (and let's face it, we humans all make errors) when you automate testing and deployment as well. Your code will be continually tested and vetted through automated pipelines, driving up quality all around. It is as if you have an angel on your shoulder—or somewhere in the cloud watching over your system 24/7.

Facilitating Independent Deployments: (One of the biggest benefits of microservices is that each service has its own life cycle.) CD (combined with DevOps) makes it easy to build, test, and deploy each service in isolation, without bringing down the entire system. So you can push a live update to one service without having to touch anything else, clean and simple.

Reducing Time to Market: Automating the build, test, and deployment process reduces the time it takes to get a new feature out the door. It's all about getting to market quicker than your competitors and getting features to your customers before they can go to the competition. Nothing else matters in today's world.

Summary

CD and DevOps—not microservices buzzwords: CD and DevOps are the core of rapid, reliable, automated software delivery. Automate building, testing, and deployment, and you gain agility, improve quality, and shrink time to market. Set up CI/CD pipelines, bring infrastructure as code, adopt a DevOps culture, and nail your best practices for monitoring, security, and performance, and your microservices will be ready for anything. Do it right, and you'll be innovating faster, responding to business needs with more agility, and adding value for your customers. Next up: Polyglot programming and how to use different languages and technologies for even more power to build the best possible solutions.

8. Polyglot Programming

In polyglot programming, you give your development team the proverbial toolbox instead of just one precarious wrench. Figure 2-7 represents how microservices are free to choose from different technical stacks or different versions of the same programming language. The microservices world is all about using the best language, tool, and technology for the task at hand, as opposed to forcing everything into the same one-size-fits-all hammer. This enables teams to pick the best tool for the job—be it faster performance, more easily scalable code, or the most maintainable software for that particular task. Polyglot programming delivers faster systems, happier developers, and better innovation. But with this flexibility comes a whole new set of issues—no pain, no gain, as the saying goes! We'll explore the ins and outs of polyglot programming, why it's important, the benefits it offers, the headaches it can sometimes cause, and how to handle it well in terms of your microservices architecture. Let's talk about why being multilingual in your codebase can actually give your app a real edge.

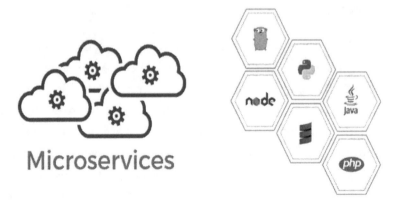

Figure 2-7. *Diagram to show that microservices are free to choose the technical stack*

Understanding Polyglot Programming

Definition and Rationale

Polyglot programming is like giving your microservices architecture a permission slip to break all the rules—for the right reasons. Instead of being restricted by one language or tech stack, you use whatever programming language, framework, or technology is best suited to implement each service. In a microservices architecture, that's like using every tool in your toolbox, rather than just a hammer. A monolithic architecture is like using a hammer to build everything from cabinets to sculptures to footwear. Instead, every service can be built with the best language for the task at hand.

So why polyglot programming? Because every programming language has its strengths, and the point here is to leverage that. It's about making your system hum, making sure everything runs smoothly, and enabling your team to do it with the best possible tools. And if you want to deal with all those different requirements, you can't do it if you're locked into a single language. Let's understand the importance of polyglot programming in Table 2-11, followed by its benefits in Table 2-12.

Table 2-11. *Importance of Polyglot Programming*

Leveraging Language Strengths	There's a sweet spot for every programming language. Python—simple, so great for prototyping, ideal for data analysis or a machine learning app; Java—strong, so good for scalable enterprise apps; your shortlist could go on. The beauty of polyglot programming is that you only code with the best language for the job—you don't use a screwdriver where a hammer is required.
Enhancing Developer Productivity	Does your development team want to be happy and productive? Of course it does! Then stop forcing them to use languages they don't like! You thought polyglot programming was about letting you use whatever languages you want? Welcome to the wonderful world of polyglot programming, where everybody's happy, because everyone gets to use the languages they're most comfortable with. And why shouldn't they be comfortable? They'll be much faster that way and much happier too. No one likes having to fight their way through a language they don't like! Instead of having to do that, you can enjoy the benefits of all the expertise you already have, and none of the need to learn new tricks. No need to slow you down with all that learning; you just want to get on with it, right?
Improving Performance	Not all programming languages are created equal, either; Node.js is great for I/O-bound apps. C++ is far better for performance-heavy operations. With polyglot programming, you get the best performance because you can use the right language for each microservice. It's like tuning a car to go faster and turn better; each part is built for optimal performance.
Encouraging Innovation	But what polyglot programming really enables is innovation. You can try out new languages, frameworks, and technologies if your stack doesn't lock you in. You'll be free to find more efficient approaches, adopt new tools, or collectively make incremental improvements to your architecture. Let your developer monkeys play with the latest and greatest, and you might just get a banana.

Table 2-12. Benefits of Polyglot Programming

Flexibility	Polyglot programming provides your team with a buffet of technological choices, not just a set menu. In other words, instead of having to use the same wrench to hit a nail, you can pick the tool that's best suited for the job. This gives you the chance to optimize performance; it can also help you adapt more easily to changing technological environments and evolving requirements.
Increased Innovation	When you let your teams experiment with different languages and technologies, magic happens. Polyglot programming turns your development environment into a playground for creativity. By trying out new tools, teams often stumble upon smarter, faster solutions and get the chance to adopt cutting-edge tech that keeps your architecture ahead of the game.
Better Resource Utilization	Different programming languages or frameworks are not all equal—some are built for specific purposes, and polyglot programming means you can use the best tools for each microservice. That means you can extract the maximum performance out of every microservice and also cut out all the unnecessary costs, just like putting the right gear on the right car engine.
Enhanced Developer Productivity	But allowing developers to remain in the languages and tools they know and love is like allowing a chef to use their favorite ingredients. They'll work faster, more productively, and, most importantly, better. Happier developers mean faster projects, faster iteration, and a faster time to market. This is exactly what every organization needs in order to stay competitive.

Challenges and Considerations

Complexity: Polyglot programming can be like handling a bunch of balls with different quirks: keeping track of your dependencies, just to make sure the various languages all play well together. But if you plan well, and use tools that help you containerize and orchestrate your applications, then you can avoid a real circus.

Skill Requirements: But let's be realistic—not every programmer is a coding superhero who can switch between Python, Java, Go, and more without breaking a sweat. Polyglot programming means your team needs to be versed in more than one language and technology—or at least willing to learn. Continuing education is a must here, because if your team doesn't have the chops, your polyglot dreams could die out pretty quickly.

Consistency: A multi-language codebase can seem like a bunch of herding cats trying to keep consistent coding styles across a few languages. It matters if you want your codebase to hold together over the long run. Establish standards and best practices up front, so you don't have to deal with chaos in mismatched styles and confusing documentation later on.

Monitoring and Troubleshooting: Once you're working with many languages and tools to deliver a service, monitoring and troubleshooting becomes more difficult. A service might have its own peculiarities, but if the developer doesn't have some central way of logging and monitoring how the service is running, it's like looking for a needle in a haystack. Effective logging, monitoring, and tracing are must-haves if you want insight into what is happening under the hood.

Best Practices for Polyglot Programming

Define Clear Service Boundaries: You'll want clearly defined boundaries so that they're loosely coupled. Every service should have the freedom to do its own thing without being caught up in the affairs of other services and, by doing so, better manage complexity, as well as to pick the best language or tool for each service.

Use Containerization and Orchestration: Containers are your best friend in a polyglot world. They help keep dependencies in check and make deployments consistent. Pair containerization with orchestration tools (hello, Kubernetes) to scale and manage your polyglot environment with ease.

Standardize Communication Protocols: If your services are speaking different languages, at least make sure they're using the same communication protocol. Standardizing things like APIs and data formats will help keep everything interoperable, even when services are written in totally different languages.

Implement Centralized Monitoring and Logging: Don't even think of trying to piecemeal troubleshooting various services without having some central logging and monitoring system in place. It will make your head explode. Not only will it help in diagnosing issues but also in monitoring performance and keeping the health of your polyglot environment in check.

Foster a Culture of Continuous Learning: Since there are so many languages and tools to consider, it's important to cultivate a learning culture. Encourage your teams to play with new tech, and make sure they have training and resources to keep their skills up to date. The more your team learns, the more creative problem solving they'll initiate.

Summary

Polyglot programming is the backbone of modern microservices architecture. With teams free to pick the best tool for each job, performance increases, developer productivity ramps up, and innovation is sparked. It also brings complexity, skill requirements, and consistency. With some careful planning, clear service boundaries, and a centralized monitoring system, polyglot programming can turn your architecture into an adaptable, efficient, and scalable beast. Give your services the freedom to speak many languages, and your system will be ready for whatever's coming over the horizon. It will deliver more value to your users.

With that discussion on polyglot programming out of the way, we can move on to service discovery, where I'll show you how microservices go about finding each other in a highly volatile and rapidly changing world. I'll show you how your services can stay connected, even as they scale and evolve!

9. Service Discovery

Service discovery is like the GPS for your microservices—helping them find each other in a vast, ever-changing landscape. In a world where services are scattered across multiple hosts, scaling up and down on demand, service discovery ensures they can locate and communicate with each other without the hassle of static configurations. No need for manually updating IPs or hardcoding locations—service discovery keeps everything fluid and adaptable. That's how you keep microservices scalable, resilient, and agile. So, let's take a closer look at service discovery and dissect why it is so important, how it works, and what best practices you need to keep your microservices connected and talking to each other in real time. After all, in this ultra-dynamic world, your services need to know where everyone else is. Even if everything's all over the place.

Figure 2-8 explains the process of service discovery for microservices architecture. Service Provider registers itself to Service Registry. It is a dynamic directory that stores information about all registered services. When Service Consumers need to communicate with a particular provider, it first asks the registry to find service. The registry provides the location of service, and Service Consumer invokes the provider and gets the functionality required. Because the location of service is dynamically looked up, it is not necessary to hardcode the service address in the consumer. This gets rid of many limitations in traditional monolithic architectures. As services grow in size and scale, consumers can query the registry to discover the services they need to interact with.

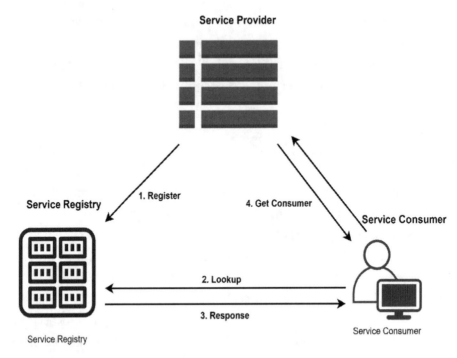

Figure 2-8. *Diagram to show service discovery*

Understanding Service Discovery

Definition and Rationale

Service discovery is like giving your microservices a handy phonebook, but with numbers that constantly update. It's the process through which services in a distributed system dynamically locate and connect with each other. Instead of hardcoding locations or manually keeping track, services register themselves in a service registry (the dynamic phonebook), which stores their network details. Whenever a service needs to talk to another one, it simply looks up the registry to get the correct address.

In the old days of monolithic apps, everything was cozy inside a single process. Communication between different functions was straightforward, predictable, and static. But in the world of microservices, things are much more chaotic—in a good way. Services are scattered across servers, containers, and cloud environments, and they're constantly scaling, stopping, or starting up again based on traffic. Relying on static configurations is like trying to use a paper map in a world where streets are constantly moving. That's where service discovery steps in, offering a dynamic solution so microservices can always find each other, no matter how much the environment shifts. Let's understand the importance of this principle in Table 2-13, followed by its benefits in Table 2-14.

Table 2-13. *Importance of Service Discovery*

Enhancing Scalability	Think of service discovery as the ultimate wingman for scaling. As your app grows and demand spikes, service instances can be spun up and down on the fly. Each new instance seamlessly registers itself with the discovery mechanism, instantly making itself available for others to use—like showing up to the party with name tags already on. No need for anyone to ask where to find you!
Improving Resilience	Service discovery is like having a backup plan (or five) at all times. If one service instance decides to call it quits, no problem—the discovery mechanism will quickly redirect traffic to a healthy instance, keeping things running smoothly. It's fault tolerance on autopilot, ensuring your app doesn't flinch even when something goes wrong.
Simplifying Configuration	Gone are the days of manually updating service endpoints or sifting through static configs. With service discovery, you don't need to know exactly where your services live at any given moment. This hands-off approach not only lightens the operational load but also minimizes configuration mistakes, which we all know can be a major pain.
Supporting Load Balancing	Service discovery isn't just good at connecting the dots; it also plays well with load balancers. By feeding real-time service locations to the load balancer, traffic gets spread out evenly across all available instances, preventing any one service from getting overwhelmed. It's like traffic control, but way less stressful (for you and the system).

Mechanisms for Service Discovery

Client-Side Discovery: Client-side discovery is when your service plays detective. The client itself queries the service registry to figure out where the other service lives (a bit like asking for directions at a crossroads). Once it has the details, it heads straight to the target service and starts communicating.

Best Practices

- Use tools like Eureka, Consul, or ETCD to manage your service registry.

- Implement a smart client library to handle querying and caching the registry, so your clients aren't lost without a map.

- Don't forget to add retry logic and fallback mechanisms—just in case the registry has a meltdown.

Server-Side Discovery: In this approach, the client doesn't bother playing detective. Instead, it throws its request to a load balancer or API gateway, which does the registry lookup and then kindly forwards the request to the right service. Think of it like asking the receptionist to call the right department for you.

Best Practices

- Use NGINX, HAProxy, or Zuul for load balancing or as a gateway.

- Integrate the load balancer with the service registry for dynamic service resolution.

- Always have health checks to make sure only healthy services are dealing with traffic. No one likes being passed on to a broken-down service.

DNS-Based Discovery: In DNS-based discovery, DNS servers play the middleman. Services register their instances with the DNS, and clients query the DNS to get the service's IP addresses. It's like your clients asking the yellow pages to give them the latest service info.

Best Practices

- Tools like Amazon Route 53 or CoreDNS are your friends for DNS-based service discovery.

- Configure short TTL (Time-To-Live) for DNS records, so updates don't get stale.

- Make sure clients are caching DNS responses to reduce lookup delays.

Implementing Service Discovery

Setting Up a Service Registry: The service registry is like the phonebook for all your services. It keeps track of who's around, so everyone knows where to find each other. Without it, your services would just be shouting into the void.

Best Practices

- Choose a reliable tool like Consul, Eureka, or ETCD for your service registry.

- Make sure it's highly available and fault-tolerant— because if the phonebook goes missing, everyone's lost.

- Automate the registration and deregistration of services.

Integrating with Load Balancers and API Gateways: Load balancers and API gateways play a vital role in server-side discovery by distributing traffic and providing a unified entry point for clients.

Best Practices

- Choose a load balancer or gateway that supports dynamic service discovery.

- Implement regular health checks to keep tabs on your service instances.

- Use smart routing rules to ensure traffic is distributed efficiently, with no congestion on the highway.

Ensuring Consistent Configuration: When dealing with a bunch of independent services, keeping everyone on the same page is vital. Consistent configuration ensures your services know what's up and can communicate smoothly.

Best Practices

- Use tools like Ansible, Chef, or Puppet to manage configurations.

- Keep configuration data in one place, like a centralized repository, so it's always up to date.

- Implement version control and change management— just like you would with code. Don't let rogue configs derail your system.

Monitoring and Health Checks: No one likes a zombie service—up but not really running. Continuous monitoring and health checks ensure only healthy services are taking requests, keeping your system robust.

Best Practices

- Health checks are a must for every service. Monitor status and availability like a hawk.

- Use tools like Prometheus, Grafana, or Datadog to collect and visualize metrics. Make it easy to see what's going on.

- Set up alerts for critical metrics, so you can jump on any issues before they become disasters.

Table 2-14. *Benefits of Service Discovery*

Dynamic Scalability	Service discovery is like your app's personal growth coach—it allows new service instances to join the party as soon as they're ready. No need for manual intervention; these instances can just pop in and start taking traffic, ensuring your system scales up (or down) depending on the load. It's the kind of flexibility you wish you had when trying to multitask!
Improved Resilience and Fault Tolerance	Think of service discovery as a traffic cop directing requests away from any service that's taking an unexpected nap (a.k.a. failed). It keeps things running smoothly by automatically rerouting traffic to healthy instances, ensuring your application keeps humming along even when a few services hit a rough patch.
Simplified Configuration Management	Static configurations? Pfft, those are so last decade. With service discovery, there's no need to painstakingly hardcode endpoints. Everything is dynamic, making configuration management as easy as pie (or at least easier than managing a monolith!). No more config errors lurking around to surprise you.
Enhanced Load Balancing	Service discovery doesn't just find services—it works hand in hand with load balancers to make sure the traffic gets evenly distributed. No single service gets swamped while others are sipping lemonade. It's like having your own personal efficiency manager making sure everything's running at optimal capacity without any bottlenecks in sight!

Challenges and Considerations

Consistency and Latency: It's a juggling act to keep everything up to date and quick. Your service registry must be able to push updates fast enough that clients can always find what they need—like making sure that Google Maps doesn't send you to a restaurant that closed two years ago. Otherwise, your clients could be ringing the wrong doorbell, and latency is definitely an issue.

Handling Failures: Service discovery is fantastic, but what happens when the discoverer itself fails? You need to have a Plan B (or C). Redundancy and failover mechanisms are key here. If your service registry goes down, it's like losing the guest list at a party—no one knows who's supposed to be where. Build in backups and failovers, or you might end up in chaos.

Security: Allowing services to find each other is great—unless unauthorized services sneak in too. Securing the service discovery process is nonnegotiable. It's like putting a bouncer at the door: you need authentication, authorization, and encryption to keep unwanted guests out and ensure the integrity of communications between services. You don't want rogue services crashing the party.

Monitoring and Observability: If you can't see it, you can't manage it, right? You also need to monitor the health and performance of your service discovery system—it's just as important as watching the services themselves. If you don't have good visibility into your registry and discovery mechanism, it's easy for problems to remain hidden until something big breaks. You want your system to be like a bank with security cameras on every corner—it's always on guard.

Summary

Service discovery isn't just a feature—it's the backbone of microservices architecture, making sure all your services can find each other and play nice together. With a solid service registry in place, smooth integration with load balancers and API gateways, and consistent configuration management, you're setting the stage for seamless communication across your system. Throw in some monitoring and health checks, and you've got yourself a dynamic, scalable, and resilient architecture that can roll with whatever comes its way. By embracing these best practices, your microservices will not only be efficient and flexible but also ready to tackle changing business needs while delivering maximum value to your users.

Speaking of keeping things running smoothly, next up we'll dive into load balancing—the unsung hero that makes sure traffic gets distributed evenly, so no service gets overloaded. Stay tuned!

10. Load Balancing

Load balancing is like the traffic cop of your microservices architecture—directing incoming requests to the right lanes so that no service gets stuck in a traffic jam. By distributing traffic evenly across multiple service instances, load balancing helps keep your system running smoothly, ensuring resources are used efficiently, response times stay snappy, and overall reliability is rock solid. Be it a simple web tier with multiple internal nodes or a grand multitier infrastructure, spanning geographically distributed regions, load balancing is your golden armor in a microservices world where services constantly scale up and down under load. It allows you to handle traffic fluctuations without breaking a sweat. In this guide, we'll take a closer look at load balancing: what it is, the different types that exist, how to set it up, and how to do it right.

Figure 2-9 depicts the principle of load balancing in a microservices architecture. The clients (desktop, mobile, or other devices) send requests to the load balancer. Then the load balancer distributes the traffic in a round-robin fashion to each service instance (Instance 1, Instance 2, and Instance 3). This method prevents a single service instance being overloaded. The system can maximize resource usages, maintain high availability, and minimize response times. In this way, the dynamic distribution of traffic helps the system handle different loads and improve scalability and reliability.

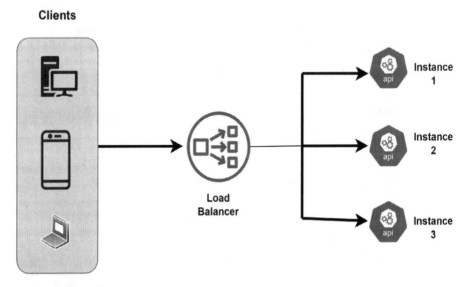

Figure 2-9. Diagram to show "how a load balancer works"

Understanding Load Balancing

Definition and Rationale

Load balancing is like the skilled traffic cop of the microservices world. It ensures that all incoming network requests are evenly distributed across multiple servers or service instances. Think of it as spreading out the workload, so no single service is burdened with too many tasks at once. This helps maintain smooth operations, avoiding bottlenecks, and ensures the system remains responsive and available.

In a microservices setup, where services are scattered across different servers and constantly scaling up or down, load balancing plays the role of a vigilant mediator. It's what keeps everything running smoothly, ensuring no one instance is doing all the heavy lifting while others take it easy.

By doing so, it helps preserve performance, keeps the system resilient, and ensures everything stays scalable as traffic grows or fluctuates. We will explore the significance of load balancing in microservices in Table 2-15, followed by an overview of its types in Table 2-16, and conclude with its benefits in Table 2-17.

Table 2-15. *Importance of Load Balancing in Microservices*

Optimizing Resource Utilization	Load balancing is like the matchmaker for your microservices—making sure no service instance is sitting alone at the dance. By spreading out traffic, it ensures that each service instance is pulling its weight, preventing overloading and keeping things running smoothly across the board.
Improving Response Times	When traffic is distributed across several instances, the system avoids long queues of requests waiting on a single, overloaded service. This keeps things snappy, meaning users get their data faster, and the overall experience feels fluid and responsive—just as it should in the fast-paced world of microservices.
Enhancing Availability and Reliability	If one of your service instances decides to take a nap (i.e., fails), load balancing steps in like a seasoned stage manager. It redirects the traffic to other active and healthy instances, ensuring that your application continues running smoothly, making failures feel like no big deal to the end user.
Supporting Scalability	Microservices grow as demand grows, and load balancing helps the system keep pace. When new service instances are added to handle increased traffic, the load balancer gets to work, making sure requests find their way to these new recruits, ensuring the system scales gracefully without breaking a sweat.

Table 2-16. *Types of Load Balancing in Microservices*

Client-Side Load Balancing	Server-Side Load Balancing
With client-side load balancing, it is the client that takes over the responsibility for spreadloading (finding multiple service instances to take on the request) by pulling a list of available instances from a service registry, picking one (with some sort of load balancing algorithm that spreads the traffic evenly among the available instances).	Conversely, server-side load balancing delegates the task to an external load balancer, like NGINX, HAProxy, or a cloud-based load balancer. The load balancer sits in front of the service instances and distributes the traffic according to some rules or algorithm.

Best Practices

- Use libraries like Netflix Ribbon or Spring Cloud LoadBalancer to handle client-side load balancing.
- Keep your service registry in check with tools like Eureka, Consul, or ETCD to maintain a fresh list of available instances.
- Make sure to implement retry logic and fallback mechanisms on the client side to avoid cascading failures.

Best Practices

- Pick a battle-tested load balancer, such as NGINX, HAProxy, or cloud-based options such as AWS ELB or the Azure Load Balancer.
- Set up health checks that continuously assess the health of your service instances and keep traffic flowing through your system.
- You should set up SSL/TLS termination at the load balancer so that you communicate using TLS without burdening the individual services.

Load Balancing Algorithms

Round Robin: Think of Round Robin like dealing cards in a game—every service instance gets its turn, one after the other, like clockwork. Requests are sent sequentially, ensuring that no one instance hogs all the action.

Least Connections: Least Connections is the load balancer's way of saying, "Let's be fair." It sends new requests to the instance that's already dealing with the least amount of traffic. No one gets overburdened, and the system stays balanced.

Weighted Round Robin: Here's Round Robin with a twist of logic. In Weighted Round Robin, you're not just sharing equally—you're sharing wisely. Instances with more capacity get more traffic, so the work is divided based on who can handle the most.

IP Hash: IP Hash is all about familiarity. It will hash the client's IP address and use the result as the identifier for which instance should handle the request. That way, the same client will always talk to the same service instance, like always ordering from the same barista rather than the first available one.

Implementing Load Balancing in Microservices

Configuring Load Balancers: When it comes to setting up load balancers, it's not just about pointing traffic somewhere and calling it a day. They need to route traffic efficiently and maintain high availability like traffic cops keeping the peace at a busy intersection.

Best Practices

- Health checks are your safety net—monitor the status of service instances and yank unhealthy ones out of rotation before they cause a jam.

- SSL/TLS termination at the load balancer ensures that data travels securely, so nothing leaks on the way.

- Choose your load balancing algorithm wisely (yes, there are different ones!) depending on the use case, to keep things running smoothly.

Integrating with Service Discovery: Load balancers should play nicely with your service discovery system. That way, they know where all the active services are without needing a static map pinned on the wall.

Best Practices

- Use dynamic service discovery tools like Consul, Eureka, or ETCD to keep track of active instances.

- Configure the load balancer to automatically query this dynamic list and update its routing table when new services pop in or disappear.

- Make sure instances register and deregister themselves without manual babysitting—it saves you the headache.

Ensuring Security: A well-configured load balancer can't be a weak link in your security chain. In fact, it should act as a guardian at the gate.

Best Practices

- Implement SSL/TLS termination at the load balancer to encrypt traffic.

- Use firewalls and security groups to control access to the load balancer.

- Monitor and log traffic to detect and respond to security threats.

Monitoring and Logging: You can't have any workhorses without knowing whether they're about to collapse under the strain or taking the wrong route like a distracted driver.

Best Practices

- Use something like Prometheus, Grafana, or Datadog to monitor it in real time.

- Centralize your logs, using systems such as the ELK stack (the ELK stack combines the power of Elasticsearch, Logstash, and Kibana to index and analyze your traffic logs).

- Set up alerts for critical metrics.

Table 2-17. *Benefits of Load Balancing in Microservices*

Enhanced Performance	Load balancing is like having a personal trainer for your microservices, making sure no instance gets overloaded and lazy. By distributing traffic evenly, it optimizes performance and keeps response times speedy. No more waiting around for an overworked server to catch its breath!
Increased Availability	When one service instance starts to falter, load balancing steps in, rerouting traffic to healthier instances, ensuring the system stays up and running. It's like having backup players ready to step in when someone on the team gets injured—keeping availability and reliability high.
Improved Scalability	As your system grows and new service instances are added, load balancing ensures the extra help doesn't go to waste. It directs traffic to those shiny new instances, allowing your system to handle increased loads without a sweat.
Efficient Resource Utilization	Essentially, load balancing makes sure you're not spinning your wheels, so to speak. If all your traffic is funneled into a single instance, you'll end up with one service as a bottleneck and others sitting idly by, twiddling their thumbs.

Summary

Whether a system is managing hundreds of users or many millions, one key behind microservices' scalability is its ability to efficiency, so that no service is overloaded while others are sitting idle, thanks to load balancing. If assigning traffic in round-robin fashion is like handing tray after tray at a cafeteria, load balancing is the unsung engine that keeps everything on schedule and makes sure no one has to wait for service, while contributing to efficiency of storage, speed of response, virtually unlimited scalability, and system availability. Now that we've covered traffic control, let's get into logging and monitoring, where we'll dive into how to keep an eye on everything that's happening in your microservices universe. Stay tuned!

11. Logging and Monitoring

Logging and monitoring are the unsung heroes of microservices architecture. They're like the backstage crew making sure the show goes on without a hitch, giving you visibility into the performance and behavior of your entire system. In a microservices world, where dozens of services are buzzing around on different hosts and containers, having effective logging and monitoring is nonnegotiable if you want to maintain reliability, performance, and security. These practices are what help teams catch issues early, troubleshoot problems efficiently, and make smart decisions based on real-time data.

Understanding Logging and Monitoring

Definition

Logging: Think of logging as your microservices environment's diary. Every time an event, error, or significant transaction is triggered, a record is stamped. This comes in handy when things go wrong, because, while microservices provide a thick cloud of abstraction, your logs provide a rich, forensic-level account of what is going on inside your microservices environment.

Monitoring: Monitoring is the white-gloved gatekeeper for your infrastructure; it measures the performance and health of everything going on inside your applications. It sends out alerts when something goes awry and records metrics to ensure that everything is running within acceptable boundaries. It's the tool that prevents you from catching fire—and that puts out those fires when they inevitably happen.

Rationale

In microservices, services are distributed across hosts, containers, and even continents, and it's difficult to know what's going on across the different services. This is where logging and monitoring become indispensable, offering the visibility you need to understand what's happening under the hood. They enable you to catch issues before your users do and to fix them before they become disasters. Now we have some background in place, we can dig a little deeper into how to use logging and monitoring and best practices to get the most out of it. Figure 2-10 represents a centralized logging system in which logs from multiple application servers are aggregated, processed, and transformed in Logstash. After that, they can be stored, indexed, and searchable in Elasticsearch, so log data can be stored and retrieved efficiently. Finally, it can be done using Kibana, a tool for analyzing, visualizing, and monitoring logs, so you can see how your system behaves and what's wrong. This allows you to keep all logs in one place. It is useful for troubleshooting, as it can help teams find out what is wrong with the system, monitor system health, and make data-driven decisions. We will explore the significance of logging and tracing in microservices in Table 2-18, followed by the benefits in Table 2-19.

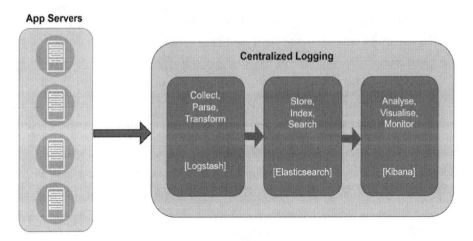

Figure 2-10. *Typical process of configuring logging*

Table 2-18. *Importance of Logging and Monitoring in Microservices*

Ensuring Reliability and Availability	Logging and monitoring are essential pillars of a microservices architecture. Keeping track of the system performance and health at all times allows your team to spot problems before they reach the user, ensuring continuous availability.
Facilitating Troubleshooting and Debugging	Logs record details about system events, errors, and transactions so that they can be later analyzed to debug issues. When systems fail, logs enable teams to find the source of problems and resolve them.
Enhancing Security	By tracking access patterns and alerting on anomalies, monitoring and logging can help prevent security incidents. They can also be used as an audit log to investigate security incidents, as well as to ensure the enterprise complies with regulation.

(continued)

Table 2-18. (*continued*)

Optimizing Performance	Such monitoring systems capture performance metrics such as resource utilization, response times, and more, which teams can use to identify bottlenecks in performance, optimize resource allocation, and ensure that services run at peak efficiency.
Supporting Scalability	Scaling microservices is enabled by sound logging and monitoring, which helps us to understand what's happening in the system as it's under different kinds of load. This helps us make good decisions about scaling services and allocating resources.

Implementing Logging in Microservices

Centralized Logging: In a microservices world, logs can quickly become a scattered puzzle—pieces of data floating across different services and hosts. Centralized logging swoops in to gather all these pieces into one tidy place, making it much easier to search, analyze, and make sense of it all. Instead of hopping between multiple locations, you have one central repository to crack the case of any bug or performance hiccup.

Best Practices

- Use centralized logging solutions like the ELK stack (Elasticsearch, Logstash, Kibana) or Graylog.

- Implement log shippers (e.g., Filebeat or Fluentd) to collect and forward logs to the central repository.

- Structure logs in a consistent format (e.g., JSON) to facilitate analysis.

Log Aggregation and Analysis: Aggregating and analyzing logs helps teams to identify patterns, detect anomalies, and gain insights into system behavior.

Best Practices

- Use log aggregation tools to bring all logs together from various sources into a single repository.

- Leverage analysis tools to filter, search, and visualize your logs for deeper insights.

- Create dashboards to keep an eye on key metrics and trends, so you're always a step ahead of potential issues.

Structuring Log Data: Logs are only as useful as their readability. Structured logs—those written in a consistent, machine-readable format—make analysis much easier. With structured logging, you won't waste time deciphering unstructured, scattered bits of data.

Best Practices

- Use a standardized log format (again, JSON works wonders).

- Add relevant metadata like timestamps, service names, or request IDs to provide context for every log entry.

- Stick to standardized log levels like DEBUG, INFO, WARN, and ERROR to indicate the severity of events clearly.

Logging Best Practices

- **Log Contextual Information:** Add request IDs, user IDs, or other context clues to your log entries to make it easier to connect the dots across services.

- **Avoid Logging Sensitive Data:** Keep things like passwords and personal data out of your logs to avoid privacy issues and comply with regulations.

- **Implement Log Rotation:** Prevent storage bloat by setting up log rotation policies to automatically manage log sizes.

- Logging in microservices isn't just about storing data—it's about giving your team the tools to make sense of a complex, distributed environment.

Implementing Monitoring in Microservices

Metrics Collection: Metrics collection is like strapping your system into a heart rate monitor and oxygen saturation monitor or putting it in the chair at the local gym and strapping another heart rate monitor around your own wrist. You want to know CPU usage, memory consumption, response times, and error rates. You want to know what your services are telling you about how they're doing. In short, your services have a Fitbit.

Best Practices

- You can use tools such as Prometheus, Grafana, or Datadog to monitor and visualize the metrics—akin to giving your system a proverbial physical.

- Instrument your services so that all the important metrics are exposed (either through APIs or exporters) so that nothing is missed.

- Obtain service-level, host-level, and container-level metrics to get a 360-degree view of what's going on under the hood.

Alerting and Notifications: Alerting, in turn, sets off a system of smoke alarms on your services. When something goes wrong, you want to know about it and as soon as possible—before things burn down. By configuring your alerting rules correctly, you can stay ahead of problems before they happen.

Best Practices

- Create smart alerting rules based on important metrics such as CPU spikes or high error rates, so you're alerted only when necessary (and not once every five minutes).

- Send you notifications through your favorite channels (email, SMS, Slack) using alerting tools.

- Have escalation policies so that critical alerts aren't ignored because, c'mon, who doesn't want to be the hero who caught the big one?

Distributed Tracing: Distributed tracing gives you an X-ray into what's happening as requests hop from one service to another, giving a holistic view of the flow of a request, identifying hotspots and the cause of breakdowns. It's a GPS for microservices.

Best Practices

- Trace all the data with something like Jaeger or Zipkin, and you'll get an X-ray of what's happening inside your services.

- Ensure each service generates some form of trace information, such as trace IDs or spans, for every request and that you can follow the breadcrumbs.

- Visualize that trace data to see the entire path that requests take, and find the places along the way where performance was lost.

Table 2-19. *Benefits of Logging and Monitoring in Microservices*

Enhanced Visibility	Imagine logging and monitoring as a pair of high-powered glasses for your microservices: it allows you to see everything—from the way your services are behaving to what's going on under the hood to when things start to get a little wonky—and then you're in a position to understand what's happening, see patterns, and make judgments early, before the situation gets out of control.
Proactive Issue Detection	With real-time monitoring and alerting, you don't have to wait for something to break to find out there's a problem; it's like a smoke alarm for your system. If something goes wrong, you know about it before your users do, and you can minimize the disruption and keep your services up and running.
Improved Troubleshooting	Detailed logs and metrics are your detective toolkit—clues that show you what happened and when and why it's happening. You don't have to spend hours furtively poking around in the dark to find the problem. You can trace back the issue to its source and apply the right patch.
Optimized Performance	But more importantly, keeping a careful eye on performance metrics—usage of resources, response times, traffic patterns—allows you to detect inefficiencies while they're still nascent and before they spiral out of control. Perhaps you need to tweak the workload distribution among resources, or maybe a particular API request is being slowed down by a bottleneck in the network tier.
Enhanced Security	However, logs are not just for debugging—they are your audit trail. By monitoring who is accessing what and when, you can look for anomalies and detect potential security violations before they become a problem. This is like having a video camera in your microservices, so you're covered in case you need to prove compliance and protect your system from intruders.

Challenges and Considerations

Managing Data Volume: Microservices are also data generation machines. Under the hood of every chat or search or profile request, there are dozens of logs and metrics generated and collected millisecond by millisecond. To avoid becoming data prisoners in your own systems, it's critical to create a log rotation system, set retention policies, and store the logs in a well-managed manner. Call it cleaning up after the party: you can't drink from a fire hose, but you can capture data from one.

Ensuring Consistency: One of the trickiest parts of logging across multiple services is getting everyone on the same page. Different teams, different services, different formats—it can turn into a mess fast. Standardizing your logging formats and monitoring practices helps keep things consistent, so you're not stuck trying to piece together a puzzle with mismatched pieces.

Balancing Overhead: Logging and monitoring are essential, but they come at a cost. They take up resources and cause latency. The trick is to find just the right amount of visibility so that you don't slow down your system. It's like putting on mirrors. That's great, but not if it makes you lose speed.

Securing Log Data: Logs can, without meaning to, become veritable goldmines of sensitive data—passwords, user information, and other goodies that black-hat hackers would pay top dollar for. Consequently, giving logs the proper love and care means protecting them at all costs. Encrypt them, lock them down with access controls, and ensure that they remain compliant with data protection regulations. Logs are an asset, not a liability.

Summary

Logging and monitoring are the lifelines of a thriving microservices architecture. You use them to understand what's happening across your distributed systems logs, gather meaningful metrics, set up automatic alerts, and tap into distributed tracing; your microservices will run smoothly, safely, and efficiently. The name of the game is to be proactive: to detect issues before they get out of hand, troubleshoot like a pro, and take smarter decisions based on real-time data. Keep to best practices, and your microservices will be a resilient, scalable, and future-proof set of services.

And next, let's delve into security, because microservices are nothing if they are not safe.

12. Security

When it comes to microservices architecture, security isn't just an afterthought; it's the bodyguard at the front door, making sure your application is safe from all the digital chaos out there. Protecting your microservices from threats and vulnerabilities is essential for maintaining the holy trinity of data—integrity, confidentiality, and availability. In a microservices world, where different services are scattered across multiple hosts and communicate over networks, security gets tricky. Each service and every interaction must be secured, no exceptions. It's like trying to lock down a neighborhood instead of just one house—more complicated, but absolutely vital. So, let's dive into the core concepts of microservices security, exploring why it's crucial, the challenges you'll face, and strategies and best practices to keep your system secure, resilient, and ready for whatever the digital landscape throws at it.

Figure 2-11 illustrates a secure microservices architecture where client requests are routed through an HTTPS load balancer, ensuring encrypted communication. The load balancer directs traffic to various APIs, which are safeguarded by an authentication database (AUTH DB). Each API service checks the user's credentials, most likely using keys or tokens, before granting access to the appropriate resources. This approach ensures that only authenticated and authorized requests are processed, maintaining security and data integrity across the system while efficiently balancing the load among services.

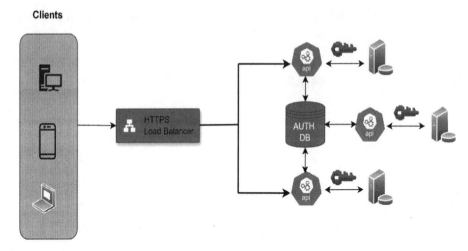

Figure 2-11. *Illustrates a secure microservices architecture*

Understanding Security in Microservices

Definition and Rationale

Security in microservices architecture is all about locking down your distributed services, data, and communication channels to keep unauthorized folks and malicious threats at bay. It covers the big security buzzwords: authentication, authorization, data protection, network security, and the essential ongoing monitoring to make sure everything stays secure.

Microservices may offer flexibility, but they also increase the attack surface. Now, instead of securing one monolith, you're dealing with a lot of independent services spread across multiple hosts, all chatting over networks. Each service needs to be fortified individually, and their communication secured, so that your sensitive data doesn't fall into the wrong hands. Besides, regulations are not getting any easier to deal with—keeping security airtight isn't just a suggestion; it's a must-have for compliance and user trust. Let's discuss the importance of security in Table 2-20.

Table 2-20. *Importance of Security in Microservices*

Protecting Sensitive Data	With microservices handling everything from personal details to payment info and proprietary business data, securing these precious bits and bytes is nonnegotiable. You don't want to be the headline for a data breach scandal—trust me.
Ensuring Compliance	The GDPR, HIPAA, PCI-DSS alphabet soup is all about keeping data safe. Skipping on proper security can lead to more than just bad press; we're talking legal fines that will make your CFO break a sweat. So, following solid security practices isn't just about safety, it's about survival in today's regulated world.
Maintaining System Integrity	Keeping your services secure ensures that no one is sneaking in to mess around with your code or data. Imagine the chaos if someone tweaks just one part of your system—safeguarding the integrity of microservices keeps the whole operation trustworthy and reliable.
Preventing Unauthorized Access	The goal is simple: keep the wrong people out. Whether it's blocking data breaches, stopping account takeovers, or preventing unauthorized transactions, securing your microservices means only the right people get in.
Enhancing User Trust	When users know their data is secure, they feel better about using your service. In today's world, where data breaches feel like weekly occurrences, solid security practices aren't just about compliance—they're also about keeping your customers loyal and confident in your product.

Strategies for Implementing Security in Microservices

Authentication and Authorization: Authentication is about figuring out who is who: it's the bouncer at the club with the ID checker. You want to know that the user and service that you're connecting with is who they say they are. Authorization is the VIP list. After you get in, you can go to only certain places (or use certain resources). Getting the right tools in place—using solid mechanisms like OAuth2 and OpenID Connect—can be a godsend.

Best Practices

- Use OAuth2 and OpenID Connect for rock-solid authentication.

- Implement RBAC (Role-Based Access Control) or ABAC (Attribute-Based Access Control) to keep things granular.

- Centralize all authentication and authorization efforts through identity providers for simplicity and security.

Secure Communication: Ever sent a postcard and worried about who might read it along the way? Yeah, don't do that with your microservices. Make sure the data traveling between services stays private and intact by encrypting it. This prevents prying eyes and meddling hands from messing with your system.

Best Practices

- Use TLS (Transport Layer Security) to encrypt data on the move.

- Implement mutual TLS (mTLS) to authenticate communication between services—because even your microservices need to know who they're talking to!

- Lock down those APIs. Don't leave internal endpoints exposed to the big, bad Internet.

Data Protection: It is like putting your jewels into a safe. When your data is at rest, it is vulnerable, as much as your jewels would be, and strong encryption will work wonders. When your data is in flight, it is vulnerable, like your jewels would be if you were wearing them on your fingers, and secure storage solutions will ensure that your secret remains secret.

Best Practices

- Use top-tier encryption algorithms to protect data at rest.

- Always use TLS for data in transit.

- Store sensitive data in secure storage systems. Skip the sticky notes.

Network Security: Imagine each microservice living in its own guarded fortress. Implementing firewalls, security groups, and segmentation creates layers of protection around your services. This way, even if one service gets compromised, the others remain shielded.

Best Practices

- Use firewalls and security groups to control who gets access.

- Segment your network to keep services isolated. If one falls, the others don't follow.

- VPNs (Virtual Private Networks) are a great way to secure remote access—like secret tunnels for your data.

Monitoring and Logging: You need eyes everywhere. Monitoring and logging give you visibility into your system's behavior, so when something weird happens (like that uninvited guest), you'll know. Alerts will help you catch potential threats early, keeping your services safe and sound.

Best Practices

- Use tools like Prometheus, Grafana, or Datadog to track security metrics in real time.

- Aggregate logs with centralized solutions like the ELK stack to keep everything in one place for easy analysis.

- Set up alerts for any fishy activities, so you're ready when security incidents strike.

Secure Development Practices: An ounce of prevention is worth a pound of cure. Build secure code by not including security holes in your code, and review your code regularly with security testing to keep it patched, clean, and safe.

Best Practices

- Corral security vulnerabilities hiding in your codebase with static code analysis tools such as SonarQube.

- Run frequent penetration tests and vulnerability scans, in order to stay one step ahead of the attacker.

- Follow secure coding practices and industry standards—don't reinvent the wheel.

Incident Response: Finally, plan. If you're being really honest with yourself, things will go wrong—and when they do, you'll want to have an incident response plan in place so that you can quickly detect, respond to, and recover from security incidents.

Best Practices

- Draft and document a solid incident response plan.

- Regularly conduct drills so that everyone knows what to do in the event of an emergency.

- SIEM (Security Information and Event Management) solutions may be helpful in identifying and responding quickly to security breach incidents.

Summary

Security is the backbone of any successful microservices architecture, ensuring that every piece of the puzzle—data, services, and communications—remains safe from threats while upholding integrity, confidentiality, and availability. To fortify your microservices, you'll need to embrace a toolkit of essential practices, such as strong authentication and authorization, encrypted communication, safeguarding data, airtight network security, vigilant monitoring, and, of course, secure development protocols. Think of it as setting up a digital fortress, where each service knows its role and has its defenses ready. But don't just stop at building your defenses—addressing security challenges head-on means that sensitive data stays exactly where it should, your organization meets compliance, and most importantly, you keep the trust of your users intact. Taking a security-first approach is not just a checkmark on a list; it's the bedrock that will support an adaptive, resilient, and scalable microservices architecture, ready to take on both today's risks and tomorrow's unknowns. Mastering these security fundamentals is key to leveraging the full power of microservices while building software systems that are as flexible and resilient as they are safe.

Conclusion

As we wrap up this chapter, it's clear that microservices architecture is like assembling a team of specialist superheroes—each independent, focused, and equipped with just the right tools for their unique job. We've tackled everything from the Single Responsibility Principle (SRP) to the magic of decentralized data management, weaving through the complexities and marvels of APIs and scalability. It's a lot, but hey, if microservices were easy, everyone would be doing them without breaking a sweat, right?

Now, before you get too comfortable basking in the glow of microservices wisdom, remember—this is just the start of your journey. We've laid the foundation, but the real fun begins in the next chapter: "Designing Microservices." Here, we'll dive into how to craft these independent units with finesse, blending art and engineering to create services that are not just functional but downright elegant. Think of it as moving from assembling building blocks to crafting intricate, efficient machinery.

And yes, we'll also discuss some common pitfalls—because what's a good design without a few "lessons learned the hard way" anecdotes? Spoiler: Design is where you learn that "simple" and "easy" are not synonyms. Stay tuned, and let's keep decoding the art of microservices!

CHAPTER 3

Designing Microservices

1. Domain-Driven Design (DDD)

Domain-Driven Design (DDD) is a fancy way of saying, "Let's keep things aligned with the real business needs," but it's much more than that. At its heart, DDD is about creating software that mirrors the core concepts of the business itself, constantly evolving with it. Now, when you take this approach and apply it to microservices, magic happens. DDD gives you a structured blueprint to design microservices that aren't just another piece of tech but actually resonate with how the business operates. It's all about designing services around the business domains, which makes the whole system more flexible and easier to maintain.

In other words, DDD is your go-to method for keeping tech and business in perfect harmony—especially when those microservices start stacking up! Let's dive into how this works in the world of microservices, making things smoother and more effective. Figure 3-1 represents the "Onion Architecture," a layered design approach often used in Domain-Driven Design (DDD). At the core is the domain, which represents the heart of business logic, isolated from external influences. Surrounding the domain is the application layer, handling tasks like coordination and validation without involving business rules. The infrastructure layer

© Sumit Bhatnagar and Roshan Mahant 2025
S. Bhatnagar and R. Mahant, *The Art of Decoding Microservices*,
https://doi.org/10.1007/979-8-8688-1267-5_3

wraps around that, responsible for external dependencies like databases, messaging systems, or APIs. At the outermost layer is the framework, which connects the infrastructure to external systems, like UI or databases, ensuring that the domain logic remains clean and decoupled from technology concerns. This design ensures that the domain remains isolated, flexible, and adaptable to changes.

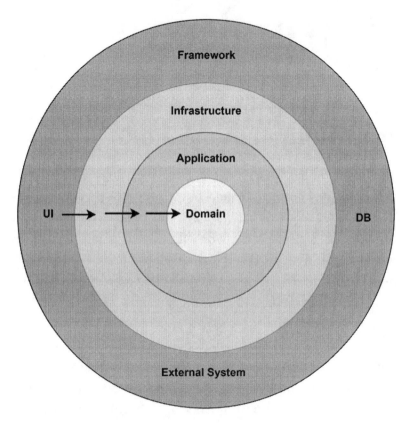

Figure 3-1. *Diagram to represent how DDD is placed within microservices architecture*

Applying Domain-Driven Design (DDD) to microservices can feel like matching puzzle pieces that finally fit. The bounded contexts from DDD naturally translate into individual microservices, making sure each service handles a specific part of the domain. This creates a system where services are tightly focused internally (high cohesion) but don't step on each other's toes (loose coupling). Here's how DDD shapes your microservices architecture.

Defining Bounded Contexts

Identification: Get cozy with your domain experts, because you'll need them to help you spot the natural splits within the business. These splits, known as bounded contexts, mark where one part of the domain ends and another begins.

Mapping: Once you've identified those contexts, it's time to map each one to a microservice. For example, in an ecommerce platform, you might break it down into "Order Management," "Inventory," and "Shipping"— each one a separate microservice with its own responsibilities.

Modeling Around Business Capabilities

Capabilities: Forget about how things get done for a minute and focus on *what* needs to get done. What are the business's core capabilities? When you zoom in on these, you design services that are way more aligned with business goals.

Services As Capabilities: Each microservice is like a little business powerhouse, offering one specific capability. Its interface? That's where the magic of the ubiquitous language kicks in, reflecting domain operations.

Integration and Communication

Asynchronous Communication: Microservices should be like great neighbors: independent, but willing to talk. Using asynchronous messaging or an event-driven architecture allows services to communicate without needing to dive into each other's data. No more prying neighbors!

Domain Events: Picture this—a new order is placed, or an item ships. These domain events ripple through the system, triggering actions across various services, ensuring everyone's on the same page without being tangled up in each other's business.

Autonomy and Decentralization

Data Ownership: Every microservice is the proud owner of its own data. This ensures data integrity, and no one else can touch it. You can think of it like owning a house—you get to make the rules inside your domain.

Decentralized Data Management: Different services, different needs. Microservices can even have their own tailored storage solutions—polyglot persistence in action. Use the right tool for the job, and you'll have services that hum along smoothly, each with its perfect fit.

By applying DDD to microservices, you create a system that is not only well structured but also closely aligned with real business needs—a win for both development and the business itself.

Challenges

Interservice Coordination: While bounded contexts do a great job of keeping things loosely coupled, they introduce the challenge of managing interactions between services. It's like juggling plates—keeping them separate yet ensuring they coordinate smoothly takes a little finesse.

Overhead of Consistency: Keeping data consistent across services without tightly coupling them is no walk in the park. You've got to work with eventual consistency, compensating transactions, or distributed sagas. It's like putting together a puzzle where the pieces keep moving, which adds some complexity to the mix.

Complexity in Governance: As microservices multiply like rabbits, managing the overall model and maintaining governance around how all those bounded contexts play nicely together becomes a growing headache. It's a classic case of "the more you have, the more you manage."

When using DDD to design microservices, we aren't just tearing apart systems into smaller chunks. Instead, we're incorporating the knowledge of domain experts, and building models of the business domain. By using business capabilities as the foundational building blocks for the microservices architecture, and connecting those capabilities to bounded contexts, the result is not only a system that will scale but one that's deeply integrated with the business. This alignment makes life a lot easier when it comes to development, maintenance, and adapting to changes as the business evolves. It's like building a system that grows and shifts in lockstep with the organization.

Imagine an online retail company as our playground. In this context, DDD shines by helping us map real-world business capabilities to distinct microservices. Think about everything involved—order management, inventory, shipping—all working harmoniously in their own bounded contexts. This setup allows the system to function seamlessly, from domain analysis all the way to implementation, illustrating how DDD transforms abstract business needs into a well-oiled microservices architecture.

Example: Online Retail Company

1. **Domain Analysis and Bounded Contexts**

   The first step is to sit down with the experts—the people who know the ins and outs of the online retail business. This means sales managers, inventory specialists, and customer service leads. After some lively workshops and discussions, a few key bounded contexts reveal themselves:

- **Product Catalog:** Manages product information, keeping everything from prices to descriptions in check

- **Inventory Management:** Tracks stock levels and handles all that behind-the-scenes restocking

- **Order Processing:** Manages customer orders, from checkout to payment

- **Shipping:** Ensures products make their way to customers

- **Customer Management:** Manages customer profiles and keeps track of interactions

2. **Mapping Bounded Contexts to Microservices**

Now, it's time to map these bounded contexts to their own microservices, giving each its own playground:

- **Product Catalog Microservice:** Responsible for adding, removing, and modifying product listings. Also retrieves all that vital product info

- **Inventory Microservice:** Keeps tabs on stock, updates levels, and lets the other microservices know when stock is low or replenished

- **Order Processing Microservice:** Handles order placements, processes payments, and tracks order status

- **Shipping Microservice:** Works with external shipping providers and keeps the delivery process in check

- **Customer Management Microservice:** Maintains customer data, preferences, and takes care of authentication and authorization

3. **Designing Communication and Integration**

These microservices need to talk to each other—often—and that's where communication strategies come into play:

- **Event-Driven Communication:** Say a customer places an order. The Order Processing Microservice sends out an "Order Placed" event, which the Inventory and Shipping microservices listen for. Inventory reserves the stock, and Shipping gears up for dispatch as soon as the order is confirmed.

- **Asynchronous Messaging:** If new products are added, the Product Catalog Microservice sends an asynchronous message to Inventory, ensuring the stock is updated without anyone needing to wait around for a response.

4. **Handling Data**

Each microservice needs to own its data—no sharing allowed here! This promotes encapsulation and autonomy:

- **Polyglot Persistence:** The Product Catalog Microservice uses a document store to handle flexible schemas and fast retrieval. Meanwhile, the Inventory Microservice prefers a speedy

141

NoSQL database, and the Customer Management Microservice opts for a relational database to keep customer transactions safe and sound.

5. **Challenges Addressed**
A few common challenges arise, but they're handled neatly:

- **Decentralization:** Each service operates independently, with clear APIs and event triggers, so there's no reliance on one big, slow central database.

- **Data Consistency:** The system embraces eventual consistency. So, if inventory runs out, the Inventory Microservice eventually catches up and stops new orders from being placed, preventing those dreaded oversells.

Summary

This online retail example showcases how Domain-Driven Design (DDD) can guide the creation of microservices. By aligning each microservice with a specific bounded context, the system stays maintainable and scalable—precisely what the business needs. Teams can work independently, focusing on their areas without stepping on each other's toes, which speeds up development and makes maintenance a whole lot easier. In the next section, we'll dive deeper into the concept of bounded contexts and service boundaries, exploring how to clearly define the lines between services and keep everything working harmoniously.

2. Bounded Contexts and Service Boundaries

In microservices architecture, getting the service boundaries just right is like setting up the perfect blueprint for a scalable, maintainable, and adaptable system. These boundaries don't just form by accident; they're shaped by an idea borrowed from Domain-Driven Design (DDD) called "bounded contexts." This concept plays a critical role in ensuring that microservices stay loosely coupled yet remain highly cohesive—kind of like the dream team of software design.

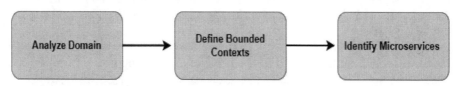

Figure 3-2. *Diagram to represent where bounded context fits within microservices architecture*

Understanding Bounded Contexts

A bounded context is one of DDD's central ideas. It draws a line around a specific domain model, saying, "This is where this model applies, and nowhere else." Within this boundary, the domain's complexity is tucked into a neat set of capabilities and data that belong together. Outside that boundary? Well, that's someone else's problem (or rather, another service's). In microservices, each bounded context usually maps to one or more microservices, which can develop, deploy, and scale independently of others. This separation makes life easier for teams, as shown in Figure 3-2, breaking a giant system into smaller, more digestible chunks that each team can work on without stepping on one another's toes.

Principles for Defining Service Boundaries

When you bring bounded contexts into the microservices world, a few key principles help define the right service boundaries:

Autonomy: Each microservice should be its own boss. It should fully own its domain logic and data, handling everything independently. This autonomy minimizes the need to rely on other services, allowing it to grow and evolve without causing a domino effect on the rest of the system.

Business Capability Alignment: Service boundaries should map directly to business capabilities. This keeps services focused on delivering specific business value, encapsulating all the logic and data they need to get their job done without meddling in someone else's work.

Model Consistency: Everything within a bounded context needs to be consistent with itself, but, and here's the kicker, nothing in the bounded context needs to map to anything in any other bounded context. This means that the different individual models can coexist within the system in relative peace; there is no universal way that all of the model pieces need to fit together.

Integration through Interfaces: Services talk to each other through well-defined interfaces, usually APIs or messaging. These interfaces act as the handshake between different bounded contexts, keeping them loosely coupled but still in sync when they need to be.

Size and Scope: Goldilocks would approve. The microservice you are designing should be "just right." Small enough to be owned by a single team, but large enough to subsume something meaningful, like a core business function. Finding the optimal point between "too fine" and "too coarse" takes some experimentation, but it's worth it.

Grounding microservice design in the notion of bounded contexts will keep microservice dependencies tidy, limit complexity, and keep systems simpler to evolve with changing business needs. After this brief introduction to bounded contexts, our next post, bounded contexts and service boundaries, will go into more detail.

Challenges in Defining Boundaries

Getting service boundaries right in microservices architecture is a tricky dance, with plenty of pitfalls along the way:

Over-segmentation: Splitting services too finely can turn your system into a tangled mess of communication lines. You might find that you're spending more time managing the overhead of orchestrating interactions than actually building features.

Under-segmentation: On the flip side, grouping too many responsibilities into a single service defeats the purpose of microservices altogether. You risk creating bloated services that are hard to scale, evolve, or maintain.

Data Duplication: Bounded contexts often need to own their data, even if that means duplicating it across services. While this keeps services autonomous, it brings its own headaches—like keeping data synchronized and consistent across those boundaries.

Integration Complexity: Fewer direct dependencies between services is a good thing, but it means you have to work harder on the integration points—event-driven architecture, asynchronous messaging, anti-corruption layer, etc. These need to be the right ones or it's all chaos.

Finding that sweet spot between autonomy and interdependence is a constant balancing act.

Let's look at how this might play out in a real-world scenario, like a bustling ecommerce platform. Picture a system where different key areas—inventory, billing, and customer management—are treated as distinct business domains. Each of these is modeled as its own bounded context and, naturally, becomes its own microservice:

Inventory Service: Responsible for managing stock levels, product information, and supplier details.

Billing Service: Takes care of pricing, discounts, invoicing, and payment processing.

Customer Service: Focused on managing customer profiles, preferences, and customer support interactions.

By clearly defining the boundaries for each of these contexts, the platform ensures that changes in one service—let's say tweaking how the inventory management system tracks stock—won't mess with the billing or customer services. This careful separation also means the system can scale independently. If the platform experiences a surge in customer traffic, for example, the customer service component can scale up without disrupting other areas.

Summary

Bounded contexts are at the heart of well-structured microservices architecture. They help tame domain complexity, making systems more manageable, scalable, and resilient. Getting your service boundaries right means you get better fault isolation, smarter scaling, and clear team ownership, all of which add up to a more flexible and robust system.

3. Microservices Design Patterns

There's no question that adopting microservices brings its own set of opportunities and challenges. As systems become more distributed, the complexity naturally ramps up. To navigate these complexities, a set of tried-and-true design patterns has emerged. These patterns offer practical solutions to the common hurdles encountered when designing, deploying, and maintaining microservices. The goal? Keeping your system scalable, resilient, and manageable, no matter how intricate the infrastructure or demanding the application becomes. The diagram showcases a wide range of microservice design patterns, categorized by specific areas such as service communication, data management, fault tolerance, deployment, scalability, security, and observability. Each category, as shown in Figure 3-3, contains essential patterns that address common challenges in building microservices. For example, patterns like Circuit Breaker and bulkhead in fault tolerance ensure resilience under failures, while patterns like API Gateway and Token-Based Authentication focus on securing service interactions. The diagram provides a clear road map for designing scalable, secure, and robust microservices architectures by leveraging these well-established patterns.

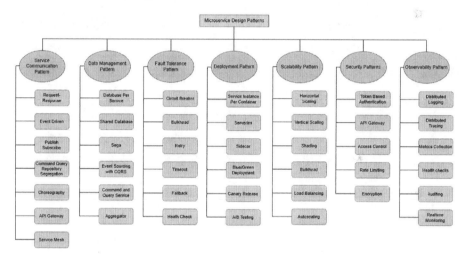

Figure 3-3. *Microservice design patterns*

Table 3-1. *Service Communication Pattern*

Service Communication Pattern			
Pattern Name	**Description**	**Use Cases**	**Challenges**
Request-Response	A classic synchronous communication model where one service sends a request to another and waits for a reply, just like how you might text a friend and sit there anxiously waiting for those three little dots to pop up.	Perfect when you need answers right now, like fetching user profiles or retrieving product details.	This approach can lead to tight coupling between services, increased latency, and if the downstream service decides to ghost you (a.k.a. it's down), it might disrupt everything.
Event-Driven	An asynchronous style where services publish events (e.g., a booking for a meeting room has been made) when something happens, and other services subscribe and act upon them (e.g., add the time to my calendar). It's like sending out a party invite and whoever wants to come, comes.	Good for decoupled systems where you're reacting to things, like processing a user action or interacting with a third-party system.	It can be difficult to keep things consistent, and it's not uncommon for events to get lost.

(*continued*)

Table 3-1. (*continued*)

Service Communication Pattern			
Pattern Name	**Description**	**Use Cases**	**Challenges**
Publish-Subscribe	Services can post messages to a channel, and anyone subscribed to that channel will receive the message. It's the microservices world's version of the group text.	Good for publishing data, such as sending an alert or updating a fleet of services when data changes.	Receiver dropout happens. Messages get jumbled. Like in a group text people might not get the memo.
Command Query Responsibility Segregation (CQRS)	CQRS divides the responsibilities of reading data (queries) and writing data (commands) so that they can scale independently.	Great for systems where reads and writes have different performance needs, like in high-traffic applications where people read far more than they update.	While the performance benefits are solid, keeping your command and query models in sync can feel like juggling while walking a tightrope.
Choreography	A decentralized communication pattern where each service does its own thing in response to events, kind of like a dance routine where everyone knows their moves without a conductor.	Works well for workflows where multiple services need to collaborate without being tightly controlled, like processing an order in an ecommerce system.	If everyone's doing their own thing, it can be difficult to track and understand the flow, and the dance routine can get out of sync.

(*continued*)

Table 3-1. (*continued*)

Service Communication Pattern			
Pattern Name	**Description**	**Use Cases**	**Challenges**
API Gateway	The one-stop-shop for client requests, directing them to the right services, and handling authentication, load balancing, caching—basically everything but making your coffee.	A lifesaver for managing multiple microservices and giving clients a simplified entry point.	If not scaled properly, the gateway can become a bottleneck, slowing down everything. Plus, it adds an extra layer of complexity to manage.
Service Mesh	A dedicated infrastructure layer for managing service-to-service communication. It's like the bouncer for your microservices, handling traffic, security, and ensuring everything goes smoothly.	Use Cases: Ideal for large-scale microservices that need robust communication management and observability.	It can introduce more operational overhead and requires specialized knowledge to implement effectively—think of it as a fancy new gadget that needs a manual.

Table 3-2. *Data Management Pattern*

Data Management Pattern			
Pattern Name	**Description**	**Use Cases**	**Challenges**
Database Per Service	Each microservice manages its own database, promoting loose coupling and autonomy.	Suitable for systems with distinct data requirements, allowing services to evolve independently.	Managing data consistency and integrity across services, often requiring data replication or event sourcing.
Shared Database	Multiple services share a single database, simplifying data management but increasing coupling.	Useful in smaller systems or where data consistency requirements are strict.	Can lead to tight coupling between services, making it harder to scale and evolve the system.
Saga	Coordinates transactions across services by breaking them into local transactions, with compensating actions if needed.	Ideal for multi-step workflows like booking systems or order fulfillment.	Requires careful design of compensating actions and management of data consistency.
Event Sourcing with CQRS	Stores state changes as events, with CQRS separating read and write models for better performance.	Great for systems needing an audit trail, such as financial applications.	Complex to implement, especially in ensuring eventual consistency across services.

(*continued*)

Table 3-2. (*continued*)

Data Management Pattern			
Pattern Name	**Description**	**Use Cases**	**Challenges**
Command and Query Services	Separates services to handle command operations (writes) and query operations (reads), aligning with CQRS principles.	Useful in scenarios where reads and writes have differing requirements, such as in high-read or high-write systems.	Maintaining consistency and synchronization between command and query services can be challenging.
Aggregator	A service that gathers data from multiple microservices to present a unified response.	Simplifies client-side interactions and reduces multiple network calls.	Can become a bottleneck if not designed for scalability, especially with increasing requests.

Table 3-3. *Fault Tolerance Pattern*

Fault Tolerance Pattern			
Pattern Name	**Description**	**Use Cases**	**Challenges**
Circuit Breaker	Acts like a switch that stops sending requests to a failing service after a certain number of failures. It "breaks the circuit" to let the service recover before trying again.	Prevents a domino effect of failures, especially useful when dealing with flaky downstream services.	Tuning the thresholds and timing for breaking and resetting the circuit can be tricky; too strict or too lenient, and you're either blocking unnecessarily or letting failures through.

(*continued*)

Table 3-3. (*continued*)

Fault Tolerance Pattern			
Pattern Name	**Description**	**Use Cases**	**Challenges**
Bulkhead	Isolates different services or functions into resource "compartments," so if one fails, it doesn't bring down the whole system—like watertight compartments in a ship.	Ideal for making sure a high-load service doesn't take down everything else.	Getting the resource allocation right is tricky—allocate too much, and you're wasting resources; too little, and the isolation doesn't help.
Retry	Automatically tries failed requests again after a short interval, usually with increasing delays (exponential backoff), to handle transient issues.	Perfect for dealing with temporary network blips or brief service outages.	If retries aren't managed well, they can actually overwhelm the system, adding load when things are already struggling.
Timeout	Limits the amount of time one service will wait for a response from another before giving up.	Helps avoid delays cascading through the system when one part is slow or failing.	Set your timeouts too low, and you risk cutting off services that are just a little slow; too high, and you're wasting resources waiting for something that won't happen.

(*continued*)

Table 3-3. (*continued*)

Fault Tolerance Pattern			
Pattern Name	**Description**	**Use Cases**	**Challenges**
Fallback	Offers an alternative action or response when the primary service fails, helping the system continue to function at a lower capacity.	Great for degraded modes, like showing cached data when live data is unavailable.	Creating useful fallback responses that don't confuse users or degrade the experience too much can be tough.
Health Check	Continuously monitors the status of services, often used by orchestration tools to automatically recover failing services.	Ensures high availability by detecting failures quickly and enabling automated recovery.	Health checks must be accurate; false positives or negatives can cause unnecessary restarts or missed outages.

Table 3-4. *Deployment Pattern*

Deployment Pattern			
Pattern Name	**Description**	**Use Cases**	**Challenges**
Service Instance Per Container	Each service instance runs in its own container, promoting isolation and independent scaling.	Ideal for microservices that require frequent updates and independent deployment.	Managing and orchestrating a large number of containers efficiently requires robust tooling.

(*continued*)

Table 3-4. (*continued*)

Deployment Pattern			
Pattern Name	**Description**	**Use Cases**	**Challenges**
Serverless	Code runs in response to events without worrying about server infrastructure, offering scalability and cost-efficiency.	Great for event-driven applications, periodic tasks, or workloads with unpredictable demand.	Cold start latency can be a problem and requires proper management.
Sidecar	Auxiliary components (e.g., for logging, security) are deployed alongside the main service in separate containers, extending functionality without modifying core logic.	Best for adding nonintrusive features like monitoring or security without altering the service itself.	Adds complexity to deployment and resource management.
Blue/Green Deployment	Two identical environments (blue and green) allow zero-downtime updates by switching traffic between them.	Ideal when uninterrupted service is essential, such as in high-availability applications.	Duplicating environments can raise infrastructure costs.
Canary Release	Updates are rolled out incrementally to a small group of users, allowing testing before a full release.	Effective for minimizing risk and testing new features before wider deployment.	Requires careful monitoring and a robust rollback mechanism in case of issues.

(*continued*)

Table 3-4. (*continued*)

Deployment Pattern			
Pattern Name	Description	Use Cases	Challenges
A/B Testing	Two versions of a service or feature are compared by splitting users into groups to measure performance, engagement, and other metrics.	Useful for testing changes to determine the impact on user behavior or performance.	Requires solid data analysis and thoughtful design to ensure valid and actionable results.

Table 3-5. *Scalability Pattern*

Scalability Pattern			
Pattern Name	Description	Use Cases	Challenges
Horizontal Scaling	Adds more service instances to spread the load, improving capacity to manage increased traffic.	Ideal for microservices with fluctuating demand, managing peak loads by spinning up additional instances.	Requires robust load balancing and orchestration to ensure traffic is evenly distributed.
Vertical Scaling	Increases resources (CPU, memory) on existing instances to handle greater demand, useful when horizontal scaling isn't practical.	Works well for resource-heavy services or when infrastructure limits horizontal scaling.	Physical resource limits and can become a single point of failure if not managed correctly.

(*continued*)

Table 3-5. (*continued*)

Scalability Pattern			
Pattern Name	Description	Use Cases	Challenges
Sharding	Splits data across multiple databases or nodes, allowing parallel processing for better load management and scalability.	Perfect for large-scale apps with heavy data use, like social platforms or ecommerce.	Complex logic needed for data partitioning and maintaining consistency across shards.
Bulkhead	Isolates system resources for different services, protecting one overloaded service from impacting others, similar to fault tolerance.	Ideal for safeguarding critical services from failures or overload in other areas.	Requires thoughtful allocation of resources to ensure optimal usage without underutilization.
Load Balancing	Spreads incoming requests across multiple service instances, optimizing performance, resource use, and ensuring availability.	Essential for high-traffic apps that need to maintain performance and reliability.	Must properly handle session persistence and stateful services to avoid inconsistencies or degraded user experience.
Autoscaling	Automatically adjusts the number of instances in real time based on demand, optimizing both performance and cost.	Ideal for apps with unpredictable traffic spikes, like seasonal events or variable workloads.	Needs precise monitoring and policies to avoid underprovisioning or excessive costs from overscaling.

Table 3-6. *Security Pattern*

Security Patterns			
Pattern Name	**Description**	**Use Cases**	**Challenges**
Token-Based Authentication	Uses tokens (e.g., JWTs) to authenticate requests, removing the need for traditional credentials like usernames and passwords.	Ideal for stateless authentication, enabling secure access across services in distributed systems.	Managing token life cycle, expiration, and securing token storage requires careful planning and robust measures.
API Gateway Authentication	Centralized authentication and authorization at the API Gateway, managing security for all incoming requests.	Perfect for simplifying security across microservices by handling authentication in a single, unified place.	Can become a bottleneck or single point of failure if the API Gateway isn't properly scaled or secured.
Access Control	Limits access to resources based on roles and permissions, ensuring only authorized users can perform specific actions.	Critical for systems managing sensitive data or needing compliance with security standards like HIPAA or GDPR.	Implementing and enforcing consistent policies across services can be complex and requires careful orchestration.

(continued)

Table 3-6. (*continued*)

Security Patterns			
Pattern Name	**Description**	**Use Cases**	**Challenges**
Rate Limiting	Limits the number of requests a user or service can make within a set time frame to prevent abuse.	Essential for defending against DDoS attacks and ensuring fair resource distribution.	Striking a balance between preventing abuse and maintaining a seamless user experience can be tricky.
Encryption	Protects data both in transit and at rest using encryption methods to ensure confidentiality.	Key for applications dealing with personal, financial, or sensitive data, ensuring regulatory compliance.	Managing encryption keys and mitigating performance overhead from encryption processes can add significant complexity.

Table 3-7. *Observability Pattern*

Observability Pattern			
Pattern Name	Description	Use Cases	Challenges
Distributed Logging	Centralizes logs from multiple services to create a unified view of system activity, helping troubleshoot issues across distributed systems.	Crucial for diagnosing problems and understanding behavior in complex, multi-service environments.	Managing log volume, filtering noise, and extracting meaningful insights require thoughtful planning and tools.
Distributed Tracing	Tracks requests as they move across services, highlighting bottlenecks, latency issues, and dependencies.	Great for optimizing performance and debugging in microservices architectures.	Tracing adds overhead and requires careful instrumentation across services for meaningful results.
Metrics Collection	Gather key performance metrics such as response times and error rates to monitor service health.	Key for proactive maintenance, capacity planning, and ensuring adherence to SLAs.	Ensuring accurate and actionable data collection can be tricky without a strong monitoring infrastructure in place.

(continued)

Table 3-7. (*continued*)

Observability Pattern			
Pattern Name	**Description**	**Use Cases**	**Challenges**
Health Checks	Continuously monitors service health to trigger automated recovery and maintain high availability.	Essential for maintaining reliability and detecting failures early in production environments.	Crafting health checks that reliably reflect the true service status without false alarms can be challenging.
Auditing	Tracks changes and access events for accountability and compliance with regulatory requirements.	Crucial for security and compliance in regulated industries like finance or healthcare.	Balancing comprehensive auditing with performance impact and managing the audit trail efficiently.
Real-Time Monitoring	Provides live insights into system behavior and performance, enabling instant response to issues.	Essential for ensuring optimal service quality in environments that require quick adjustments and optimizations.	Requires advanced tools and infrastructure capable of processing and visualizing data in real time without overwhelming teams.

Let's deep dive into the most used design patterns in detail.

Key Microservices Design Patterns

1. API Gateway Pattern

The API Gateway pattern is like the front door to your microservices universe. It's the go-to point where client requests are funneled in, but it does much more than just open the door. Acting as the middleman, the API Gateway smartly directs traffic to the right backend services while taking care of those behind-the-scenes chores like authentication, logging, rate limiting, and caching as shown in Figure 3-4. Think of it as the helpful concierge that keeps everything in check so clients don't have to deal with the messiness of a hundred different microservices. This approach not only streamlines client interaction but also brings order to the chaos, offering a single, unified interface to manage the complexity.

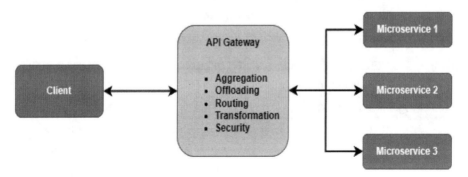

Figure 3-4. *API Gateway pattern*

Why Use the API Gateway Pattern?

Unified Entry Point: Instead of juggling multiple microservice endpoints, clients get the simplicity of a single gateway, like a front desk that knows exactly where to direct you.

Load Balancing: Think of it as traffic control for microservices—spreading out incoming requests so no single service gets overwhelmed, keeping things fast and smooth.

Security: All those security concerns—authentication, authorization—handled in one place, like having a bouncer at the front door, checking credentials for all.

Rate Limiting: It's like crowd control, ensuring your backend services aren't flooded by too many requests at once. Everyone gets in, but at a manageable pace.

Response Aggregation: If clients need data from multiple services, the API Gateway pulls it all together, wrapping up a neat, single response instead of several back-and-forth calls.

Caching: Frequently requested data gets cached, reducing the workload on backend services. It's like having pre-prepared meals at a buffet—you're served faster because it's already there.

Monitoring and Logging: All the activity is tracked in one place, making it much easier to debug issues or monitor performance, like having CCTV footage of every interaction.

Core Concepts

Client: The end-user app, whether it's web, mobile, or desktop, making the requests.

API Gateway: The doorkeeper of your microservices, handling routing, aggregating responses, and managing all those cross-cutting concerns.

Backend Services: The individual microservices that actually do the heavy lifting—handling business logic and processing data.

How It Works

Request Routing: Clients knock on the API Gateway's door, and it figures out which backend service should handle the request, then forwards it on.

Response Aggregation: When a client needs info from more than one service, the API Gateway collects the responses, bundles them up, and sends just one neat response back to the client.

Cross-Cutting Concerns: Whether it's checking if someone is allowed to make a request, limiting how often they can make it, or caching popular data, the API Gateway handles it all seamlessly.

Benefits of the API Gateway Pattern

Simplified Client Interaction: The client only has to deal with one endpoint—no need to remember which service does what.

Centralized Cross-Cutting Concerns: All those annoying-but-essential tasks—authentication, caching, logging—are handled in one place.

Improved Performance: By aggregating responses and caching frequently requested data, the API Gateway keeps things running fast.

Enhanced Security: Centralized security checks reduce the chances of vulnerabilities slipping through.

Scalability: It's built to handle lots of requests and distribute them efficiently across multiple backend services.

Challenges and Considerations

Single Point of Failure: The API Gateway can become a weak link. If it goes down, nothing works—so redundancy and load balancing are musts.

Increased Latency: The extra hop through the API Gateway can slow things down a little—worth keeping an eye on.

Complexity: There's a bit of a learning curve in configuring and managing the gateway effectively.

Scalability: As your traffic grows, the gateway needs to keep up—make sure it's designed to scale.

Summary

The API Gateway pattern is like the Swiss Army knife of microservices—it does a little bit of everything: routing, securing, caching, you name it. It simplifies life for the client, juggles all those cross-cutting concerns like a pro, and keeps your backend services running smoothly. Sure, it has its quirks, like the risk of being a single point of failure (let's hope it doesn't catch a cold!) and adding a bit of latency (nobody's perfect, right?). But overall, it's a superhero in your architecture, quietly saving the day while your microservices shine. With tools like Spring Cloud Gateway, even setting it up in Java feels less like a chore and more like a power move.

2. Circuit Breaker Pattern

The Circuit Breaker pattern is a smart way to avoid those dreaded system meltdowns in distributed systems. Imagine it as a safety valve that prevents a small glitch from snowballing into a full-blown disaster. In microservices, where services depend on one another like a domino chain, one failure could potentially bring down the whole system. Enter the Circuit Breaker pattern, designed to stop that domino effect and handle faults with grace and style. To add another layer of resilience, a fallback method can be used to handle requests when the Circuit Breaker is in an Open state. This fallback method acts as a backup plan, providing either a cached response or an alternative workflow to keep the system running, even if it's at a reduced capacity.

Figure 3-5 describes the life cycle of a Circuit Breaker in a microservices architecture. The Circuit Breaker starts in a Closed state, allowing a request to flow through. If failures occur but remain below a set threshold, the Circuit Breaker stays closed and continues accepting requests. However, once the failure count exceeds the threshold, the Circuit Breaker transitions to an Open state, blocking further requests to prevent overwhelming the service. After a timeout, the Circuit Breaker

165

moves to a Half-Open state, allowing a limited number of test requests. If the connection succeeds, it returns to the Closed state. If it fails, the Circuit Breaker stays Open, giving the service more time to recover. This mechanism helps ensure system resilience by managing faults gracefully.

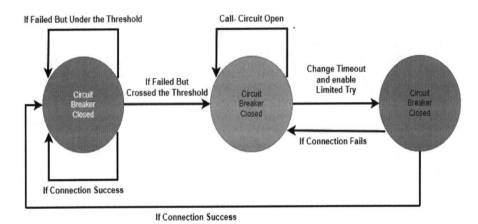

Figure 3-5. *Typical Circuit Breaker pattern*

Why Use the Circuit Breaker Pattern?

Fault Tolerance: Think of it as the system's "nope" button. It stops trying the same failing operation over and over, preventing a total system collapse.

Resilience: It helps the system stay functional even when parts of it are temporarily on the fritz.

Latency and Timeout Management: It's like knowing when to give up early if a service isn't available, so you don't keep waiting forever.

Improved Stability: It helps struggling services by reducing the pressure on them, giving them a chance to catch their breath and recover.

Core Concepts

Closed State: Everything is normal; requests flow as usual. Failures? Just a minor hiccup being counted.

Open State: Uh-oh, too many failures! The circuit breaks, and new requests are stopped before they even start.

Half-Open State: After a short break, the circuit tests the waters by allowing a few requests. If they succeed, things go back to normal (closed). If they flop, back to open it goes.

How It Works

Request Flow: Requests pass through the Circuit Breaker in its normal, closed state.

Failure Detection: It keeps an eye on how many requests are failing and how long each one takes.

State Transition: Based on its rules, it shifts between closed, open, and half-open states.

Fallback Mechanism: When the circuit is open, the system fails fast and triggers a fallback plan—keeping things graceful, not chaotic.

Benefits of the Circuit Breaker Pattern

Improved Fault Tolerance: It stops one failing service from dragging the rest of the system down with it.

Enhanced Stability: It keeps things running smoothly by giving overloaded services a break.

Resilience: It helps the system gracefully bounce back from failures.

Latency Management: If a service is down, it knows to move on quickly, saving users from endless loading screens.

Challenges and Considerations

Configuration Complexity: Getting the settings just right—balancing how many failures are okay before the circuit opens—takes some finesse.

Fallback Handling: Creating smart fallback options can be tricky but essential for making failure feel less, well, like failure.

Monitoring and Tuning: Like any good safety system, the Circuit Breaker needs regular checkups to make sure it's doing its job without slowing everything down.

Summary

The Circuit Breaker pattern is like having a safety net for your microservices architecture. It stops minor failures from turning into big problems and helps keep the system running smoothly. Tools like Resilience4j (`https://resilience4j.readme.io/docs/getting-started`) make implementing this pattern in Java pretty straightforward. When used thoughtfully, the Circuit Breaker can be a game-changer for building resilient, fault-tolerant systems. So, go ahead, break the circuit—before your system breaks itself!

3. Event-Driven Architecture Pattern

Event-Driven Architecture (EDA) as shown in Figure 3-6, is like the rockstar of software design patterns, thriving in dynamic environments where systems need to stay scalable, responsive, and loosely coupled. Instead of components chatting directly with each other, they shout out "events" into the void (or, you know, an event bus), and other components pick up the pieces when they need to. It's like a well-coordinated but completely hands-off conversation happening across a crowded room.

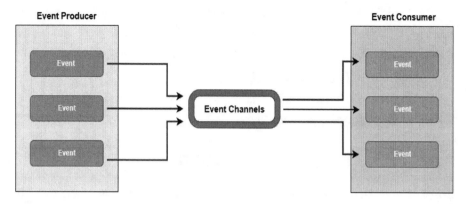

Figure 3-6. *Typical EDA pattern*

Core Concepts

Event: A noteworthy change in state. Think of it as the system's version of a gossip—big or small, it's worth spreading the word. Events are immutable and contain info about what happened.

Event Producer: The one who starts the gossip—this component generates and publishes events.

Event Consumer: The ones who listen in on the gossip, subscribing to and reacting to these events.

Event Channel: The "rumor mill" where the events are transmitted from producers to consumers.

Event Bus/Broker: The middleman who ensures the events are reliably delivered, no matter how juicy or mundane the details.

Why Use Event-Driven Architecture?

Scalability: EDA scales horizontally, handling event processing in parallel like a well-oiled machine.

Loose Coupling: Components mind their own business, leading to a modular, manageable system.

Responsiveness: The system reacts in real time, giving it that zippy feel users love.

Flexibility: Want to add a new event consumer? Go ahead, without touching the producers. Freedom!

Resilience: EDA isolates issues—so if one component fails, the whole system doesn't come crashing down.

Types of Event-Driven Architecture

Simple Event Processing: When an event happens, it's processed. Simple. Great for straightforward use cases like logging.

Complex Event Processing (CEP): This one's for the pros, handling complex event patterns. Use it when detecting fraud or monitoring financial transactions.

How It Works

Simple Event-Driven Example: Order Processing System

Event Producers

- **Order Service:** Generates an "Order Created" event when a new order is placed

- **Payment Service:** Generates a "Payment Processed" event when a payment is successfully completed

Event Consumers

- **Inventory Service:** Subscribes to "Order Created" events to update inventory levels

- **Shipping Service:** Subscribes to "Payment Processed" events to initiate the shipping process

Event Flow

- The Order Service publishes an "Order Created" event to the Event Bus.

- The Event Bus routes the event to the Inventory Service, which updates the stock. The Payment Service processes the payment and publishes a "Payment Processed" event. The Event Bus routes the event to the Shipping Service, which begins the shipping process.

Benefits of Event-Driven Architecture

Scalability: Since events can be processed independently, scaling up or down is a breeze.

Decoupling: Producers and consumers don't have to know each other—they are strangers, ships passing in the night.

Real-Time Processing: Get the info you need the moment it happens.

Flexibility: Add new consumers to the mix without rewriting everything.

Resilience: If one component is down, the others just keep doing their thing.

Challenges and Considerations

Event Ordering: Ensuring events are processed in the correct order can be challenging.

Event Duplication: Handling duplicate events to ensure idempotency is necessary.

Event Schema Evolution: Managing changes to event structures over time without breaking consumers.

Complexity: EDA can introduce complexity in understanding and managing the event flow.

Debugging and Monitoring: Tracking and debugging events in a distributed system requires robust monitoring and logging tools.

Real-Life Example: Online Retailer

Consider an online retailer that uses an event-driven architecture to handle customer orders.

Event Producers

- **User Service:** Publishes events like "User Registered" and "User Logged In"

- **Order Service:** Publishes events like "Order Placed" and "Order Canceled"

- **Payment Service:** Publishes events like "Payment Completed" and "Payment Failed"

Event Consumers

- **Email Service:** Subscribes to "User Registered" events to send welcome emails and "Order Placed" events to send order confirmations

- **Inventory Service:** Subscribes to "Order Placed" events to update stock levels

- **Analytics Service:** Subscribes to various events to track user behavior and generate reports

Event Flow

- A user registers on the site, triggering the User Service to publish a "User Registered" event.

- The Email Service consumes the event and sends a welcome email to the new user.

- The user places an order, causing the Order Service to publish an "Order Placed" event.

- The Inventory Service consumes the "Order Placed" event and updates stock levels.

- The Payment Service processes the payment and publishes a "Payment Completed" event.

- The Analytics Service consumes various events to generate insights and reports.

Summary

Event-Driven Architecture is the MVP (minimum viable product) of scalability, flexibility, and resilience. By decoupling components and letting them communicate via events, EDA lets you build systems that can easily grow, adapt, and recover from failures without falling apart. Sure, it adds some complexity to the mix, but with great power comes... Well, you know the rest. For modern distributed applications, EDA is a game-changer that makes scaling and managing complexity a whole lot easier.

4. Sidecar Pattern

The Sidecar pattern is a clever design approach often seen in microservices architecture, especially when containers and Kubernetes are involved. Picture it as a trusty sidekick, deployed alongside the main application, ready to handle all the auxiliary tasks like logging, monitoring, configuration, and even network communication. This setup lets the primary service do what it does best—focus entirely on its core business logic—while the sidecar takes care of the important but often distracting supporting roles. It's like having an ever-reliable assistant who manages the day-to-day operations, so the hero (your main app) can shine.

Figure 3-7 illustrates the Sidecar pattern in a containerized environment, typically used in Kubernetes. In this setup, a main container runs the primary application, while a sidecar container handles auxiliary tasks like logging, monitoring, or configuration. Both containers are part of the same pod, sharing the same disk, file system, and network resources. This approach allows the primary application to focus solely on its core functionality, while the sidecar takes care of essential supporting services, enhancing the overall efficiency and maintainability of the system.

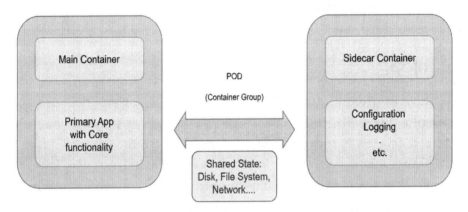

Figure 3-7. *Illustration of how Sidecar pattern works*

Why Use the Sidecar Pattern?

Separation of Concerns: It's like letting the main app be the star of the show, focusing solely on business logic, while the sidecar handles all those behind-the-scenes tasks like logging and monitoring.

Reusability: Think of the sidecar as that multi-tool you bring to every job. It works with different services without needing a tweak, cutting down on redundancy.

Scalability: You can scale the sidecar independently of the primary app, meaning you can give it more resources when needed without blowing up the whole deployment.

Consistency: It's your go-to for uniform logging and monitoring across services—no more "every service for itself."

Ease of Maintenance: You can update or fix your sidecar without even touching the core app, keeping everything running smoothly without any drama.

Core Concepts

Primary Application: The main show. This is your microservice dealing with heavy business logic.

Sidecar Component: The trusty sidekick that handles the supporting tasks—think logging, monitoring, or config management.

Deployment Unit: Usually, a pod in Kubernetes that houses both the main app and its sidecar, keeping them cozy and close.

How It Works

Deployment: Both the primary app and the sidecar are deployed together in the same pod or container. They share the same network and can communicate as if they're neighbors.

Communication: The primary app passes off the grunt work to the sidecar via HTTP APIs, shared volumes, or other methods.

Functionality: The sidecar handles its specific job—whether it's logging, monitoring, or acting as a proxy—then sends back the results, keeping the main app lean and mean.

Benefits of the Sidecar Pattern

Separation of Concerns: Cleaner code, because each part handles its own job.

Reusability: One sidecar to rule them all—use it across services without duplication.

Flexibility: You can update or scale sidecars independently, making tweaks without a complete system overhaul.

Consistency: Logging, monitoring, and config management stay uniform across your ecosystem.

Enhanced Functionality: Add new abilities to your app without rewriting its core code.

Challenges and Considerations

Resource Management: Be mindful of sidecars hogging too many resources and slowing down the main app.

Complexity: Adding sidecars means more moving parts, which can make deployments trickier.

Communication Overhead: There can be extra latency from the back-and-forth between the app and the sidecar.

Deployment Coordination: Make sure both the main app and sidecar are in sync, so they don't end up speaking different languages.

Security: Ensure safe and secure communication, especially if sensitive data is involved.

Summary

The Sidecar pattern is like having an assistant who takes care of the routine tasks, leaving your primary app to focus on what it does best—running the business logic. It brings added functionality, scalability, and consistency without burdening the core service. Sure, it adds some complexity to deployments, but in a well-oiled microservices environment, it's a pattern worth embracing for the long-term gains.

5. Backends for Frontends (BFF) Pattern

The Backends for Frontends (BFF) pattern is like giving each type of client (whether it's web, mobile, or desktop) its own personal backstage crew. Instead of all clients being forced to deal with the same generic backend, the BFF pattern creates a tailored backend service for each frontend, ensuring smoother interactions. This setup boosts performance, tightens up security, and—perhaps most importantly—makes life a lot easier for developers by providing exactly what each frontend needs without unnecessary complexity. It's like crafting a custom suit for each client rather than one-size-fits-all.

Figure 3-8 illustrates the Backends for Frontends (BFF) pattern in action, showing how different frontends—Android, iOS, and Web apps—each have their own dedicated backend services (Android BFF, iOS BFF, Web BFF) tailored to their specific needs. These BFFs communicate with common backend services like Cart, Product, Customer, and Order services, which interact with a shared database. This setup ensures optimized communication for each platform, enhancing performance, simplifying frontend logic, and ensuring a better user experience by tailoring responses to each client type.

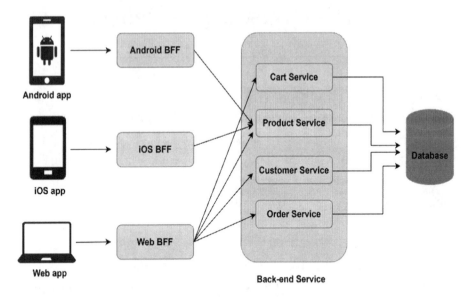

Figure 3-8. *Illustration of how BFF pattern works*

Why Use the BFF Pattern?

Client-Specific APIs: By tailoring APIs to fit each frontend's exact needs, the BFF pattern eliminates the extra baggage of unnecessary data and simplifies the overall interaction, leading to smaller payloads and better efficiency.

Improved Performance: It's like giving your frontend a personal trainer—BFFs optimize how data is retrieved, transformed, and delivered, which means less time waiting around and more time enjoying a seamless user experience.

Separation of Concerns: You wouldn't stuff your living room with kitchen appliances, right? Similarly, BFFs keep frontend-specific logic out of general APIs, keeping things cleaner and easier to maintain.

Flexibility: Want to tweak your mobile app without touching the web version? With BFF, you can independently evolve both frontends and backends, keeping everyone happy without causing unnecessary drama.

Security: By dedicating specific backend services to frontends, you can better control security, reducing exposure to attacks and giving you more peace of mind.

Core Concepts

Frontend: The face of the application, whether it's a mobile, web, or desktop app—the user's interaction point.

Backend for Frontend (BFF): The trusted sidekick of the frontend, handling data fetching, transformation, and all those behind-the-scenes tasks, making sure the frontend gets exactly what it needs, when it needs it.

General-Purpose API: This is where all the magic happens—business logic, data access, and heavy lifting. The BFF communicates with these backend services to get things done.

How It Works

Frontend Requests: Instead of bombarding the general backend, the frontend sends its requests to its own BFF—a service tailor-made for its needs.

BFF Processing: The BFF takes those requests, aggregates data, transforms formats, adds any relevant business logic, and ensures proper authentication.

Response to Frontend: The BFF returns the data, perfectly wrapped and ready for the frontend to display, optimized for that specific client.

Benefits of the BFF Pattern

Optimized Performance: With tailored data responses, the frontend doesn't have to sift through unnecessary info, leading to faster loading times and a smoother user experience.

Custom Tailoring: Like a bespoke suit, each frontend gets data presented just the way it needs—whether it's for a mobile app, web app, or desktop version.

Enhanced Security: BFF lets you apply security measures specific to each frontend, reducing the attack surface and helping you sleep better at night.

Simplified Frontend Logic: The frontend doesn't need to worry about complex transformations or heavy business logic—it just focuses on looking good and being fast, while the BFF does the heavy lifting.

Independent Evolution: Want to revamp the web app but keep the mobile app as is? No problem. BFF gives you the flexibility to evolve different front ends independently.

Challenges and Considerations

Increased Complexity: With great power comes great responsibility—adding multiple BFFs means more services to manage and maintain.

Duplication of Logic: Some logic may end up being repeated across BFFs, which can make maintenance a little trickier.

Coordination: Frontend and BFF teams need to stay in sync, making sure APIs are tailored exactly to what each frontend needs.

Deployment Overhead: With more BFFs come more deployments, meaning you'll need to manage the extra overhead.

Summary

The Backends for Frontends (BFF) pattern is like having a personal assistant for each client type—whether it's a mobile app, web app, or desktop. It optimizes interactions with backend services, ensuring that each frontend gets exactly what it needs in the most efficient way possible. Though managing multiple BFFs can increase complexity, the improved performance, flexibility, and security make it well worth the effort. So, if you want to keep your front ends happy and your backend services running smoothly, the BFF pattern is your new best friend in modern microservices architectures.

6. Security Pattern

Microservices Security Patterns are like security guards at the entrance of your home—they might not be visible, but they are constantly working, keeping your data secure, your services safe, and your hackers at bay. When the Circuit Breaker pattern prevents system failure, security patterns protect against vulnerabilities that could affect the confidentiality and integrity of your application. The distributed nature of microservices creates many opportunities for vulnerabilities (i.e., "back doors"), and using security patterns is like adding a high-security lock and a CCTV system for each one.

Let's dive into how Microservices Security Patterns work their magic, ensuring that your microservices architecture stays resilient, safe, and, most importantly, hacker-free.

Why Use Microservices Security Patterns?

Enhanced Protection: In a microservices setup, security needs to be distributed across all services. These patterns ensure every service is shielded from unauthorized access and data leaks.

Isolation: Microservices operate independently, which means you need to isolate security concerns so that a breach in one service doesn't expose the whole system.

Adaptability: As microservices evolve, security patterns help scale protection alongside, ensuring that security doesn't become a bottleneck.

Reduced Attack Surface: By enforcing strict security measures at every service entry point, you reduce the overall exposure of your architecture to attacks.

Core Security Patterns

1. **Token-Based Authentication**

   What It Does:

   Authentication: It relies on tokens (JSON Web Tokens, or JWTs) to identify users. After the user has been identified, a token is created and sent to the user to authenticate all their subsequent requests. Once this token is presented with the request, the user can access the protected resources.

   Why Use It: Why ask for sensitive credentials back and forth when you can simply use tokens, which are secure, stateless, self-contained, and suitable for distributed systems such as microservices.

   Challenges: Keeping track of token expiration, storage, and refreshing can be tricky. Tokens also need to be secure.

2. **API Gateway Authentication**

   What It Does: Centralized authentication at the API Gateway, where all requests are funneled through before they reach the internal services.

   Why Use It: Simplifies security management by putting the security checks (like verifying tokens, rate limiting, and authentication) at the entry point.

   Challenges: The API Gateway becomes a potential single point of failure if not properly managed. Scaling the gateway to handle high traffic is essential.

3. **Rate Limiting**

    What It Does: Limits the number of requests that a user, service, or client can issue in a given timeframe to prevent abuse, DDoS attacks, and exhaustion of resources.

    Why Use It: Imagine someone continually refreshing your website—without rate limiting, they could swamp your system. This pattern prevents a system from becoming overloaded by repeated requests.

    Challenges: Because it's possible to block malicious traffic while letting good users through, it can be difficult to attain the right balance.

4. **Encryption**

    What It Does: Provides encryption for data in transit (as it travels between services) and at rest (when it's stored in a database or file system).

    Why Use It: Encryption can make the data useless to an attacker, even if they gain access to it, because the information is scrambled without the decryption keys. It's like giving someone a box to unwrap, but not the key to open it.

    Challenges: Storing encryption keys securely, ensuring you don't lose them, and keeping encrypted data flowing at acceptable performance levels can be a balancing act.

How It Works

Authentication Flow: Clients first authenticate through the API Gateway, which checks for valid tokens. If authenticated, requests are routed to the appropriate backend services.

Token Management: Tokens are validated at each service level, ensuring that every service involved in a transaction only accepts requests from authenticated users or other services.

Rate Limiting: The API Gateway or a dedicated rate-limiting service monitors traffic, ensuring no single user or service overloads the system.

Data Encryption: Sensitive data is encrypted before storage or while being transmitted across services, ensuring that even if intercepted, the information remains protected.

Benefits of Microservices Security Patterns

Improved Security Posture: By enforcing security at each microservice, you reduce the likelihood of a breach affecting your entire system.

Scalability: Security patterns are flexible and scalable, adapting as your microservices architecture grows and new services are added.

Layered Defense: By combining different security patterns, such as token authentication with encryption, you create a multilayered defense system—because when it comes to security, redundancy is your friend.

Resilience to Attacks: Rate limiting and API Gateway Authentication work together to prevent attacks like DDoS from overwhelming your services, while encryption protects your sensitive data.

Challenges and Considerations

Token Expiration: Token-based authentication is fantastic, but you need to plan for token expiration and refreshing mechanisms. What happens when a token expires mid-request? You need to handle that seamlessly.

Security Overhead: More security means more overhead—processing tokens, encrypting/decrypting data, and managing rate limits can add latency. Careful tuning is required to ensure security doesn't slow down your system.

API Gateway Bottleneck: While centralizing security at the API Gateway simplifies things, it can also become a bottleneck if not scaled properly. Plus, if the gateway goes down, the whole system could be impacted.

Summary

Microservices Security Patterns are the invisible armor that protects your distributed system from a wide range of threats. They ensure that each service is secure, isolated, and protected from potential breaches.

By integrating patterns like token-based authentication, API Gateway security, rate limiting, and encryption, you create a secure and resilient architecture that can withstand attacks without sacrificing performance. Sure, it adds a bit of complexity, but in the wild world of microservices, security is nonnegotiable. With tools like Spring Security and JWT libraries, implementing these patterns in Java is straightforward, giving you the peace of mind that your system is both scalable and secure. After all, you don't want to leave the backdoor open to your microservices—especially when it's so easy to lock it up tight!

7. Observability Pattern

Microservices Observability Pattern is your backstage pass to your entire distributed system, seeing everything that is happening, diagnosing the problems, and immediately spotting errors. Running a number of microservices can be quite chaotic, and without the right tools it is like looking for a needle in a haystack. Observability patterns are the way to make sense of it all, providing real-time insights into the health, performance, and behavior of your microservices architecture. Think X-ray vision for your system, without the supervillain vibes.

Why Use the Observability Pattern?

Real-Time Visibility: In microservices, every request hops from service to service, and tracing that request's journey is all you need to know about what's going on under the hood. Observability is all about following the path and catching anything that goes wrong.

Performance Monitoring: Slow apps are the most annoying ones. Since no one loves slow apps, except sloths, observability helps you to track performance metrics, such as response times, memory consumption, and throughput, so that you can optimize before things go south.

Fault Detection: What's worse than a bug? A bug you didn't know existed. Observability catches faults early, before they snowball into major outages.

Root Cause Analysis: When something breaks (it will) observability patterns give you a granular trail to figure out why and where.

Proactive Maintenance: Seeing where something is going wrong before a disaster strikes, keeping your system up and your users happy.

Core Observability Patterns

1. **Distributed Logging**

   What It Does: Gather and consolidate logs from different microservices into one place, so you get a unified narrative of what's happening across your system.

Why Use It: Without distributed logging, you'd be trudging around from server to server like a homicide detective, trying to piece together logs. This pattern simplifies that by bringing everything to one place.

Challenges: Logging can be noisy and large in volume. Handling log noise and storing large amounts of data can be a challenge.

2. **Distributed Tracing**

    What It Does: Tracks a request as it flows through multiple services, showing you each hop, time taken, and where things slow down.

    Why Use It: It's like having GPS for your microservices. You can see the full journey of a request from start to finish, perfect for pinpointing bottlenecks or failures.

    Challenges: Implementing tracing across all your services can require a lot of instrumentation. And just like with GPS, sometimes the signal can get a little messy.

3. **Metrics Collection**

    What It Does: Gathers quantitative data on service health, such as CPU usage, memory consumption, error rates, and request latencies.

    Why Use It: Metrics are your pulse. By gathering performance metrics, you can keep a constant heartbeat on the health of your system.

Challenges: Turning metrics into meaningful information—the hard part is knowing what to measure and how to understand the numbers.

4. **Health Checks**

What It Does: Continuously checks the operational health of each microservice, often using a simple HTTP endpoint that returns whether the service is functioning properly.

Why Use It: Think of this as a service's daily wellness check. If a service is struggling, the health check will tell your orchestrator to stop sending traffic its way.

Challenges: Make sure your health checks are ... well, healthy. They need to go beyond "is the service responding?"—they should check that the service is functioning as we expect.

5. **Real-Time Monitoring**

What It Does: Provides real-time dashboards and alerts to monitor system performance and detect anomalies.

Why Use It: Real-time monitoring lets you identify problems as they are forming, not just after they are done forming.

Challenges: Implementing effective alerts can be a balancing act. If you have too few, you miss something important. But if you have too many, your team will get alert fatigue.

6. **Auditing**

   What It Does: Who did what and when. It's your recording angel, the system that keeps track of changes and events related to access, security, and accountability.

   Why Use It: In regulated industries, an audit trail is not a nice-to-have, it's a must-have. You need to be able to prove compliance and traceability.

   Challenges: With lots and lots of data generated by auditing, you really want to keep the information secure but also accessible.

How It Works

Logging in Action: A service logs each event it deals with, such as an incoming request, an error, or the completion of a process. This information is then streamed into a centralized, distributed logging platform (such as an ELK Stack or Splunk) for easy searching, analyzing, and trend visualization.

Tracing the Journey: Distributed tracing walks a request through all the services it touches as it moves through the system. Each request starts with a unique ID. As the request moves between services, the ID gets passed along, tracking the entire route that the request takes. Visualize this flow with a tool like Jaeger or Zipkin to understand where latencies or failures are occurring.

Health and Metrics Monitoring: For each service, a pair of health checks and metrics endpoints are returned. The health check endpoint returns a status on the health of the service, while the metrics endpoint returns data such as memory consumed, CPU load, or request counts.

The data from health and metrics endpoints are then scraped by monitoring tools like Prometheus, Grafana, and Datadog, which convert the data into real-time dashboards.

Auditing for Compliance: User activities and developer operations (such as updates, testing, deployments, etc.) are recorded in an audit log to enable traceability if there are any doubtful activities or unauthorized changes.

Benefits of Observability Patterns

Improved Fault Detection: Observability means detecting faults before they cause a catastrophe. Metrics, request tracing, and logs will tell you when and where something breaks.

Faster Debugging: When you run into some kind of problem, you don't have to guess at the cause or spend hours looking through the code. Tracing and logging will show a trail to get you to the cause of the problem quickly.

Better Performance Insights: Metrics and real-time monitoring allow you to know how your services are performing. You can scale out resources or optimize code just when you need to.

Enhanced Security: You can audit everything that transpires and have a record of who is doing what to whom, whenever the need arises, providing both security and accountability.

Challenges and Considerations

Data Overload: Logging, tracing, and metrics collection generate massive amounts of data. Managing, storing, and making sense of it all can be overwhelming. You'll need a strategy to deal with log noise and irrelevant metrics.

Instrumenting Traces: Setting up distributed tracing across all services requires careful instrumentation, and ensuring every service passes along the trace IDs correctly can get tricky.

Alert Fatigue: Too many alerts can lead to false positives or, worse, ignored alerts. You'll need to fine-tune your monitoring system to only alert on meaningful issues.

Summary

The Microservices Observability Pattern is what holds most modern distributed systems together. Without it, you would be blind in a complex, ever-changing environment, where problems could be happening anywhere, at any given time. With it, you get a deep insight into how your system behaves, performs, and is secure. You will find and fix problems faster, optimize for performance, and run more reliably. With distributed logging and tracing, real-time monitoring, and health checks, these patterns will become an inseparable part of your architecture for creating resilient, scalable microservices. Sure, getting observability is a bit of work, but once you have those real-time dashboards and automatic alerts in place, you'll be wondering how you survived without them. What could possibly be better than knowing exactly what is going on inside your system without having to dive into logs?

Conclusion

As we bring this chapter to a close, take a moment to admire how far you've come in navigating the maze of designing microservices. We've covered the art and science of aligning microservices with business capabilities, taming complexity with Domain-Driven Design, and crafting architectures that are both scalable and resilient. By now, you're probably seeing microservices not just as buzzwords but as dynamic pieces of a larger symphony—each service playing its unique tune while harmonizing with the others.

But let's be real, design is only half the story. It's like planning the perfect road trip—figuring out the destinations and mapping the route is great, but someone's got to start the car, pack the snacks, and handle the bumps along the way. That's where the next chapter, "Developing Microservices," takes the spotlight. Here, we'll shift gears to the hands-on, nitty-gritty process of bringing your designs to life. Expect discussions on building robust APIs; handling dependencies; writing clean, maintainable code; and, of course, embracing failures (because in software development, failure is just another feature waiting to be debugged).

So buckle up, grab your virtual toolbelt, and get ready to turn those beautifully crafted designs into functional, efficient, and downright impressive microservices. It's where the magic truly happens—and where your expertise as a seasoned microservices architect will shine brightest. Let's get developing!

CHAPTER 4

Developing Microservices

Let's dive into this chapter and discover how choosing the right technology stack can transform your microservices architecture. Choosing the right technology stack, when preparing a microservices architecture, isn't just important, it's transformational. Which technology you adopt will either make your app more efficient, faster, scalable, and generally easier to manage, or it will become a jumble. Microservices don't rely on the standard monolith; you can stack different technologies in different services. But flexibility begets responsibility! It's a matter of making the right decisions to make sure you don't turn that adaptability into wrack.

Factors to Consider

When diving into microservices architecture, choosing the right tech stack can make or break your project's success. First off, business requirements take the front seat—what exactly are you solving for? From expected traffic to low-latency needs, ensure that each service fits the business like a glove. Then, think about your team—team expertise matters. Sticking with what they know might just save you from hours of Googling and endless debugging marathons. But don't stop there! Community and support are your secret weapons. Go with technologies that come with an active,

© Sumit Bhatnagar and Roshan Mahant 2025
S. Bhatnagar and R. Mahant, *The Art of Decoding Microservices*,
https://doi.org/10.1007/979-8-8688-1267-5_4

vibrant community. More hands-on deck means more libraries, better frameworks, and quicker problem resolution.

Of course, there's performance and scalability to weigh in. Different services call for different strengths, and some stacks excel at specific tasks—whether you need a CPU-cruncher or a lightning-fast I/O handler, choose wisely. Don't forget about compatibility and integration—microservices don't exist in a vacuum. They need to communicate, sync, and play nice with other parts of your system, so pick tools that integrate smoothly. Finally, keep an eye on the operational complexity. Some tech choices come with added layers of deployment and monitoring headaches. Unless you're into that sort of thing, aim for simplicity where possible.

Technology Stack Components

When deciding on a tech stack for microservices, you're just choosing the tools for the task at hand with flexibility and scalability in mind. Architectural Decision Records (ADRs) play a crucial role here, documenting why specific technologies are chosen, ensuring decisions are transparent, and providing a historical context for future teams. The programming languages such as Java and.NET tend to be the preferred choice for enterprises as they're highly flexible, while Python and Node. js can be utilized for speed in more complex systems. Data storage is generally a matter of each microservice having its own database to remain decoupled, and you may opt for SQL (PostgreSQL or MySQL) or NoSQL (MongoDB (`https://www.mongodb.com/`) or Cassandra (`https://cassandra.apache.org/`)) depending on your data and consistency requirements. Interfacing with services requires communication protocols, RESTful APIs, gRPC, or a messaging protocol such as Kafka (`https://kafka.apache.org/`) or RabbitMQ (`https://www.rabbitmq.com/`) tend to be preferred options depending on whether you need synchronous or asynchronous interaction.

Infrastructure components like containerization using Docker and orchestration using Kubernetes simplify deployment and scaling, and cloud platforms like AWS (https://aws.amazon.com/), Azure (https://azure.microsoft.com/), or Google Cloud (https://cloud.google.com/) deliver managed services which remove overhead. Lastly, DevOps tools (Jenkins (https://www.jenkins.io/), GitLab (https://about.gitlab.com/), or CircleCI (https://circleci.com/) for the CI/CD pipelines, and monitoring and logging systems (Prometheus (https://prometheus.io/), Grafana (https://grafana.com/), and the ELK stack (https://www.elastic.co/elastic-stack)) keep your microservices healthy and up and running. All of these features combined provide a complete, scalable, and efficient microservices platform. By combining these thoughtfully chosen technologies, documented through ADRs, you establish not only a complete and scalable microservices platform but also a system where decisions are guided, consistent, and easily adaptable as needs evolve.

Best Practices

- **Start Small:** Begin with a minimal set of technologies and expand as required. This approach helps in understanding the impact of each technology choice on the system.

- **Consistency Where Possible:** While different services can use different stacks, standardizing where possible can reduce complexity. For instance, using the same programming language or database technology across several services can simplify maintenance.

- **Evaluate Regularly:** As the project evolves and scales, regularly reevaluate the technology choices to ensure they still meet the business needs and operational capabilities.

Summary

Selecting the right technology stack for microservices is a careful balancing act—it's about finding the best tool for each service's unique needs without overwhelming the system with unnecessary complexity. The ideal stack boosts both productivity and performance while keeping operational headaches to a minimum. Flexibility is key, allowing you to adjust and evolve your choices as requirements change, ensuring your architecture stays agile and efficient.

Building RESTful Services

REST (Representational State Transfer) is an architectural style that follows key principles designed to make web services scalable and maintainable. First, it emphasizes statelessness, meaning each client request must include all necessary information for the server to process it without relying on stored session data. It also follows a client-server model, where clients and servers operate independently, only interacting through requests and responses. REST encourages cacheable responses to enhance performance, allowing certain responses to be stored and reused. Lastly, RESTful services must adhere to a uniform interface, ensuring consistent and standardized communication across the system. These principles together provide a solid foundation for building efficient and flexible web services.

REST with its stateless, client-server, and cache-safe architecture is the current standard for creating web services that do their job only. Let's say you're requesting coffee online (who needs caffeine anyway?). You tell the coffee server (a.k.a. the RESTful API), "I'd like a double shot latte, please!"—that's the request. The server processes your order, makes the coffee (or calls the barista service), and hands it back to you—this is the response. But here's the thing: you need to give all the details

196

every time (stateless), because the coffee server isn't keeping track of your previous orders or how many shots you prefer. Every interaction is fresh. Meanwhile, the server is focusing solely on the coffee-making, not worrying about anything else (client-server separation).

Setting Up a Spring Boot Project

Spring Boot is an excellent framework for building RESTful services with Java. It simplifies the development process by providing a suite of tools and default configurations. To get started, create a new Spring Boot project.

Step 1: Set Up Spring Boot Project
First, create a new Spring Boot project. You can do this using the Spring Initializer (https://start.spring.io/) or by setting up the project manually.

Dependencies

- Spring Web

- Spring Test

- Spring DevTools

Sample pom.xml

```
<dependency>
        <groupId>org.springframework.boot</groupId>
        <artifactId>spring-boot-starter-web</artifactId>
</dependency>
<dependency>
        <groupId>org.springframework.boot</groupId>
        <artifactId>spring-boot-devtools</artifactId>
        <scope>runtime</scope>
        <optional>true</optional>
</dependency>
```

```
<dependency>
    <groupId>org.springframework.boot</groupId>
    <artifactId>spring-boot-starter-test</artifactId>
    <scope>test</scope>
</dependency>
```

Step 2: Create the Item Class with Getters and Setters

```
public Item (Long id, String name) {
    this.id = id;
    this.name = name;
}
public Long getId() {
    return id;
}
public void setId(Long id) {
    this.id = id;
}
public String getName() {
    return name;
}
public void setName(String name) {
    this.name = name;
}
```

Step 3: Create the Controller

Create an ItemController class to handle HTTP requests:

```
@RestController
@RequestMapping("/api/items")
public class ItemController {
    private List<Item> itemList = new ArrayList<>();
    @GetMapping
```

```java
public List<Item> getAllItems() {
    return itemList;
}
@GetMapping("/{id}")
public Optional<Item> getItemById(@PathVariable Long id) {
    return itemList.stream().filter(item -> item.getId().
    equals(id)).findFirst();
}
@PostMapping
public Item createItem(@RequestBody Item item) {
    item.setId((long) (itemList.size() + 1));
    itemList.add(item);
    return item;
}
@PutMapping("/{id}")
public Optional<Item> updateItem(@PathVariable Long id,
@RequestBody Item itemDetails) {
    return itemList.stream().filter(item ->
        item.getId().equals(id)).findFirst().map(item -> {
        item.setName(itemDetails.getName());
        return item;
    });
}

@DeleteMapping("/{id}")
public void deleteItem(@PathVariable Long id) {
    itemList.removeIf(item -> item.getId().equals(id));
}
}
```

Step 4: Create the Main Application Class

Create a Spring Boot Rest Application main class to bootstrap the application:

DemoApplication.java:

```
@SpringBootApplication
public class DemoApplication {
    public static void main(String[] args) {
        SpringApplication.run(DemoApplication.class, args);
    }
}
```

Step 5: Run the Application

Run the application by executing the main method in DemoApplication. The application will start and listen for HTTP requests on port 8080.

Step 6: Test the RESTful Service

You can use tools like Postman or curl to test the RESTful endpoints:

- **Get all items**: curl -X GET http:// localhost:8080/api/items

- **Get an item by ID**: curl -X GET http:// localhost:8080/api/items/1

- **Create a new item**: curl -X POST http:// localhost:8080/api/items -H "Content-Type: application/json" -d '{"name":"Item 1"}'

- **Update an item**: curl -X PUT http://localhost: 8080/api/items/1 -H "Content-Type: application/ json" -d '{"name":"Updated Item 1"}'

- **Delete an item**: curl -X DELETE http:// localhost:8080/api/items/1

EXERCISE CHAPTER 4-1

1. Build the above example in any IDE of your choice like IntelliJ or Eclipse.

2. Add 10 items to the list and delete items 7 and 9.

3. Add validation annotations to the Item class:

   Ensure that name and description are not empty or null when creating/updating an item.

   Add validation in the ItemController and handle validation errors using @Valid.

4. Write test cases to verify that validation works correctly, such as ensuring that creating an item without a name returns an appropriate error response.

5. Print list of items.

Explanation of Annotations

Let's go over the annotations used in the provided Spring Boot RESTful service example:

@RestController

- **Explanation:** It combines @Controller and @ResponseBody, which means that the class will handle HTTP requests, and the return values of its methods will be written directly to the HTTP response body as JSON (or another format).

@RequestMapping

- **Explanation:** In the example, it's used at the class level to define the base URL for all the endpoints in the controller. The path specified in @RequestMapping ("/api/items") will prefix all the other paths defined in the controller.

  Example: @RequestMapping("/api/items")

@GetMapping

- **Explanation:** It's used to map HTTP GET requests to specific handler methods. In the example, @GetMapping is used to handle requests to retrieve items.

  Example: @GetMapping("/{id}")

@PostMapping

- **Explanation:** It's used to map HTTP POST requests to specific handler methods. In the example, @PostMapping is used to handle requests to create a new item.

@PutMapping

- **Explanation:** It's used to map HTTP PUT requests to specific handler methods. In the example, @PutMapping is used to handle requests to update an existing item.

  Example: @PutMapping("/{id}")

@DeleteMapping

- **Explanation:** It's used to map HTTP DELETE requests to specific handler methods. In the example, @DeleteMapping is used to handle requests to delete an item.

Example: @DeleteMapping("/{id}")

@PathVariable

- **Explanation:** It indicates that a method parameter should be bound to a URI variable. In the example, @PathVariable Long id binds the value of the {id} path variable in the URL to the id method parameter.

@RequestBody

- **Explanation:** It indicates that a method parameter should be bound to the body of the HTTP request. In the example, @RequestBody Item item binds the JSON body of the request to the item parameter.

Example: @RequestBody Item item

@Autowired

- **Explanation:** It allows Spring to resolve and inject collaborating beans into your bean. In the example, @Autowired is used to inject the ItemService and ItemRepository instances into the controller and service classes, respectively.

@SpringBootApplication

- **Explanation:** It combines three annotations— @Configuration, @EnableAutoConfiguration, and @ComponentScan. It enables auto-configuration and component scanning in a Spring Boot application. In the example, @SpringBootApplication is used to mark the SpringBootRestApplication class as the main entry point of the Spring Boot application.

These annotations are key components of Spring Boot, enabling developers to build RESTful web services efficiently and effectively by simplifying configuration and boilerplate code.

Summary

For our examples, we've seen how to develop RESTful services using Java and Spring Boot. Now you know how to create a project, specify a quick model, implement REST endpoints using annotations, and launch your service. Writing RESTful services is one of the key skills of any backend developer because it helps you develop scalable, maintainable, and interoperable web APIs. Test different endpoints, handle more complicated data structures, and see what else Spring Framework has to offer for your REST services.

Synchronous vs. Asynchronous Communication

In software development, how systems talk to each other—whether they like to chat in real time (synchronous) or prefer leaving messages for later (asynchronous)—makes a huge difference. These communication modes can shape how components manage requests, juggle resources, and respond under pressure. In the world of microservices, where many small services have to play nice together, getting communication right is nonnegotiable. Synchronous communication is like a direct phone call between services: one calls, the other answers, and both wait until the conversation is over. Asynchronous communication is more like leaving a voice message—services can go about their business while waiting for a reply as represented in Figure 4-1. Understanding when to use each of these styles is key to designing microservices that don't buckle under the weight of too many conversations and stay resilient even when one service gets stuck in traffic.

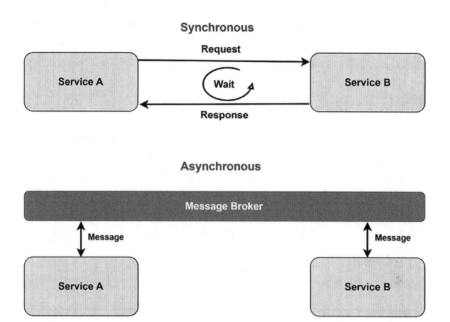

Figure 4-1. This diagram shows two microservice communication styles: **Synchronous** (Service A waits for a response from Service B) and **Asynchronous** (Services A and B communicate via a message broker, operating independently)

Synchronous Communication

Synchronous communication works similar to direct phone call—the client makes a request to the server, waits for the response, then exits. This interaction is instantaneous and tightly coupled so that the client has no choice but to wait until the server gets a response. The perks of synchronous communication? Well, it's pretty simple to grasp and implement. You get immediate feedback since the client knows right away if the request was successful or not. Plus, debugging is easier since everything happens in a neat, linear sequence. But the limitations are equally apparent. Then there is the delay—because the client is waiting on the response, it slows down. Scalability is also vulnerable; if you have a large number of concurrent requests, it will overwhelm the server, which is an unavoidable bottleneck. Fault tolerance is another issue; if the server fails, all dependent services may go down, leading to system-wide disruption.

Example in Java

Here is an example of synchronous communication using REST with Spring Boot:

```
@GetMapping("/{id}")
  public Optional<Item> getItemById(@PathVariable Long id) {
      return itemList.stream().filter(item -> item.getId().
      equals(id)).findFirst();
  }
```

In this example, when the client makes a GET request to **/orders/{id}**, it waits until the server returns the order data. This is the same example we have discussed in the previous section.

Asynchronous Communication

Asynchronous communication operates in a way that lets the client send a request to the server and keep on with its business without waiting for an instant reply. Think of it like firing off an email—you send it, go about your day, and wait for a response whenever it arrives. The reply typically comes through a callback, message queue, or event system.

One of the major perks is that it's nonblocking, meaning the client can juggle other tasks instead of sitting idly by. This makes it ideal for handling a high volume of requests efficiently, boosting scalability. Plus, it enhances fault tolerance—systems can retry failed requests or fall back on alternate solutions when things go awry.

However, asynchronous communication isn't all sunshine and roses. It comes with added complexity, both in terms of implementation and understanding. Feedback is delayed, so you won't get that instant gratification of knowing whether your request succeeded. And let's not forget debugging—tracing the flow of messages can feel like navigating a maze, adding another layer of challenge.

Example in Java

Here is an example of asynchronous communication using REST with Spring Boot. For asynchronous communication, we have to integrate some messaging queues which can store the messages and process them in order so that your main controller can continue to process other items in parallel. For this example, we are using RabbitMQ (https:// www.rabbitmq.com/), but you could also consider using other messaging services like Apache Kafka (https://kafka.apache.org/) to stream data in real time; Amazon SQS (https://aws.amazon.com/sqs/), which is fully managed and perfect for AWS applications; or Apache Pulsar (https:// pulsar.apache.org/), which includes geo-replication and storage in layers.

You choose your messaging system depending on what you need from your application—scalability, message retention, or order guarantees. Below example uses RabbitMQ to show how we can do asynchronous communication with a Spring Boot application.

Add RabbitMQ dependencies in pom.xml:

```
<dependency>
    <groupId>org.springframework.amqp</groupId>
    <artifactId>spring-rabbit-test</artifactId>
    <scope>test</scope>
</dependency>
<dependency>
    <groupId>org.springframework.amqp</groupId>
    <artifactId>spring-rabbit</artifactId>
    <version>3.1.3</version>
</dependency>
```

Configuration class:

```
@Configuration
public class RabbitConfig {
    @Bean
    public Queue queue() {
        return new Queue("rabbitQueue");
    }
    @Bean
    public TopicExchange exchange() {
        return new TopicExchange("orderExchange");
    }
    public Binding binding(Queue queue, TopicExchange
    exchange) {
        return BindingBuilder.bind(queue).to(exchange).
        with("orderRoutingKey");
    }
}
```

Create a dummy OrderReceiver class:

```
@Component
public class OrderReceiver {
    @RabbitListener(queues = "orderQueue")
    public void receiveOrder(Order order) {
        System.out.println("Received Order: "+order);
    }
}
```

Create a dummy OrderSender class:

```
@Component
public class OrderSender {
    @Autowired
```

```
    private RabbitTemplate rabbitTemplate;
    public void sendOrder(Order order) {
        rabbitTemplate.convertAndSend("orderExchange",
        "orderRoutingKEy", order);
    }
}
```

Explanation

In this example, the client sends an order message to RabbitMQ, and the receiver processes it asynchronously. The client does not wait for the order to be processed and can continue executing other tasks.

Binding Bean: Binds the queue (rabbitQueue) to the exchange (orderExchange) using the routing key "orderRoutingKey." This allows messages sent to the exchange with this routing key to be directed to the queue.

@RabbitListener: Tells Spring to listen for messages from the "orderQueue" queue.

sendOrder Method: This method sends an Order object to the "orderExchange" using the routing key "orderRoutingKey." The RabbitTemplate converts and sends the order message to RabbitMQ.

EXERCISE CHAPTER 4-2

1. Build the above example in any IDE of your choice like IntelliJ or Eclipse.

2. Place 1000 orders sequentially and print all of them and compare the program start time and end time between synchronous and asynchronous programs.

Choosing the Right Communication Style

Choosing the right communication style for your system really boils down to your specific needs and constraints. Synchronous communication works best when you need an immediate response, the operations are quick and lightweight, and you're aiming for simplicity in implementation. On the flip side, asynchronous communication shines when tasks are resource-heavy or time-consuming, scalability and fault tolerance are top priorities, and your system needs to handle a high volume of requests without breaking a sweat.

Summary

Mastering the nuances between synchronous and asynchronous communication is key to building responsive, efficient systems. With Java's powerful frameworks like Spring Boot, you've got the tools to handle both styles of communication like a pro. Picking the right communication model isn't just about functionality; it's about making your system smarter, faster, and more scalable. By choosing wisely, you'll keep everything running smoothly while meeting those all-important operational goals and user expectations.

Event-Driven Architecture and Messaging

Event-Driven Architecture (EDA) is like the cool, laid-back sibling of traditional software patterns, where instead of services constantly poking each other for updates, they sit back and wait for things to happen— reacting only when events occur. It revolves around the creation, detection, and consumption of these events, allowing different parts of your system to communicate without being tightly coupled. In EDA, events are small, self-contained packets of information that describe significant happenings within the system, like a customer placing an order or an item running out of stock. This pattern is ideal for distributed systems where flexibility, scalability, and responsiveness take center stage.

With messaging as the backbone of this architecture, services can focus on their tasks while asynchronously listening for events that might interest them. Think of it as a system where everyone is minding their own business but remains ready to jump in when something important comes their way.

Key Concepts, Benefits, and Drawbacks

Event-Driven Architecture (EDA) is based on a few concepts that make it a cost-effective and open way to create distributed systems. Events are actually actual meaningful events that happen to the system—for example, an order being received or payment received. They are produced by event producers, the components that generate these events. In contrast, there are event consumers, the items that react to them by doing something such as updating a database or publishing a message. An event broker or messaging system (the middleware), which acts as a communication channel between producers and consumers, takes care of delivering and receiving events.

EDA brings significant benefits. Decoupling allows components to be loosely tied together, so each can be developed, deployed, and scaled independently. This decoupling makes scalability a natural advantage, as events can be processed by multiple consumers distributed across different services. The system's flexibility shines here, too, since you can easily add or modify producers and consumers without disrupting the entire system. Plus, EDA improves resilience, as event brokers can replay events or persist them, ensuring that failures don't result in data loss and that processes can be retried when needed.

However, EDA is not without its challenges. The complexity of managing asynchronous communication and event flows can increase, especially in large systems. Event duplication or out-of-order processing requires additional handling to ensure consistency. Also, latency can be a drawback in scenarios where real-time responses are critical, as the decoupled nature introduces delays. Lastly, debugging and tracing the flow of events through a distributed system can be more difficult, making troubleshooting more complex than in tightly coupled architectures.

Example in Java Using Spring Boot and Apache Kafka

Let's create a simple event-driven system where an OrderService generates events when an order is created, and a NotificationService listens to these events and sends notifications.

Add Kafka dependencies to pom.xml

```xml
<dependency>
    <groupId>org.springframework.kafka</groupId>
    <artifactId>spring-kafka</artifactId>
</dependency>
<dependency>
    <groupId>org.springframework.kafka</groupId>
    <artifactId>spring-kafka-test</artifactId>
    <scope>test</scope>
</dependency>
```

Configure Kafka

application.properties:

```
#Kafka Configuration
spring.kafka.bootstrap-servers= localhost:9092
spring.kafka.consumer.group-id= order-group
spring.kafka.consumer.auto-offset-reset= earliest
```

Create Order Event Model

```
public class OrderEvent {

    private String orderId;
    private String orderStatus;

    public OrderEvent(String orderId, String orderStatus) {
        this.orderId = orderId;
        this.orderStatus = orderStatus;
    }

    public String getOrderId() {
        return orderId;
    }

    public void setOrderId(String orderId) {
        this.orderId = orderId;
    }

    public String getOrderStatus() {
        return orderStatus;
    }

    public void setOrderStatus(String orderStatus) {
        this.orderStatus = orderStatus;
    }
}
```

Create OrderService to Produce Events

```
@Service
public class OrderService {
    private final KafkaTemplate<String, OrderEvent>
kafkaTemplate;
```

213

```
    public OrderService(KafkaTemplate<String, OrderEvent>
    kafkaTemplate) {
        this.kafkaTemplate = kafkaTemplate;
    }
    public void createOrder(String orderId) {
        OrderEvent event = new OrderEvent(orderId, "CREATED");
        kafkaTemplate.send("orders", event);
        System.out.println("Order event sent for orderId: " +
        orderId);
    }
}
```

Configure Kafka Producer

```
public class KafkaConfig {
    @Bean
    public ProducerFactory<String, OrderEvent>
    producerFactory() {
        Map<String, Object> config = new HashMap<>();
        config.put(ProducerConfig.BOOTSTRAP_SERVERS_CONFIG,
        "localhost:9092");
        config.put(ProducerConfig.KEY_SERIALIZER_CLASS_CONFIG,
        StringSerializer.class);
        config.put(ProducerConfig.VALUE_SERIALIZER_CLASS_
        CONFIG, JsonSerializable.class);
        return new DefaultKafkaProducerFactory<String,
        OrderEvent>(config);
    }

    public KafkaTemplate<String, OrderEvent> kafkaTemplate() {
        return new KafkaTemplate<>(producerFactory());
    }
}
```

Create NotificationService to Consume Events

```
@Service
public class NotificationService {
    public void consume(OrderEvent event) {
        System.out.println("Received order event: " + event.
        getOrderId() + " with status: " + event.getOrderStatus());
    }
}
```

Configure Kafka Consumer

```
@Configuration
public class KafkaConsumerConfig {
    @Bean
    public ConsumerFactory<String, OrderEvent>
    consumerFactory() {
        Map<String, Object> config = new HashMap<>();
        config.put(ConsumerConfig.BOOTSTRAP_SERVERS_CONFIG,
        "localhost:9092");
        config.put(ConsumerConfig.GROUP_ID_CONFIG,
        "order-group");
        config.put(ConsumerConfig.KEY_DESERIALIZER_CLASS_CONFIG,
        StringDeserializer.class);
        config.put(ConsumerConfig.VALUE_DESERIALIZER_CLASS_
        CONFIG, JsonDeserializer.class);

        return new DefaultKafkaConsumerFactory<String,
        OrderEvent>(config);
    }

    @Bean
    public ConcurrentKafkaListenerContainerFactory<String,
    OrderEvent> kafkaListenerContainerFactory(){
```

```
    ConcurrentKafkaListenerContainerFacto
    ry<String, OrderEvent> factory = new
    ConcurrentKafkaListenerContainerFactory<>();
    factory.setConsumerFactory(consumerFactory());
    return factory;
  }
}
```

Expose an API Endpoint

```
@RestController
@RequestMapping("/orders")
public class OrderController {

    @Autowired
    OrderService orderService;

    @GetMapping("/{id}")
    public ResponseEntity<Order> getOrder(@PathVariable
    Long id){
        ResponseEntity<Order> resp = null;
        try {
                Order order = orderService.getOrder(id);
                resp = new ResponseEntity<Order>(order,
                HttpStatus.OK);
        }catch(OrderNotFoundException e) {
            throw e;
        }
        return resp;
    }

    @PostMapping
    public ResponseEntity<Order> createOrder(@RequestBody
    Order order){
```

```
    Order savedOrder = orderService.saveOrder(order);
    return ResponseEntity.status(HttpStatus.CREATED).
    body(savedOrder);
  }
}
```

Explanation

This is just an easy Spring Boot/Apache Kafka event-driven program. There are two services that the application is consuming, OrderService and NotificationService.

OrderService: Order Service that processes orders. When you place an order, the order event (OrderEvent) is created with the order information, like orderId and orderStatus. Then it propagates this event to a Kafka topic named "orders" with KafkaTemplate.

NotificationService: This service will listen for "orders" topic events. It logs the order data whenever it consumes an OrderEvent, showing it received the event and the orderId and orderStatus.

Kafka Setup: The program sets up Kafka producers and consumers on Spring Kafka. KafkaConfig creates the producer factory and template to pass events to, and KafkaConsumerConfig creates the consumer factory and listener container to listen to Kafka events.

ConsumerConfig.KEY_DESERIALIZER_CLASS_CONFIG: This specifies the deserializer class for the keys of the Kafka messages. Kafka serializes data before sending it so a deserializer is required to convert it back into a usable format.

ConsumerConfig.VALUE_DESERIALIZER_CLASS_CONFIG: This specifies the deserializer class for the values of the Kafka messages. The JsonDeserializer class is used here, which converts the message value (stored as bytes) into a JSON object or a POJO (Plain Old Java Object) based on the target data type.

Order Event Model: OrderEvent is an easy model storing order data like ID, status, etc.

OrderController: This controller exposes the REST API endpoints for order administration. The GET request gets an order ID and the POST request adds a new order, and it sends createOrder function to the OrderService, sending the Kafka event.

This implementation describes a minimal event-driven system where services communicate through Kafka, asynchronously, offering a scaled, decoupled framework for handling and responding to events.

EXERCISE CHAPTER 4-3

1. Build the above example in any IDE of your choice like IntelliJ or Eclipse.

2. Build a similar program based on the event-driven approach using Spring Boot and Apache Kafka of User Registration and Notification System. This system manages user registration events and sends notifications when a user successfully registers. It follows the same structure and principles as the order processing system.

Summary

EDA and messaging are the twins of modern software architecture and a great way to create scalable, loosely coupled systems capable of asynchronous communication. Event brokers such as Apache Kafka and Java-based event producers and consumers help programmers build performant, scalable applications that handle high-throughput events. It is not just nice-to-have but absolutely essential to understand EDA basics of messaging systems in today's tech-enabled world. It enables you to build flexible, scalable, and robust architectures that are ready for real-time events.

Service Discovery and Load Balancing

Service Discovery and Load Balancing are like the dynamic duo of modern distributed systems, working together to ensure efficient communication between microservices while keeping the whole operation scalable and reliable. In a microservices architecture, where services are constantly being deployed, scaled, or updated, these components ensure that services can seamlessly find each other and distribute the load without overloading any single instance.

Service Discovery is the system's GPS and helps services find each other dynamically (without having to hardcode dependencies). Service Registry: This is one of the primary components of Service Discovery, which is a single-entry point to keep track of all services, location in the network, and metadata. While the Service Discovery Client is the system component that searches through this registry to identify the services it wants to interface with to facilitate fast and fluid interservices communications. But Service Discovery's major limitation is that it opens the door to Service Registry being a centralized source of failure. When it crashes, services can't find each other anymore, causing communication disruption.

However, Load Balancing is a traffic manager and distributes incoming requests among different service instances so that one of them does not get overwhelmed. This ensures that system resources are used efficiently, response times are kept as low as possible, and there is no service instance that overflows. Load Balancing has different approaches, like Round Robin where the request is evenly spread over multiple instances; Least Connections, which sends requests to the instance with the fewest connection(s); Random, which randomly places service instances to receive new requests; and Weighted Round Robin, where larger instances receive more requests. While it's a good thing, Load Balancing can be problematic. Tracking stateful services, for example, can be very problematic because requests that are needed to be processed by the same instance may be flung out somewhere else, and it can break things.

Though both Service Discovery and Load Balancing are important for scalability and performance, they are not without their challenges. Service Discovery makes things harder to manage (secure) the registry, and Load Balancing creates latency or unbalanced distribution if not properly done. The right amount of balance between these elements will ensure a strong, reliable system capable of adapting to the changes in a distributed microservices architecture.

Implementing Service Discovery in Java

To illustrate Service Discovery in Java, we'll use Netflix Eureka for Service Discovery. Don't worry about Load Balancing, we will learn that in the next section.

Set up Eureka server in pom.xml:

```
<dependency>
    <groupId>org.springframework.cloud</groupId>
    <artifactId>spring-cloud-starter-netflix-eureka-server</
artifactId>
</dependency>
```

Create an application class:

```
@SpringBootApplication
@EnableEurekaServer
public class EurekaServerProjectApplication {
    public static void main(String[] args) {
        SpringApplication.run(EurekaServerProjectApplication.
        class, args);
    }
}
```

application.properties:

```
spring.application.name=EurekaServerProject
server.port=8761
eureka.client.register-with-eureka=false
eureka.client.fetch-registry=false
```

Register a Client Service with Eureka
pom.xml:

```
<dependency>
    <groupId>org.springframework.cloud</groupId>
    <artifactId>spring-cloud-starter-netflix-eureka-client</
artifactId>
</dependency>
```

application.properties:

```
spring.application.name=order-service-client
# Eureka Details
eureka.client.service-url.defaultZone = http://
localhost:8761/eureka
eureka.instance.instance-id=${spring.application.
name}:${random.value}
```

Client Application Class:

```
@SpringBootApplication
public class EurekaClientProjectApplication {
    public static void main(String[] args) {
        SpringApplication.run(EurekaClientProjectApplication.
        class, args);
    }
}
```

Client Service:

```
@RestController
@RequestMapping("/client")
public class EurekaClientController {
    @Autowired
    private RestTemplate restTemplate;
    public String getOrder() {
        return restTemplate.getForObject("http://order-service/
        orders", String.class);
    }
}
```

Create a Config Template:

```
@Configuration
public class RestTemplateConfig {
    @Bean
    public RestTemplate restTemplate() {
        return new RestTemplate();
    }
}
```

Explanation

@EnableEurekaServer: Activates the Eureka Server, making this application act as a service registry where other services can register and discover each other.

spring.application.name: Sets the application name for this Eureka server instance.

server.port=8761: Configures the server to run on port 8761 (the default port for Eureka).

eureka.client.register-with-eureka=false: Prevents the Eureka server itself from registering with another Eureka instance.

eureka.client.fetch-registry=false: Instructs the server not to fetch the registry since it is the registry itself.

spring.application.name=order-service-client: Names the client service as order-service-client.

eureka.client.service-url.defaultZone: Points the client to the Eureka server located at http://localhost:8761/eureka for service registration and discovery.

@RestController: Marks this class as a REST controller that handles HTTP requests.

@RequestMapping("/client"): Sets up a base path /client for this controller.

RestTemplate: A Spring-provided class for making HTTP requests.

getOrder Method: Makes a request to another service (order-service) to fetch orders. The service URL (http:// order-service /orders) uses Eureka for client-side load balancing and resolving the service instance URL.

Eureka Server: The EurekaServerProjectApplication acts as a service registry. It allows other services to register and discover each other.

Eureka Client: The order-service-client registers with the Eureka server. It can also discover other services registered in the Eureka registry.

Service Communication: The EurekaClientController uses a RestTemplate to call another service (order-service) by its name, relying on Eureka for service discovery and client-side load balancing.

Summary

In conclusion, Service Discovery and Load Balancing are the backbone of scalable and resilient microservices architectures. With tools like Netflix Eureka and Ribbon in your Java toolbox, you can seamlessly implement dynamic service registration, discovery, and smart load balancing across instances. Grasping these concepts allows you to build distributed systems that aren't just robust, but also agile and well equipped to handle the scaling challenges of today's ever-evolving digital landscape. It's all about keeping those microservices talking and thriving—without breaking a sweat.

API Gateways and Rate Limiting

API Gateways serve several important functions in a microservices system—they provide the entry point to customers, but also handle multiple backend services. They handle authentication and authorization, which helps in limiting access of non-auth-authorized users or services to highly sensitive backend data, which makes it more secure. The first thing an API Gateway provides is rate limiting, the limit of the number of requests in a day, so that the services are not overloaded, misused, and clients are getting a reasonable share of resources. Another fundamental role is load balancing where the traffic is dynamically distributed across several instances of the service for increased performance, availability, and reliability. Monitoring and logging are also provided by API Gateways with the help of metrics and logs that provide rich system behavior information that allows us to quickly diagnose, analyze, and optimize resource consumption.

However, API Gateways come with their own challenges. One of the most significant drawbacks is the potential to become a single point of failure. If the gateway goes down, access to all backend services is disrupted, making redundancy and failover mechanisms critical. API Gateways can also introduce added latency, as they add an extra hop in the request-response cycle. This complexity extends to management as well, as maintaining an API Gateway adds another layer of architectural intricacy. Lastly, scalability is a concern—if the gateway isn't designed to scale with increasing traffic and services, it can quickly become a bottleneck, impacting overall system performance.

Implementing Spring Cloud API Gateway

Add dependencies to pom.xml:

```
<dependency>
    <groupId>org.springframework.cloud</groupId>
    <artifactId>spring-cloud-gateway-server</artifactId>
    <version>4.1.5</version>
</dependency>
```

Application.properties:

```
#Gateway properties
server.port=80
spring.application.name=GATEWAY-SERVICE
# Eureka Details
eureka.client.service-url.defaultZone = http://
localhost:8761/eureka
```

Configure Spring Cloud Gateway:

```
public class GatewayRoutingConfig {
    public RouteLocator locator;
    @Bean
    public RouteLocator customRouteLocator(RouteLocatorBuilder
    builder) {
        return builder.routes()
            .route("order-service", p -> p
            .path("/orders/**").uri("lb:// order-service"))
            .build();
    }
}
```

In this example, any request that starts with **/orders/**** will be routed to the order-service. The **lb://** prefix indicates that Spring Cloud Gateway should use a load balancer to route the request to an instance of order-service registered in Eureka.

To implement rate limiter, let's create a simple program using Spring Cloud API Gateway and Redis.

Add Redis to dependencies:

```
<dependency>
    <groupId>org.springframework.data</groupId>
    <artifactId>spring-data-redis</artifactId>
    <version>3.1.9</version>
  </dependency>
```

Apply Rate Limiter to Gateway Service:

```
public class GatewayRoutingConfig {
    public RouteLocator locator;
    @Bean
    public RouteLocator customRouteLocator(RouteLocatorBuilder
    builder) {
        return builder.routes()
            .route("order-service", p -> p
                .path("/orders/**")
                .filters(f -> f.requestRateLimiter(c-> c.setRate
                Limiter(redisRateLimiter())))
                .uri("lb:// order-service"))
            .build();
    }
    public RedisRateLimiter redisRateLimiter() {
        return new RedisRateLimiter(10,20);
    }
}
```

In this configuration, the rate limiter is applied to the `order-service` route, limiting the requests to 10 per second with a burst capacity of 20.

Summary

Using Spring Cloud Gateway to implement an API Gateway is a smart move for managing traffic to your microservices with ease. Adding rate limiting on top of that ensures your services don't get overwhelmed and remain efficient, even under heavy load or potential misuse. Spring Cloud Gateway's rich feature set gives you the flexibility to create a robust, scalable, and resilient architecture that can grow with your system's needs. This foundational setup not only handles traffic but also paves the way for you to incorporate essential cross-cutting concerns like security, logging, and monitoring—helping you build a complete and more dependable microservices environment.

Resilience and Fault Tolerance

In a microservices model, services span multiple servers or even data centers and can scale easily but come with some challenges. These include latency, partial failures, and limiting the number of resources. Resilience and fault tolerance become important to ensure the system will be able to take this in graceful fashion and keep functioning despite failures of certain components. Resilience can be defined as the system's capacity to overcome failure and continue to function, and fault tolerance is the system's ability to function correctly under the impact of failure. In order to get those features for microservices, developers use various methods.

Another is to have retries. When a service request is canceled due to some short-term problem, the process retries it automatically. Retries recover from short-term glitches but are also an added burden on the system that may escalate to larger issues if handled incorrectly. Another critical pattern is the Circuit Breaker, which prevents repeated execution of failing operations by "opening the circuit" after a certain number of failures. This strategy allows failing services time to recover without overwhelming them with requests. However, configuring the thresholds for when to open and close the circuit requires careful tuning, as improper settings could either block requests unnecessarily or fail to provide enough time for recovery.

The bulkhead pattern involves isolating different parts of the system so that failures in one area don't cascade and affect others. This isolation can enhance the overall resilience of the system, but it also adds complexity, as resources must be carefully allocated to ensure each bulkhead is appropriately sized and managed.

Finally, implementing fallbacks provides alternative solutions when a service fails, such as default responses or cached data. While fallbacks ensure that the system remains responsive, they can degrade the user experience if the fallback responses are insufficient or outdated.

Despite these strategies, there are potential drawbacks to consider. Retries, if overused, can increase latency and system load. Circuit breakers can disrupt services if misconfigured, and bulkheads require thoughtful planning to prevent inefficient resource utilization. Fallback mechanisms, while useful, can lead to inconsistent user experiences if not designed carefully. Balancing these strategies is essential for creating resilient, fault-tolerant microservices systems that can gracefully handle the inevitable failures that come with distributed architectures.

Implementing Resilience4j

Add dependency to pom.xml:

```
<dependency>
    <groupId>org.springframework.cloud</groupId>
    <artifactId>spring-cloud-starter-circuitbreaker-resilience4j
    </artifactId>
</dependency>
```

Configure Resilience4j in your application.properties:

```
resilience4j.circuitbreaker.configs.default.register-health-
indicator=true
resilience4j.circuitbreaker.configs.default.permitted-number-
of-calls-in-half-open-state=3
resilience4j.circuitbreaker.configs.default.sliding-window-
type=TIME_BASED
resilience4j.circuitbreaker.configs.default.minimum-number-
of-calls=5
resilience4j.circuitbreaker.instances.backendB.
waitDurationInOpenState=10000
resilience4j.circuitbreaker.instances.backendB.
failureRateThreshold=50
resilience4j.retry.instances.backendA.maxAttempts=3
resilience4j.retry.instances.backendA.waitDuration=500
resilience4j.bulkhead.instances.backendA.maxConcurrentCalls=10
resilience4j.bulkhead.instances.backendB.maxWaitDuration=10ms
resilience4j.bulkhead.instances.backendB.maxConcurrentCalls=20
```

Configuration class:

```
@Configuration
public class AppConfig {
    @Bean
    public RestTemplate restTemplate() {
        return new RestTemplate();
    }
}
```

Implementing Bulkhead
Service class:

```
public class ExternalService {
    private final RestTemplate restTemplate;
```

229

```
@Autowired
public ExternalServiceImpl(RestTemplate restTemplate) {
    this.restTemplate = restTemplate;
}

@Bulkhead(name="serviceBulkhead")
@CircuitBreaker(name="serviceCB", fallbackMethod="fallback")
@Retry(name="serviceRetry")
public String callExternalService() {
    return restTemplate.getForObject("http://external-
    service/api", String.class);
}

public String fallback(Throwable t) {
    return "Fallback response due to: " + t.getMessage();
}
}
```

Create a Rest Controller class to test resiliency:

```
@RestController
@RequestMapping("/api")
public class ApiController {

    @Autowired
    private ExternalService externalService;
    @GetMapping("/external")
    public String callExternal() {
        return externalService.callExternalService();
    }
}
```

In This Example

- The **@CircuitBreaker** annotation is used to wrap the callExternalService method. If the method fails repeatedly, the circuit breaker will open, preventing further calls until the service recovers.

- The **@Retry** annotation automatically retries the callExternalService method if it fails.

- The fallback method provides a fallback response when the circuit breaker opens.

- The **@Bulkhead** annotation limits the number of concurrent calls to callExternalService to five.

- If more than five concurrent calls are made, additional calls will wait up to one second before failing.

- When you make a GET request to /api/external, the ExternalService will be called with resilience patterns applied.

- resilience4j.circuitbreaker.configs.default.register-health-indicator=true: Enables the health indicator for the default circuit breaker configuration, allowing it to be monitored via Spring Actuator.

- resilience4j.circuitbreaker.configs.default.permitted-number-of-calls-in-half-open-state=3: Specifies the number of test calls allowed when the circuit breaker is in the half-open state to decide whether to transition back to closed or remain open.

- resilience4j.circuitbreaker.configs.default.sliding-window-type=TIME_BASED: Configures the circuit breaker to use a time-based sliding window for evaluating metrics like failure rate.

- resilience4j.circuitbreaker.configs.default.minimum-number-of-calls=5: Sets the minimum number of calls that must be made before the circuit breaker starts evaluating metrics like failure rate.

- resilience4j.circuitbreaker.instances.backendB.waitDurationInOpenState=10000: Specifies the duration (in milliseconds) the circuit breaker will remain in the open state before transitioning to half-open. Here, it's ten seconds.

- resilience4j.circuitbreaker.instances.backendB.failureRateThreshold=50: Sets the failure rate threshold (in percentage). If 50% or more of the calls fail, the circuit breaker will open.

- resilience4j.retry.instances.backendA.maxAttempts=3: Defines the maximum number of retry attempts for backendA before giving up.

- resilience4j.retry.instances.backendA.waitDuration=500: Specifies the wait time (in milliseconds) between retry attempts for backendA. Here, it waits 500ms between retries.

- resilience4j.bulkhead.instances.backendA.maxConcurrentCalls=10: Limits the maximum number of concurrent calls allowed for backendA to prevent overload.

- resilience4j.bulkhead.instances.backendB. maxWaitDuration=10ms: Sets the maximum time (10 milliseconds) that a call can wait in the queue if the bulkhead's concurrent call limit is reached.

- resilience4j.bulkhead.instances.backendB. maxConcurrentCalls=20: Specifies the maximum number of concurrent calls allowed for backendB.

Summary

Crafting resilient and fault-tolerant Java applications is like building a system with a built-in superhero cape—ready to swoop in and save the day when things go wrong (which they inevitably will). In distributed environments, where services can fail or slow down, these principles become the glue that holds everything together. Implementing patterns like the trusty Circuit Breaker or adding retry mechanisms is like giving your app a second chance to succeed. These techniques help minimize disruptions and keep things running smoothly, even when the unexpected strikes.

And here's where frameworks like Resilience4j and Spring Retry come in, turning these strategies into easy-to-apply solutions for boosting reliability. By weaving resilience into the fabric of your Java applications, you're not just preventing total system meltdowns—you're also ensuring that when things go south, your app knows how to bounce back with style and grace. High availability? Check. Calm in the storm? Double-check.

Conclusion

Congrats, you've completed one of the most critical steps in this microservices journey! This chapter went from figuring out what technology stack to go with, creating RESTful services using Spring Boot, and even getting in the communication lane to know synchronous vs.

asynchronous interactions. We dived into the firepower of event-driven architecture, highlighted service discovery and load balancing, and concluded with an overview of resilience design patterns such as retries, circuit breakers, and bulkheads. Quite the whirlwind, isn't it? But now you have a solid starting point for an efficient and secure microservices ecosystem. This isn't the end of the story! It's not all about creating microservices. We now proceed to the equally important step: testing, deployment, and scaling. This chapter was about creating services, but the next chapter is about "how do we make these services work in the real world?"

We will dive into unit testing and integration testing to verify individual services and interactions. So put on your work gloves, load up your testing tools, and take a look into the seamless deployments and scalable architectures. It's still a long ride, and believe me, it'll be worth every line of code.

CHAPTER 5

Testing, Deploying, and Scaling Microservices

Testing microservices is like shepherding a flock of wild and naughty cats. Each service is its own—autonomously created, delivered, and scaled—yet they all must operate perfectly. Where monoliths have a little bit easier testing, microservices have the added challenge of making each service integrate with others. The goal is not merely that one service does function, but that it communicates, handles failures gracefully, and doesn't doom the system like dominoes.

Let's dive into this chapter and see how to solve the testing problems in microservices. Testing microservices isn't as fun as swinging chainsaws, and using the right strategies and resources, you can build a testing process that's robust, effective, and, yes, fun. Buckle up because we're going to pack your microservices for the wild without stressing out your day.

© Sumit Bhatnagar and Roshan Mahant 2025
S. Bhatnagar and R. Mahant, *The Art of Decoding Microservices*,
https://doi.org/10.1007/979-8-8688-1267-5_5

Unit Testing

Unit testing acts as your individual performance evaluation of each microservices puzzle. When working with microservices, unit testing involves being able to focus on individual pieces—tiny units of functionality—and verifying they are doing what they're supposed to do by themselves. This is testing them in isolation, where they don't interact with any other component of the system, ensuring each one works exactly as intended. Consider it as a prevention for problems when all the bells and whistles are working together.

For microservices, where every service runs in isolation but must integrate with the ecosystem, unit testing is even more essential. Not only checking that a function returns the correct value, but making sure your microservices are able to stand on their own when deployed out in the world. The benefit of microservices unit testing is that you can be assured of the quality of your code before it gets to other integrated tests. Plus, catching errors early in the process means less stress later down the road—and who doesn't want that?

Example: Unit Testing with JUnit and Mockito

Add Dependencies

```
<dependency>
    <groupId>org.springframework.boot</groupId>
    <artifactId>spring-boot-starter-test</artifactId>
    <scope>test</scope>
</dependency>
```

Create a Simple Service Class
ItemService.java:

```java
public interface ItemService {
    public List<Item> getAllItems();
    public Optional<Item> getItemById(Long id);
    public void addItem(Item item);
}
@Service
public class ItemServiceImpl implements ItemService {
    private List<Item> items = new ArrayList<>();
    @Override
    public List<Item> getAllItems() {
        return items;
    }

    @Override
    public Optional<Item> getItemById(Long id) {
        return items.stream().filter(item -> item.getId().
        equals(id)).findFirst();
    }

    @Override
    public void addItem(Item item) {
        items.add(item);
    }
}
```

Create Unit Tests

```java
public class ItemServiceTest {

    @InjectMocks
    private ItemService itemService;
```

```
@BeforeEach
public void setup() {
   MockitoAnnotations.openMocks(this);

   Item item1 = new Item(1L, "Item 1");
   Item item2 = new Item(2L, "Item 2");
   itemService.addItem(item1);
   itemService.addItem(item1);
}

@Test
public void testGetAllItems() {
   List<Item> items = itemService.getAllItems();
   assertEquals(2, items.size());

}

@Test
public void testGetItemById() {
   Optional<Item> item = itemService.getItemById(1L);
   assertTrue(item.isPresent());
   assertEquals("Item 1", item.get().getName());
}
}
```

Breakdown of the Code

- **@InjectMocks Annotation:** The itemService object is annotated with **@InjectMocks**, which tells Mockito to inject any necessary dependencies into ItemService when creating the instance. It facilitates the testing of ItemService in isolation.

- **setup() Method:** This method is annotated with **@BeforeEach**, meaning it will run before each test case, setting up the necessary test environment.

- The method calls MockitoAnnotations. openMocks(this); to initialize the mocks and inject dependencies into itemService.

- **spring-boot-starter-test:** This dependency is a comprehensive testing toolkit provided by Spring Boot. It includes a set of libraries and tools to support different types of testing, such as unit testing, integration testing, and more, for example, JUnit (primary framework for writing and running tests), Mockito (framework for creating and managing mock objects), AssertJ (fluent assertion library for making test assertions more readable and expressive), etc.

EXERCISE CHAPTER 5-1

---

1. Build the above example in any IDE of your choice like IntelliJ or Eclipse.

2. Write the JUnits for all the controllers we have created so far.

Integration Testing for Microservices in Java

Integration testing for microservices involves testing interactions between microservices components or with external dependencies such as databases or other services.

Integration testing verifies that different parts of the application work together as expected.

Example: Integration Testing with Spring Boot

Create a Simple REST Controller

```
@RestController
@RequestMapping("/api/items")
public class ItemController {
    private List<Item> itemList = new ArrayList<>();

    @GetMapping
    public List<Item> getAllItems() {
        return itemList;
    }

    @GetMapping("/{id}")
    public Optional<Item> getItemById(@PathVariable Long id) {
        return itemList.stream().filter(item -> item.getId().
        equals(id)).findFirst();
    }

    @PostMapping
    public Item createItem(@RequestBody Item item) {
        item.setId((long) (itemList.size() + 1));
        itemList.add(item);
        return item;
    }

    @PutMapping("/{id}")
    public Optional<Item> updateItem(@PathVariable Long id,
    @RequestBody Item itemDetails) {
```

```
        return itemList.stream().filter(item -> item.getId().
        equals(id)).findFirst().map(item -> {
            item.setName(itemDetails.getName());
            return item;
        });
    }

    @DeleteMapping("/{id}")
    public void deleteItem(@PathVariable Long id) {
        itemList.removeIf(item -> item.getId().equals(id));
    }
}
```

Create Integration Tests

```
@SpringBootTest
@AutoConfigureMockMvc

public class ItemControllerIntegrationTest {
    @Autowired
    private MockMvc mockMvc;
    @Test
    public void testGetAllItems() throws Exception {
        mockMvc.perform(get("/api/items"))
                .andExpect(status().isOk())
                .andExpect(content().contentType(MediaType.
                APPLICATION_JSON))
                .andExpect(jsonPath("$", org.hamcrest.Matchers.
                hasSize(0)));
    }

    @Test
    public void testAddAndGetItem() throws Exception {
        Item item = new Item(1L, "Item1");
```

```
    mockMvc.perform(post("/api/items")
                    .contentType(MediaType.
                    APPLICATION_JSON)
                    .content(new ObjectMapper().
                    writeValueAsString(item)))
            .andExpect(status().isOk());

    mockMvc.perform(get("/api/items"))
            .andExpect(status().isOk())
            .andExpect(content().contentType(MediaType.
            APPLICATION_JSON))
            .andExpect(jsonPath("$", org.hamcrest.Matchers.
            hasSize(1)))
            .andExpect(jsonPath("$[0].name").
            value("Item 1"));
    }
}
```

Short Explanation

@Autowired MockMvc: MockMvc is used to simulate HTTP requests and test the web layer without starting the entire server. It allows for testing controllers directly.

@SpringBootTest: Loads the full application context, including repositories and services. Use this for full end-to-end integration tests.

@AutoConfigureMockMvc: Enables MockMvc in the context.

End-to-End Testing for Microservices in Java

End-to-end testing verifies the entire application flow, involving multiple services, to ensure that everything works together as expected.

Example: End-to-End Testing

**Create End-to-End Test Class
ItemEndToEndTest.java:**

```java
@SpringBootTest
@AutoConfigureMockMvc
public class ItemEndToEndTest {

    @Autowired
    private MockMvc mockMvc;

    @Test
    public void testEndToEnd() throws Exception {
        Item item = new Item(1L, "Item 1");

        mockMvc.perform(post("/api/items")
                        .contentType(MediaType.
                        APPLICATION_JSON)
                        .content(new ObjectMapper().
                        writeValueAsString(item)))
                .andExpect(status().isOk());

        mockMvc.perform(post("/api/items"))
                .andExpect(status().isOk())
                .andExpect(content().contentType(MediaType.
                APPLICATION_JSON))
                .andExpect(jsonPath("$", org.hamcrest.Matchers.
                hasSize(1)))
                .andExpect(jsonPath("$[0]. name").
                value("Item 1"));
    }
}
```

Explanation

The test checks if the entire flow of adding an item and retrieving it works as expected by simulating API calls and verifying that the response matches the expected outcome. This ensures that the ItemController behaves correctly under real-world conditions, validating both the input processing and the output response structure.

Summary

Wrapping things up, unit testing and integration testing are nonnegotiable when it comes to building reliable, high-performing microservices. These practices aren't just about checking a box—they're about catching issues early, before they snowball into bigger problems. The sooner bugs are squashed, the smoother your services run, and the happier your users will be. Getting a solid grasp of how to apply these testing strategies in your Java microservices arsenal can seriously boost the scalability and resilience of your applications, making sure they hit both technical and business targets head-on. So, test early, test often, and make your microservices bulletproof!

Contract Testing

In microservices architecture, reliable communication between services is the glue that holds the system together. Contract testing steps in to ensure these interactions are validated without the heavy lift of traditional integration testing. Unlike full-blown integration tests where services directly communicate, contract testing focuses on the agreements—or contracts—between a service provider and a consumer. Think of it like making sure everyone's agreed on the plan before diving into execution. This approach reduces integration issues and allows services to be developed and deployed independently.

Why Contract Testing Matters

One of the primary benefits of contract testing is the early detection of issues. By validating service interactions during development, teams can catch integration problems before they make their way into production. This proactive approach helps avoid the dreaded last-minute scramble to fix broken connections right before a release.

Contract testing also supports independent development. Since each service has its own contract, teams can develop and deploy services without having to wait on each other. This separation of concerns speeds up development cycles and ensures that when services finally interact, they'll do so smoothly.

Stability is another key advantage of contract testing. With services adhering strictly to predefined contracts, there's less risk of unexpected behavior once everything is in production. It's like having a solid handshake agreement in place that ensures everyone is playing by the same rules.

Finally, contract testing fits beautifully into continuous integration and delivery (CI/CD) pipelines. Fast feedback from contract tests helps developers know right away if something isn't aligning between services, making automated deployments smoother and more reliable.

The Challenges

Of course, contract testing isn't without its hurdles. One major challenge is maintaining the contracts themselves. As services evolve and change, keeping contracts up to date can become a real task. If the contracts don't reflect current service interactions, their usefulness quickly diminishes.

Tooling complexity is another challenge. Integrating contract testing into CI/CD pipelines can sometimes feel like a balancing act. Depending on the tools and technologies in play, getting everything to work seamlessly can require some effort and fine-tuning.

Finally, there's the issue of service dependencies. During testing, you may have to deal with external services or databases, which adds layers of complexity. Simulating those dependencies accurately while keeping the tests isolated can be tricky.

Typically, contract tests are written by the service provider and shared with the consumer to ensure both sides are on the same page. It's a bit like agreeing on the rules before playing the game—once everyone's aligned, things move forward much more smoothly.

Let's create a sample Java program to understand how contract testing works. We'll create a simple scenario where a consumer service calls a provider service to fetch a list of products. If your service ecosystem is using only Spring Boot, then you can use spring-cloud-starter-contract-verifier, but if other consumers are using other languages like Node.js, Python, etc., then they will likely face difficulties with it. Companies with diverse technology stacks may face challenges in standardizing contract testing. They often rely on polyglot-friendly tools (e.g., Pact, Postman, or OpenAPI contracts). Let's see how to implement contract testing using a simple Pact example.

Example: Contract Testing Using Pact

Set Up the Provider Service

Create a Spring Boot project for the provider service:

```
<dependency>
    <groupId>au.com.dius.pact.provider</groupId>
    <artifactId>junit5</artifactId>
    <version>4.5.5</version>
    <scope>test</scope>
</dependency>
```

Create a REST controller in the provider service.

Product.java:

```java
public class Product {
    private Long id;
    private String name;
    private String description;
    public Product() {}
    public Product(Long id, String name, String description) {
        super();
        this.id = id;
        this.name = name;
        this.description = description;
    }
    public Long getId() {
        return id;
    }
    public void setId(Long id) {
        this.id = id;
    }
    public String getName() {
        return name;
    }

    public void setName(String name) {
        this.name = name;
    }
public String getDescription() {
        return description;
    }
    public void setDescription(String description) {
        this.description = description;
    }
}
```

ProductController.java:

```
@RestController
@RequestMapping("/api/products")
public class ProductController {
    public List<Product> getAllProducts(){
        return Arrays.asList(
                new Product(1L, "Product 1", "Description 1"),
                new Product(2L, "Product 2", "Description 2")
                );
    }
}
```

Consumer Side: Pact Test

```
<dependencies>
    <dependency>
        <groupId>au.com.dius.pact.consumer</groupId>
        <artifactId>junit5</artifactId>
        <version>4.6.5</version>
        <scope>test</scope>
    </dependency>
    <dependency>
        <groupId>io.rest-assured</groupId>
        <artifactId>rest-assured</artifactId>
        <version>5.3.0</version>
        <scope>test</scope>
    </dependency>
</dependencies>
```

This test creates a Pact contract where the consumer expects the /api/ products endpoint to return a list of products with specific fields.

```
import au.com.dius.pact.consumer.dsl.PactDslWithProvider;
import au.com.dius.pact.consumer.junit5.PactConsumerTestExt;
import au.com.dius.pact.consumer.junit5.PactTestFor;
import au.com.dius.pact.consumer.dsl.PactDslJsonArray;
import au.com.dius.pact.core.model.annotations.Pact;
import au.com.dius.pact.core.model.PactSpecVersion;
import io.restassured.RestAssured;
import org.junit.jupiter.api.Test;
import org.junit.jupiter.api.extension.ExtendWith;

import java.util.Map;

import static org.hamcrest.Matchers.equalTo;

@ExtendWith(PactConsumerTestExt.class)
public class ProductConsumerPactTest {

    @Pact(consumer = "ProductConsumer", provider =
    "ProductProvider")
    public au.com.dius.pact.core.model.RequestResponsePact
    createPact(PactDslWithProvider builder) {
        return builder
                .given("Products exist")
                .uponReceiving("A request to get all products")
                .path("/api/products")
                .method("GET")
                .willRespondWith()
                .status(200)
                .body(PactDslJsonArray.arrayMinLike(2)
                        .object("id", 1L)
```

```
                            .stringType("name", "Product 1")
                            .stringType("description",
                            "Description 1"))
                    .toPact();
    }

    @Test
    @PactTestFor(providerName = "ProductProvider", pactVersion
    = PactSpecVersion.V3)
    public void testGetAllProducts(MockServer mockServer) {
        RestAssured
                    .given()
                    .baseUri(mockServer.getUrl())
                    .when()
                    .get("/api/products")
                    .then()
                    .statusCode(200)
                    .body("[0].name", equalTo("Product 1"))
                    .body("[0].description",
                    equalTo("Description 1"));
    }
}
```

Provider Side: Pact Verification Test

```
<dependency>
    <groupId>au.com.dius.pact.provider</groupId>
    <artifactId>junit5</artifactId>
    <version>4.6.5</version>
    <scope>test</scope>
</dependency>
```

Provider Pact Test Code

```
import au.com.dius.pact.provider.junit5.
PactVerificationContext;
import au.com.dius.pact.provider.junit5.PactVerificationTest;
import org.junit.jupiter.api.BeforeEach;
import org.junit.jupiter.api.TestTemplate;
import org.junit.jupiter.api.extension.ExtendWith;

@ExtendWith(PactVerificationTest.class)
public class ProductProviderPactTest {

    @BeforeEach
    void setup(PactVerificationContext context) {
        context.setTarget(new HttpTestTarget("localhost",
        8080, "/"));
    }

    @TestTemplate
    @ExtendWith(PactVerificationTest.class)
    void pactVerificationTestTemplate(PactVerificationContext
    context) {
        context.verifyInteraction();
    }
}
```

Steps to Execute

1. **Run Consumer Test:** Execute
   ProductConsumerPactTest to generate a Pact file in
   the target/pacts folder.

2. **Share the Pact File:** Share the generated .json Pact
   file with the provider team.

3. **Run Provider Test:** Start your application (e.g., ProductController). Execute ProductProviderPactTest to verify the provider adheres to the consumer expectations.

Explanation

The provided code demonstrates contract testing using Pact to ensure that the consumer (ProductConsumer) and provider (ProductProvider) adhere to an agreed-upon contract for the /api/products endpoint. On the consumer side, the Pact test defines the expected interaction with the provider, specifying that a GET request to /api/products should return a 200 status and a JSON array of products with specific fields (ID, name, description). It uses Rest Assured to validate the response against these expectations. On the provider side, the Pact verification test ensures that the actual implementation of the provider meets the expectations defined in the Pact file generated by the consumer test. This ensures compatibility between the microservices without direct integration during development.

@ExtendWith(PactConsumerTestExt.class): Used in consumer tests to integrate Pact's consumer test functionality with JUnit 5.

@Pact: Marks a method as defining a Pact interaction. It is used to specify the consumer-provider contract, including request and response details.

@PactTestFor: Specifies the provider name and the Pact specification version (e.g., V3) to be used during the test. It also configures the mock server that simulates the provider during the consumer test.

@BeforeEach: A standard JUnit 5 annotation that runs the annotated method before each test. In the provider test, it sets up the Pact verification context with the target provider URL.

@TestTemplate: A JUnit 5 annotation used to define reusable test templates. In Pact, it's used for running the interaction verification for all the Pact interactions in the contract.

@PactVerificationTest: Extends the JUnit 5 test with Pact's provider-side verification functionality to validate that the actual provider implementation adheres to the consumer's expectations.

Summary

Contract testing is a powerful tool for ensuring that your microservices play nice with each other, sticking to their promises (or contracts) like a well-behaved orchestra. With Spring Cloud Contract, you can take the guesswork out of service interactions, automatically generating and validating contracts to keep everything in harmony. This approach not only makes your microservices more reliable but also keeps integration issues at bay. In this guide, we scratched the surface with a simple example to help you kickstart contract testing in a microservices setup using Java and Spring Boot. Now you're all set to take your services from good to gold!

Deploying and Scaling Microservices

Containers and orchestration are changing how modern software is written, deployed, and operated. It's no longer clunky installations where application transfer was an effort. With containerization today, the software deployment has become a bit like putting together an optimally structured suitcase—light, fast, portable, and quick. The leading technologies driving this change are Docker and Kubernetes—the two technologies which, when combined, allow you to handle containers and deploy them at scale seamlessly. This chapter covers containers, Docker, and Kubernetes in brief and shows how you can use them with an easy Java example.

Containers are boxes that come together as a unit and bundle up your app along with its dependencies, libraries, and settings. This means your app will work properly every time regardless of where it is—whether it's on your home machine, test server, or production server. Docker makes deploying, managing, and creating these containers easy. It makes it easy for you to develop, ship, and consume your apps in any destination, with little to no effort.

With Docker, it's all about building blocks. The first are images, which are read-only templates for container design. You can see the image as a schematic of what is inside the box. Once you have an image, you create a container, which is a live instance of the image running in a single lightweight container. This is another essential feature of Docker; this is the recipe that Docker consumes to create your image. And finally, there's Docker Hub, a giant registry of premade Docker images to share. So, it's a store where you can buy pictures and get projects started or sell your own.

One of the reasons that Docker has become a popular choice among developers is because of its stability. It removes the "works on my machine" flaw in your application by ensuring your app always performs the same regardless of the place it's deployed. In addition, Docker isolates you so your apps don't communicate with one another or with the host system. Portability of Docker is incredible—move your app from your laptop to the cloud and do not miss a beat. Furthermore, with Docker being light, you can deploy more containers on the same hardware to get the most out of the available resources.

We've now got the basics of Docker in our hands, so let's dive right into Kubernetes, the orchestration platform that turns container management into a finely tuned ballet. Kubernetes will let you deploy, scale, and manage your containers in a distributed infrastructure while keeping them neat and organized.

In this Docker and Kubernetes journey, we're only starting but it's only the beginning!

Kubernetes for Orchestration

In container orchestration, Kubernetes is the container's air traffic controller. Docker helps you bundle your applications into containers, but Kubernetes takes over container management. It automatically does deployment and scaling and even does the hardest thing—handling containers on clusters of nodes so they work together.

Pods, the smallest deployable unit, are the foundation of Kubernetes. Think of them like mini ships carrying one or more containers that need to work together. They might be small, but Pods are mighty—they encapsulate your containers and ensure they run with the right configuration. But managing a fleet of Pods is where Deployments come into play. These ensure your Pods always match the desired state, no matter what. If one Pod crashes, the Deployment controller will launch a new one to keep things running smoothly.

But wait, how do all these Pods talk to each other or the outside world? That's where Services come in. Services expose your application running inside Pods, making sure it's discoverable, whether it's talking to other services within your cluster or to external clients. And when you need external access to your internal services, Kubernetes brings out the big guns with Ingress. Ingress manages how traffic from outside the cluster gets routed to your services, complete with load balancing, SSL, and virtual hosting if you need it.

In essence, Kubernetes isn't just managing containers—it's orchestrating an entire symphony of services, making sure everything from scaling, load balancing, to self-healing is done automatically. It's the engine that keeps your containerized applications running smoothly, even as your environment scales and grows more complex.

To understand it fully, let's create a sample project using Docker. Let's create a simple Java application and containerize it using Docker.

255

Example: Kubernetes with Docker

1. **Java Application:** Create a basic Java application with a REST endpoint using Spring Boot.

```
@RestController
@SpringBootApplication
public class DockerDemoProjectApplication {
    public static void main(String[] args) {
        SpringApplication.run(DockerDemoProject
        Application.class, args);
    }
    @GetMapping("/")
    public String hello() {
        return "Hello, World!";
    }
}
```

Install Docker locally from https://docs.docker.com/.

Dockerfile: Create a Dockerfile to package the Java application into a Docker image.

```
FROM openjdk:11-ea-17-jre-slim
WORKDIR /app
COPY target/DockerDemoProject-1.0.jar /app/hello-world-app.jar
EXPOSE 8080
CMD ["java", "jar", "hello-world-app.jar"]
```

Build Docker Image: Build the Docker image using the Docker CLI.

```
docker build -t hello-world-app
```

Run Docker Container: Run a Docker container from the built image.

```
docker run -p 8080:8080 hello-world-app
```

Access: Access the application at http://localhost:8080 to see the "Hello, World!" message.

Explanation: This Dockerfile uses an OpenJDK 17 base image, copies the compiled JAR file (hello-world-app.jar), exposes port 8080, and specifies the command to run the application.

Example: Kubernetes Deployment

Install Minikube (minikube is local Kubernetes, focusing on making it easy to learn and develop for Kubernetes) from `https://minikube.sigs.k8s.io/` to set up a cluster locally. Also, install kubectl (a command-line tool for interacting with your Kubernetes cluster) from `https://kubernetes.io/`.

Start Minikube from the command prompt: `minikube start`

Use the above built application in this Kubernetes example. Tag the image created above:

```
docker tag hello-world-app <your-dockerhub-username>/hello-world-app:latest
```

Push the image to the Minikube cluster: `docker build -t hello-world-app`

Create Kubernetes configuration files:

```
apiVersion: apps/v1
kind: Deployment
metadata:
  name: hello-world-deployment
spec:
  replicas: 2
  selector:
    matchLabels:
      app: hello-world
  template:
```

```
metadata:
  labels:
    app: hello-world
spec:
  containers:
  - name: hello-world-app
    image: <your-dockerhub-username>/hello-world-
    app:latest  # Change this to your image name
    ports:
    - containerPort: 8080
```

Create a service file:

```
apiVersion: v1
kind: Service
metadata:
  name: hello-world-service
spec:
  selector:
    app: hello-world
  ports:
    - protocol: TCP
      port: 8080
      targetPort: 8080
  type: NodePort
```

Apply the Kubernetes Files

- Apply the deployment: kubectl apply -f hello-world-deployment.yaml

- Apply the service: kubectl apply -f hello-world-service.yaml

- Verify that the deployment and service are running:

```
kubectl get deployments
kubectl get pods
kubectl get services
```

Using **Minikube**, you can access the service directly using `minikube service hello-world-service`.

Explanation

- **replicas:** Specifies that two instances (pods) of the application will be deployed.

- **image:** Use the Docker image from your Docker Hub or local Minikube registry.

- **containerPort:** Specifies that the container listens on port 8080.

- **selector:** Selects the pods labeled app: hello-world to route traffic to.

- **ports:** Maps port 8080 of the service to port 8080 of the container.

- **type:** The NodePort service exposes the application on a port accessible from outside the cluster.

You have now set up Kubernetes configurations for a simple Spring Boot application using Docker. You created

- A Deployment (hello-world-deployment.yaml) to manage the application pods.

- A Service (hello-world-service.yaml) to expose the application on port 8080.

This setup enables you to run, scale, and access the Dockerized Spring Boot application in your local Kubernetes cluster.

EXERCISE CHAPTER 5-2

1. Update the replicas count in the hello-world-deployment.yaml file to three and reapply the configuration.

2. Verify that the number of pods has increased above example.

3. Modify the **hello-world-app** application (e.g., change the message it returns) and rebuild the Docker image.

4. Update the image version in the deployment file and redeploy the application to see the updated version.

Summary

Containers and orchestration with Docker and Kubernetes have changed the way we think about deploying, scaling, and managing applications. With Docker, you can package your app into a compact, lightweight container that runs smoothly across different environments without the "but it worked on my machine" problem. Kubernetes takes it one step further by orchestrating these containers—automating deployment, scaling, and cluster application management. Take these two and you have the most powerful combination of tools to keep your Java applications easily distributed between development, testing, and production and scalable and resilient in the face of ever more demand. For learning to use Docker and Kubernetes in your Java applications, it is like getting a sneak peek at creating efficient, agile, modern cloud-native architectures that scale as you need.

Scaling Microservices

Scaling microservices is a critical part of ensuring your system performs well and makes the most of available resources, especially in dynamic environments where demand can change rapidly. Kubernetes steps in here with tools like the Horizontal Pod Autoscaler (HPA), automating scaling decisions based on workload metrics. To really master scaling strategies for microservices, it's important to grasp the key differences between horizontal and vertical scaling, particularly when using something like HPA.

Horizontal Scaling: You scale by building more pods (instances) of your microservices. This replicates the load across many nodes which is great for high volume, fault tolerance, and availability. Consider it as the same as multiplication: the more pods you have, the more traffic you can serve without overloading one instance. The advantage of this is it's highly scalable and elastical, making it load balancing and fault-tolerant. This, of course, adds additional overhead, more moving pieces to deal with, and a distributed design.

Vertical Scaling: Here, you don't build more pods but provide each current pod with an extra amount of capacity (CPU or memory). This is useful when you want to perform heavier computation on one instance and makes managing this easy. It doesn't require your service to hold a set of instances (which can be particularly convenient for stateful services). The flip side? You have a limit of the physical resources of the node, and going vertical may bring a few seconds of downtime as resources are relocated.

Both approaches have their merits, and choosing between them—or using a combination of both—depends on the specific needs of your microservices architecture. Horizontal scaling gives you more flexibility, but vertical scaling can be a simpler, albeit sometimes temporary, fix for resource-hungry applications.

Summary

Grasping the differences between horizontal and vertical scaling, especially when using Kubernetes' Horizontal Pod Autoscaler (HPA), is key to crafting a truly scalable and efficient microservices architecture. With HPA taking care of horizontal scaling—adjusting the number of pods based on metrics like CPU usage—and vertical scaling fine-tuning the resources within individual pods, you can dynamically adapt to workload fluctuations without breaking a sweat. This smart scaling approach boosts performance and availability while keeping resource use in check, making Kubernetes an invaluable tool for creating resilient, cloud-native microservices that thrive under pressure.

Conclusion

As we wrap up this chapter, it's clear that testing, deploying, and scaling microservices is no walk in the park—it's more like managing a bustling café where every barista needs to work independently yet harmoniously. We've explored the nitty-gritty of unit testing, where each service proves it can stand on its own two feet, and integration testing, which ensures the whole team plays nicely together. Add contract testing to the mix, and you've got a safety net to catch any misunderstandings between services before they lead to a comedy of errors in production.

Deployment and scaling brought Docker and Kubernetes to the forefront—tools that transform microservices from fragile experiments into robust, scalable entities. Docker packs your applications into tidy, portable containers, while Kubernetes orchestrates them like a maestro leading a symphony. Whether it's spinning up new instances with horizontal scaling or beefing up existing ones with vertical scaling, you now have the tools to ensure your microservices perform gracefully under pressure.

Remember, these strategies aren't just about technical mastery; they're about delivering value—building systems that are resilient, efficient, and prepared for the unpredictable. With your expertise in the intricacies of microservices architecture, you're not just adopting best practices; you're setting the standard for what modern, scalable applications can achieve.

What's Next?

Buckle up for the next chapter, where we delve into the critical pillars of security, maintenance, and logging. We'll tackle topics like fortifying service-to-service communication, managing logs like a pro with centralized solutions, and ensuring your microservices aren't just functional but also compliant with industry standards. Think of it as the next step in your journey to microservices mastery—because building is only half the battle; protecting and maintaining is where the real art lies. See you there!

CHAPTER 6

Microservices Security, Monitoring, and Maintenance

When it comes to microservices, security is like the sturdy lock on the front door of a digital house—it's absolutely essential. Two basic pillars of this security structure are authentication and authorization. They provide a safe path for users and systems to work with apps and data. In this chapter, let's dive into what they are, why we should care about them, and how you can use them in a Java microservices solution with Spring Security.

Authentication and Authorization

Think of authentication as the Internet equivalent of ID verification. Just trying to see if the user/system attempting to access an app is the person they appear to be. And this happens by means of usernames, passwords, tokens, or even biometric information—fingerprints anyone?

Authentication is proving identity. Authorization is deciding what a verified user/system does once in. It's like, "Oh yeah, you're in the building now, what rooms can you access?" Authorization will identify if a user has access to a particular resource or can do certain action based on their roles or characteristics.

© Sumit Bhatnagar and Roshan Mahant 2025
S. Bhatnagar and R. Mahant, *The Art of Decoding Microservices*,
https://doi.org/10.1007/979-8-8688-1267-5_6

Why It Matters

Authentication and authorization are the lifeblood of microservices security as shown in Figure 6-1. Without them, it would be a general public house anyone could come and poke around. With solid authentication and precise authorization, you are not only locking out unsolicited visitors but also making sure everyone is adhering to the norms of engagement.

Implementing these security measures within a Java microservice? Spring Security has made this super easy as they provide a great tool to build authentication and authorization functions within seconds. Well, don't be afraid; securing your microservices doesn't have to be a scary proposition. With the right equipment and knowledge, you can erect a fortress that is as secure as it is effective.

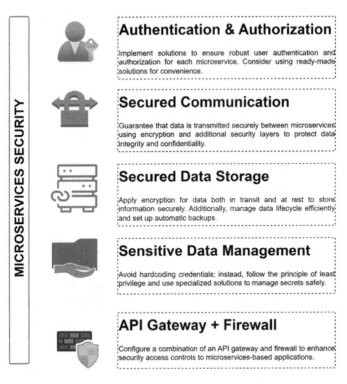

Figure 6-1. *Key security measures in microservices architecture—a breakdown of essential strategies*

Ways of Authentication

Simple Authentication: The simplest authentication there is, entering a username and password into the headers. Yes, it's base64 encoded, but don't get too excited; it's not even the safest option.

Token Authentication: This is more advanced. It's using tokens such as JWT (JSON Web Tokens) or OAuth tokens. Tokens are distributed like VIP cards and enrolled for login without constantly retyping usernames and passwords.

OAuth: Another classic, OAuth delegates the authentication to an outsider (e.g., Google, Facebook). You just wave your Google badge; it's like you can use different services without multiple credentials.

Ways of Authorization

Role-Based Access Control (RBAC): This mechanism allocates rights based on user roles. So, for instance, an "admin" can see everything (lucky them), and a "user" can only see or edit certain resources.

Attribute-Based Access Control (ABAC): A bit more specialized, ABAC works by taking the user's attributes such as location, company, or title to filter out what they can see. A user of "finance," for example, might only be able to see financials, and a "marketing" employee will only be able to see campaign data.

Policy-Based Access Control (PBAC): This model is basically a use of prebuilt policies to allow or deny access on a certain time of day or at any given level of security.

Implementing Authentication and Authorization in Java

Add Spring Security Dependency: Include Spring Security in your Maven pom.xml file.

```
<dependency>
    <groupId>org.springframework.boot</groupId>
    <artifactId>spring-boot-starter-security</artifactId>
</dependency>
```

Configure Spring Security: Create a configuration class to customize security settings.

```
@Configuration
@EnableWebSecurity
public class SecurityConfig {
    String str = "hello";
        @Bean
        public UserDetailsService userDetailsService(){
            UserDetails user1 = User.builder()
                    .username("user")
                    .password(bCryptPasswordEncoder().
                    encode("user"))
                    .authorities("ROLE_USER")
                    .build();

            UserDetails admin = User.builder()
                    .username("admin")
                    .password(bCryptPasswordEncoder().
                    encode("admin"))
                    .authorities("ROLE_ADMIN")
                    .build();
```

```
        return new InMemoryUserDetailsManager(user1,admin);
}

@Bean
public SecurityFilterChain securityFilterChain
(HttpSecurity http) throws Exception{
 http

                .headers(header -> header.frameOptions
                (HeadersConfigurer.FrameOptionsConfig::
                disable))
                .csrf(AbstractHttpConfigurer::disable)
                .formLogin(AbstractHttpConfigurer::disable)
                .authorizeHttpRequests(req -> req.
                requestMatchers("/user/**").hasRole
                ("USER"))
                .authorizeHttpRequests(req -> req.
                requestMatchers("/admin/**").hasRole
                ("ADMIN"))
                .authorizeHttpRequests(req -> req.
                requestMatchers("/**").hasAnyRole
                ("USER", "ADMIN"))
                .authorizeHttpRequests(req -> req.
                anyRequest().authenticated())
                .httpBasic(Customizer.withDefaults());
        return http.build();
}

@Bean
public BCryptPasswordEncoder bCryptPasswordEncoder(){
        return new BCryptPasswordEncoder();
}

}
```

Create a Spring Boot Application: Develop a simple Spring Boot application with REST endpoints.

```
@RestController
public class AuthExampleController {
    @GetMapping("/")
    public String home() {
        return "Welcome to the home page!";
    }

    @GetMapping("/user")
    public String user() {
        return "Welcome User!";
    }

    @GetMapping("/admin")
    public String admin() {
        return "Welcome Admin!";
    }
}
```

Explanation

@EnableWebSecurity enables Spring Security's web security features. A custom UserDetailsService is defined to create two in-memory users (user with role USER and admin with role ADMIN), with passwords encoded using **BCryptPasswordEncoder**. The **securityFilterChain** method configures security settings. It sets up authorization rules: paths starting with /user require ROLE_USER, /admin requires ROLE_ADMIN, and other paths can be accessed by users with either role. This setup secures the application, restricting access to different parts based on user roles, and uses in-memory users for testing and demonstration purposes.

EXERCISE CHAPTER 6-1
---

1. Add a new role called **"ROLE_MANAGER"** and create a new user with this role. Add a new endpoint /manager in the AuthExampleController that only users with the **"ROLE_ MANAGER"** can access. Update the security configuration to authorize this new role accordingly.

2. Test the new role by creating an additional user and checking access to the /manager endpoint. Build the above example in any IDE of your choice like IntelliJ or Eclipse.

Summary

Securing applications with authentication and authorization is like setting up the bouncer and the VIP list for your software—only the right folks get in, and they can only access what they're supposed to. These mechanisms are fundamental in keeping your application safe from unauthorized access and malicious activity. By leveraging robust frameworks like Spring Security in Java, developers can implement secure login processes, manage user permissions effectively, and enforce strict access controls over sensitive resources. It's not about ticking a security checkbox, but rather establishing trust with your users, keeping their data safe, and demonstrating that your app follows the law in terms of compliance. It's not only smart to be aware of these principles and build them into your software, it's the key to a reliable and secure system users can trust.

Securing Service-to-Service Communication

This is not an optional advice to keep the communication between services secured in microservices, it is a requirement. As sensitive information is transmitted between multiple services, high-level security is essential to build trust and make sure that data cannot be intercepted or tampered with by an unintended third party. Let's dive into the basic principles behind secure service-to-service communication, some common issues that you might encounter, and a Java example using Spring Boot to enable HTTPS and standard authentication.

Understanding What We Need: Service-to-Service Communication Security

What's essential to secure service-to-service communication is that data is secret, intact, and verified when it is being transferred. Most importantly, secrecy involves encoding information so that only the intended recipient can decrypt and read it, preventing unauthorized access. It is like writing a letter locked and only the receiver can open it.

Then there is integrity—the idea that data should arrive exactly where it left off at its origin without being changed in the process. Think of it as a form of assurance that the message was not falsified in transit. Authentication, finally, lets the sharing services authenticate each other before data transfers begin. The digital thumbs up says, "Yes, we are both who we say we are," before any information comes out.

The Implications of Securing Service Communication -

Even such security comes with challenges. Network security is one of the most difficult aspects. When services exchange information over public or nonsecure lines, the potential is for information to be leaked. Like when you send a postcard, without encryption, anyone can read the letter as it goes along. That is why it is so important to have strong encryption to protect the data.

Identity management is another major hurdle. When the distributed system exists, each service must be able to identify and authenticate the other to avoid a break-in. This calls for an infrastructure that will manage identity verification dynamically and securely without breaking the integrity of the exchange.

Thirdly, key management has its own complications. Security Keys and Certificates: Cryptographic keys and certificates are necessary for encryption, but having to keep them safe (store, distribute, and rotate on a regular basis) can be like holding delicate valuable things in your hand and navigating through them with extreme caution. Mismanagement can undermine the entire security layer, so there should be best practices in securing these keys over the lifetime.

After learning about these foundational principles and the problems with them, developers can deploy secure communication techniques that keep the microservices equilibrating data (be it static updates or mission-critical data).

Summary

Ensuring secure communication between services is nonnegotiable in today's microservices landscape. Protecting data integrity and confidentiality while making sure only authorized services are chatting with each other helps maintain a robust and trustworthy system. By leveraging HTTPS and basic authentication in Java applications using frameworks like Spring Boot, developers can set up a solid foundation of security. This not only protects sensitive data flowing between microservices but also keeps the entire architecture safer and more reliable—like setting up a security guard at every doorway to check IDs before letting anyone in.

Centralized Logging with ELK Stack

Centralized logging is an absolute must to monitor and troubleshoot distributed systems and microservices. Consider looking for a needle in a haystack—then, say the haystack is in various places. That's how finding problems in microservices is handled without centralized logs. Enter the ELK stack (Elasticsearch, Logstash, Kibana), a highly scalable combination that makes log consolidation, storage, and visualization simple, if not fast. We will see how you can integrate the ELK stack with your Java applications to clean up your logs and translate it into useful data in this guide.

The ELK Stack at Work

Let's begin with a breakdown of the ELK stack power providers and their role in the log ecosystem as shown in Figure 6-2.

Elasticsearch is the brain of the operation. It's a distributed, REST-based search and analytics system built to index logs in a flash. It's like the library of your logs, categorizing logs in such a way that, if you're looking for specific problems or trends, you can get to the data in a split second.

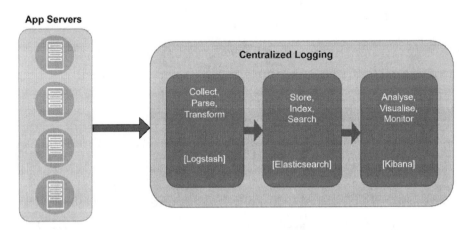

Figure 6-2. *Basic logging strategy for a microservice environment*

Then there is Logstash, the data controller. This flexible data processing pipeline loads logs from anything, from a file, a TCP/UDP stream, or even lightweight log shippers such as Beats, and converts them for delivery to Elasticsearch. You can think of it as a customs checkpoint on your logs where everything gets organized and labeled before being stored in the storage and later processed.

And then there's the art-world genius: Kibana. Kibana is your savior for plotting and browsing all that cleanly structured data. It provides real-time reports and live dashboards that you can see trends, investigate anomalies, and activate alerts all from an intuitive user interface. And with Kibana, you are not just viewing logs, but also turning them into story-driven dashboards to show you how your services are running and healthy.

It's not just a matter of a simple hooking up the ELK stack to your Java apps, it's about an elegant integration with the way logs flow from your app into searchable, visually appealing format. Logstash allows you to set up pipelines to consume logs from your Java app's logging framework, such as Logback or Log4j. Those logs are fed to Elasticsearch which indexes them and publishes them to be querying. Finally, Kibana unifies the three and lets you visualize logs in ways that uncover patterns and spot problems more quickly—no more wading through endless log files.

Now, with the ELK stack built-in, you can have visibility into your whole distributed system in a single view, so you can troubleshoot faster, more effectively, and without making guesses. Whether you're debugging a performance bug, tracing a failed transaction, or simply inspecting your microservices for general state of health, the ELK stack is the toolkit you need to avoid errors and ensure the longevity of your infrastructure.

The ELK stack—your trusty sidekick in the grand quest for centralized logging and analytics! At the heart of this dynamic trio (Elasticsearch, Logstash, Kibana) lies Beats, those lightweight yet mighty data collectors that make sure no log, metric, or network packet escapes your watchful eye. Each Beat has its own personality and purpose, like members of an eccentric yet highly functional superhero team.

Take **Filebeat**, for instance. It's like the intern who never sleeps, tirelessly tailing log files from web servers, applications, or even that obscure system log you forgot existed. Then there's **Metricbeat**, your fitness tracker for servers and applications—keeping tabs on CPU usage, memory, and even how hard your Docker containers are sweating. Think of it as your infrastructure's personal trainer, but without the guilt trips.

Packetbeat is your network detective, nosing around network traffic to sniff out latency issues or protocol-level bottlenecks. It's like the Sherlock Holmes of your stack, minus the pipe and hat. Meanwhile, **Winlogbeat** plays the role of a bouncer, standing at the door of your Windows systems, logging every suspicious move, failed login, or shady error message—just in case things get rowdy.

If you're more of a "paranoid sysadmin" type, you'll love **Auditbeat**, the Beat that lets you sleep soundly knowing it's watching user activity and monitoring file integrity. On the flip side, **Heartbeat** is your uptime cheerleader, constantly pinging APIs, websites, or services to confirm they're alive and kicking. You could say it's like your overly attached tech friend who won't stop checking in: "Hey, are you there? How about now? Now?"

For the cloud-savvy among us, **Functionbeat** has your back, collecting logs and metrics from serverless functions like AWS Lambda. It's proof that even in the cloud, someone's watching (comforting or creepy, depending on your perspective). And let's not forget **Journalbeat**, the Linux hipster that only hangs out with journald logs. It's minimalistic, efficient, and always up to date on what your system services are up to.

Together, these Beats form the ultimate data-ingestion squad, ensuring that no matter what you're monitoring—be it systems, services, or networks—you're covered. Integrating Beats into your stack is like adding extra horsepower to an already well-oiled engine. It's the kind of efficiency that doesn't just solve problems—it anticipates them. And let's face it, who doesn't want a sidekick that works smarter, not harder?

Setting Up ELK Stack

Install and Configure Elasticsearch

- Download and install Elasticsearch from Elasticsearch Downloads.

- Configure Elasticsearch settings (elasticsearch.yml) for cluster and node configurations.

Install and Configure Logstash

- Download and install Logstash from `https://www.elastic.co/downloads/logstash`.

- Configure Logstash pipelines (logstash.conf) for input, filter, and output plug-ins to process and forward logs to Elasticsearch.

Install and Configure Kibana

- Download and install Kibana from `https://www.elastic.co/downloads/kibana`.

- Configure Kibana (kibana.yml) to connect to Elasticsearch and specify settings for visualization.

Integrating Java Application with ELK Stack

To demonstrate centralized logging with ELK stack using a Java application, let's consider a basic Spring Boot application logging events to Logstash, which then forwards them to Elasticsearch for storage and Kibana for visualization.

Add dependencies:

```
<dependency>
    <groupId>net.logstash.logback</groupId>
    <artifactId>logstash-logback-encoder</artifactId>
    <version>7.4</version>
    <scope>runtime</scope>
</dependency>
```

Configure Logback for Logstash Appender

Create logback-spring.xml in src/main/resources to configure Logback with Logstash appender:

```
<configuration>
    <include resource="org/springframework/boot/logging/
    logback/defaults.xml" />
    <appender name="logstash" class="net.logstash.logback.
    appender.LogstashTcpSocketAppender">
    <destination>logalhost:5000</destination>
    <encoder class="net.logstash.logback.encoder.
    LogstashEncoder"></encoder>
    </appender>
    <root level="INFO">
      <appender-ref ref="logstash"/>
    </root>
</configuration>
```

Run Logstash

Start Logstash with a configuration (logstash.conf) to listen on TCP port 5000, parse incoming logs, and send them to Elasticsearch.

1. **Run Elasticsearch and Kibana**

   Start Elasticsearch and Kibana to interact with and visualize logs stored in Elasticsearch.

2. **Generate Logs in Java Application**

   Create a simple controller in your Spring Boot
   application to generate logs:

```java
@RestController
public class HelloWorldController {
    private static final Logger logger = LoggerFactory.
    getLogger(HelloWorldController.class);
    @GetMapping("/hello")
    public String hello() {
        logger.info("Hello World! Logging from Spring
        Boot application");
        return "Hello World!";
    }
}
```

3. **View Logs in Kibana**

   - Access Kibana at http://localhost:5601.

   - Create index pattern myapp-* to visualize logs
     stored in Elasticsearch.

   - Explore logs with various visualizations and
     dashboards provided by Kibana.

Summary

Centralized logging using the ELK stack provides powerful tools for
gathering, storing, and visualizing logs from distributed systems and
microservices. By integrating Java applications with ELK through
frameworks like Spring Boot, Logback, and Logstash, you set the stage
for efficient log management, quick troubleshooting, and comprehensive
performance monitoring. With the ELK stack's capabilities, teams gain

improved operational visibility, making debugging less of a scavenger hunt and more of a guided tour. This approach ensures your microservices architecture remains scalable, reliable, and efficient. Mastering centralized logging with the ELK stack equips developers and operations teams with the insight needed to manage, maintain, and optimize cloud-native applications with confidence and ease.

Monitoring Health and Performance

Maintaining health and performance of Java apps is more than best practice—it's survival, to make sure that your systems function, bugs get pounded early, and resources get spent efficiently. When everything is distributed and changing, monitoring all parts' health is essential in a microservices environment. In this chapter, you'll learn how to implement health checks, collect metrics, and check on your Java application with Spring Boot Actuator, among other useful features.

Health checks are just like doctor's visits for your app; they check if it is in good health by examining key components like databases and dependencies. Health checks deliver endpoints indicating the state of the application in case something's wrong, helping developers and operators see the problem early before it becomes out of hand.

Metrics collection, by contrast, is a process of keeping track of the in-depth stuff. From JVM memory to HTTP request latency, you can monitor it all. As you track such metrics, you'll be able to see how your app is performing and if it's utilizing resources effectively. It's your computer equivalent of a fitness monitor—only that in this case you don't want to know when the software is burning too much "calorie" (i.e., memory) or slowing down under load.

All of this data has to be gathered by monitoring systems, such as Prometheus, Grafana, and Micrometer. These tools do not only collect and save metrics, but can display them in real-time through interactive dashboards. You can also configure your own custom health metrics and endpoints to get the full visibility into your application performance. With these tools, your app transforms from a black box into an open and transparent environment where every performance blip and blop can be spotted, analyzed, and addressed—keeping your services healthy and responsive.

Implementing Health Checks with Spring Boot Actuator

Add Spring Boot Actuator Dependency

Include Spring Boot Actuator in your pom.xml:

```
<dependency>
    <groupId>org.springframework.boot</groupId>
    <artifactId>spring-boot-starter-actuator</artifactId>
</dependency>
```

Configure Health Indicators

```
import org.springframework.boot.actuate.health.Health;
import org.springframework.boot.actuate.health.HealthIndicator;
import org.springframework.stereotype.Component;
import org.springframework.web.client.RestTemplate;
import org.springframework.web.client.HttpStatusCodeException;

@Component
public class ApiHealthIndicator implements HealthIndicator {

    private static final String API_URL = "https://api.example.
    com/health";
```

```java
@Override
public Health health() {
    if (isApiUp()) {
        return Health.up().withDetail("Message",
        "API is up").build();
    } else· {
        return Health.down().withDetail("Message",
        "API is down").build();
    }
}

private boolean isApiUp() {
  //Add code to check if API is up and running
        return true; // If no exception, the API is up
    } catch (HttpStatusCodeException e) {
        // Log the error or handle specific HTTP
        status codes
        System.err.println("API is down: " +
        e.getStatusCode());
    } catch (Exception e) {
        // Handle other exceptions like timeouts
        System.err.println("API is down: " +
        e.getMessage());
    }
    return false; // Return false if an exception occurs
  }
}
```

Enable Actuator Endpoints

Configure Actuator endpoints in application.properties or application.yml:

```
# application.yml
management:
  endpoints:
    web:
      exposure:
        include: '*'
```

Access health endpoint: http://localhost:8080/actuator/health

Explanation

The application exposes Actuator endpoints by configuring them in application.yml to include all ('*'). This allows access to various built-in endpoints, such as /actuator as shown in Figure 6-3, followed by /actuator/ health as shown in Figure 6-4.

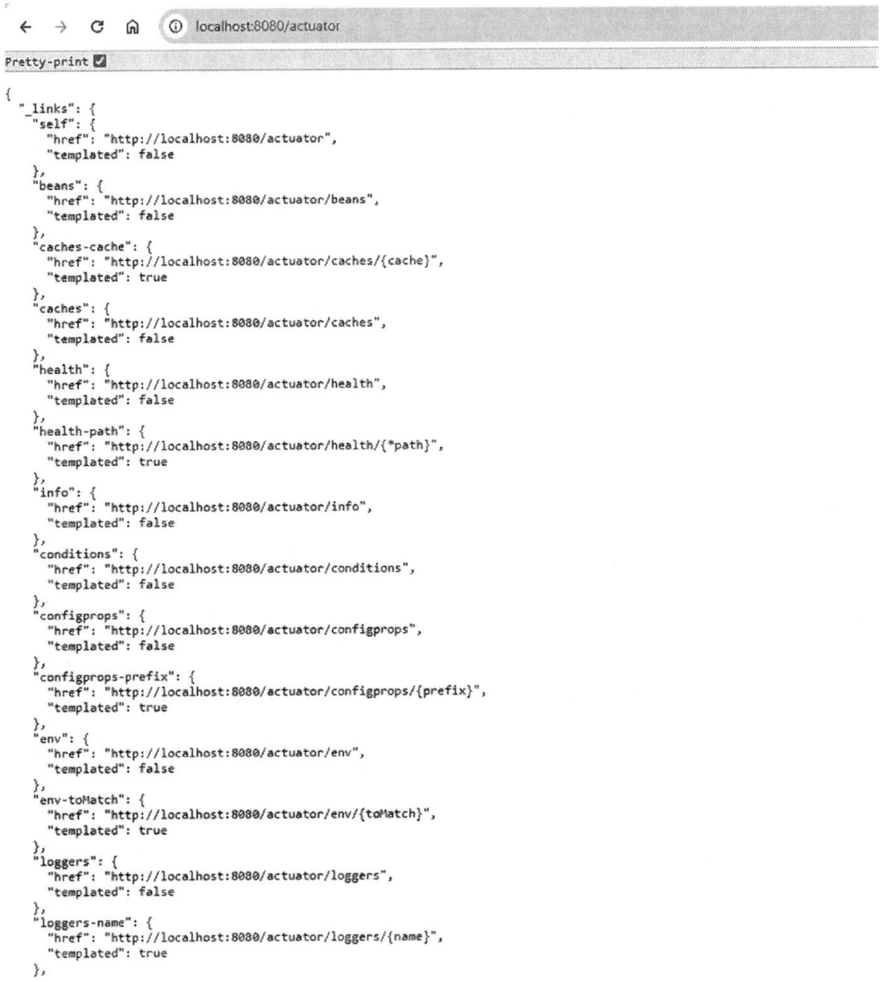

```
←  →  C  ⌂  ⓘ  localhost:8080/actuator

Pretty-print ☑

{
  "_links": {
    "self": {
      "href": "http://localhost:8080/actuator",
      "templated": false
    },
    "beans": {
      "href": "http://localhost:8080/actuator/beans",
      "templated": false
    },
    "caches-cache": {
      "href": "http://localhost:8080/actuator/caches/{cache}",
      "templated": true
    },
    "caches": {
      "href": "http://localhost:8080/actuator/caches",
      "templated": false
    },
    "health": {
      "href": "http://localhost:8080/actuator/health",
      "templated": false
    },
    "health-path": {
      "href": "http://localhost:8080/actuator/health/{*path}",
      "templated": true
    },
    "info": {
      "href": "http://localhost:8080/actuator/info",
      "templated": false
    },
    "conditions": {
      "href": "http://localhost:8080/actuator/conditions",
      "templated": false
    },
    "configprops": {
      "href": "http://localhost:8080/actuator/configprops",
      "templated": false
    },
    "configprops-prefix": {
      "href": "http://localhost:8080/actuator/configprops/{prefix}",
      "templated": true
    },
    "env": {
      "href": "http://localhost:8080/actuator/env",
      "templated": false
    },
    "env-toMatch": {
      "href": "http://localhost:8080/actuator/env/{toMatch}",
      "templated": true
    },
    "loggers": {
      "href": "http://localhost:8080/actuator/loggers",
      "templated": false
    },
    "loggers-name": {
      "href": "http://localhost:8080/actuator/loggers/{name}",
      "templated": true
    },
```

Figure 6-3. *This diagram represents how an actuator endpoint will look like on a browser*

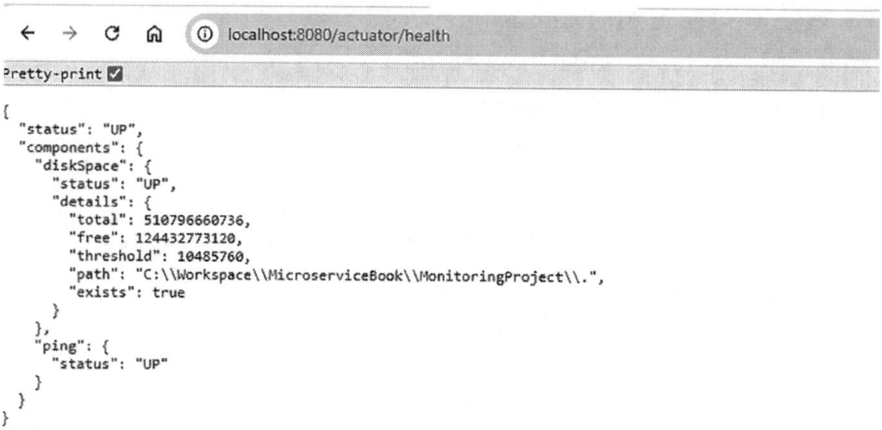

```
←  →  C  ⌂  ⓘ  localhost:8080/actuator/health
Pretty-print ☑
{
  "status": "UP",
  "components": {
    "diskSpace": {
      "status": "UP",
      "details": {
        "total": 510796660736,
        "free": 124432773120,
        "threshold": 10485760,
        "path": "C:\\Workspace\\MicroserviceBook\\MonitoringProject\\.",
        "exists": true
      }
    },
    "ping": {
      "status": "UP"
    }
  }
}
```

Figure 6-4. *This diagram represents how a health endpoint will look like on the browser from actuator*

Actuator with Kubernetes

In the case of a Spring Boot application deployed on Kubernetes, the Actuator module can be used to generate readiness and liveness probes for Kubernetes health monitoring. Such probes help Kubernetes track the health of the application and detect if the container is available for traffic or it needs to be restarted.

Endpoints in Spring Boot for Kubernetes

Spring Boot provides Actuator health endpoints that can be used directly for readiness and liveness checks:

1. **Liveness Probe Endpoint:** This endpoint indicates whether the application is still running and should not be restarted. Default endpoint: /actuator/health/liveness.

2. **Readiness Probe Endpoint:** This endpoint indicates whether the application is ready to serve requests. Default endpoint: /actuator/health/readiness.

285

Configuration in application.properties

Activate the readiness and liveness probes:

   management.endpoint.health.probes.enabled=true management. endpoints.web.exposure.include=health

   This ensures that the /health/liveness and /health/readiness endpoints are exposed for Kubernetes to access.

Kubernetes YAML Example

You can configure the probes in your Kubernetes Deployment YAML file like this:

```
livenessProbe:
  httpGet:
    path: /actuator/health/liveness
    port: 8080
  initialDelaySeconds: 5
  periodSeconds: 10

readinessProbe:
  httpGet:
    path: /actuator/health/readiness
    port: 8080
  initialDelaySeconds: 10
  periodSeconds: 5
```

   initialDelaySeconds: Time to wait before the probe starts after the container starts

   periodSeconds: Frequency of probe checks

How They Work in Kubernetes

1. **Liveness Probe:** If the application becomes unresponsive or enters a "broken" state, Kubernetes will use this probe to determine if the container should be restarted.

2. **Readiness Probe:** Indicates whether the application is ready to serve requests. Kubernetes will not route traffic to a pod until the readiness check passes.

Metrics Collection and Monitoring with Prometheus and Grafana

Especially for microservices, metrics and monitoring serve as a lifeline. You can't forget about the performance of your applications when you have a bunch of different services that need to follow along like a choreographed dance. That is, if you take Prometheus and Grafana, the free-floating set of open source monitoring frameworks that have made this all possible. Together, these two provide a single, complete, and easy way to gather and visualize app metrics that help developers and ops maintain their systems' availability and performance.

Prometheus is a time-series database designed with monitoring in mind. It gathers metrics from tracked targets by scraping HTTP endpoints periodically. Imagine it is a constant worker bee, constantly checking in and collecting information to see how everything is working. And it doesn't just collect data, but also stores that data effectively and has a query language called PromQL that lets you do real-time analytics and accurate monitoring.

Grafana, however, is the musician of this collaboration. It's a data visualization and monitoring solution that transforms the metrics that Prometheus collects into gorgeous, customizable dashboards. It visualizes data across different sources and lets you monitor your services' status in real time, with dynamic graphs and alerts customized to your requirements.

Let's dive into how these tools work together with a Java application. Prometheus, like a curious observer, will scrape metrics from your application's endpoints, storing all the essential data. Grafana steps in to create dashboards that visualize these metrics, helping you not just see but understand the performance patterns and any anomalies in your services. You can set up Prometheus to track things like request rates, error counts, memory usage, and anything else you want to keep an eye on. Grafana then transforms this data into interactive, user-friendly visuals, making your monitoring experience not just informative but genuinely engaging.

Understanding the components of this stack is key. Prometheus is your data collector and analyzer, purpose-built for handling time-series metrics with efficiency and flexibility. Grafana is your visualizer, turning numbers into insightful dashboards that provide clarity and control over your system's performance. Together, they create an invaluable toolset for anyone working with cloud-native applications, ensuring that your microservices not only work well but work smart.

Setting Up Prometheus

1. **Download and Install Prometheus**

   - Download Prometheus from Prometheus Downloads.

   - Extract the downloaded archive and configure prometheus.yml for scraping targets.

2. **Configure in pom.xml**

```xml
<dependency>
    <groupId>io.micrometer</groupId>
    <artifactId>micrometer-registry-prometheus
    </artifactId>
    <scope>runtime</scope>
</dependency>
```

3. **Configure prometheus.yml**

   Example configuration to scrape metrics from a Java application:

```yaml
global:
scrape_interval: "15s"
scrape_configs:
  - job_name: 'java-app'
    metrics_path: '/actuator/prometheus'
    static_configs:
      - targets: ['localhost:8080']
```

   Configure Prometheus to scrape metrics from localhost:8080/actuator/prometheus endpoint exposed by the Java application.

4. **Run Prometheus**

   Start Prometheus server by running prometheus.exe (on Windows) or prometheus (on Linux/Mac):

```
./prometheus --config.file=prometheus.yml
```

   Access Prometheus at http://localhost:9090 to explore metrics and execute queries using PromQL.

Visualizing Metrics with Grafana

1. **Download and Install Grafana**

   - Download Grafana from Grafana Downloads.

   - Install and configure Grafana according to your operating system.

2. **Add Prometheus Data Source**

   - Access Grafana at http://localhost:3000 (default port).

   - Add Prometheus as a data source (Configuration ➤ Data Sources ➤ Add data source).

     - URL: http://localhost:9090

     - Access: Direct

3. **Create Grafana Dashboards**

   - Create a new dashboard (+ ➤ Dashboard ➤ Add new panel).

   - Select Prometheus data source and use PromQL queries to visualize metrics.

   - Example: Create a panel to monitor JVM thread count (jvm_threads_current) over time.

Example Java Application Metrics Dashboard in Grafana

- Dashboard Example

- Visualizes JVM metrics (jvm_threads_current) and HTTP request metrics (http_server_requests_seconds_count) from the Java application.

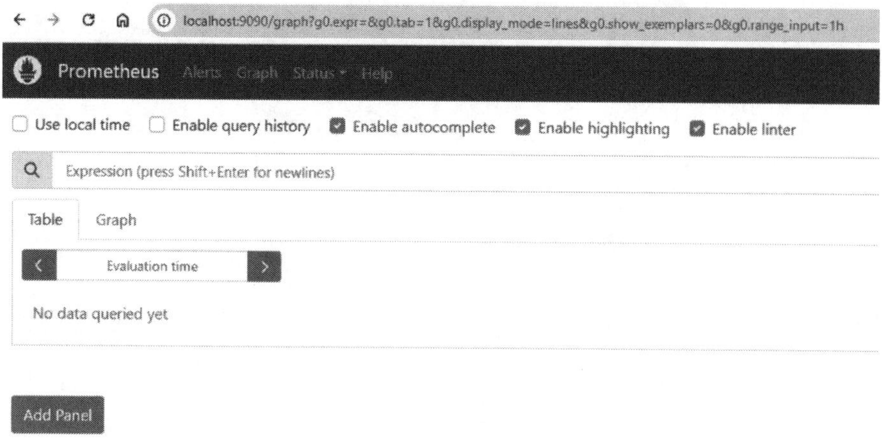

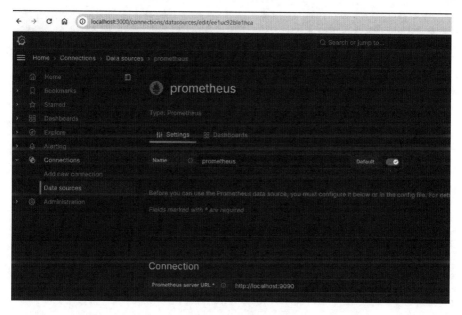

Figure 6-5. *This diagram shows Prometheus home page running on port 9090*

Figure 6-6. *This image shows Grafana home page running on port 3000*

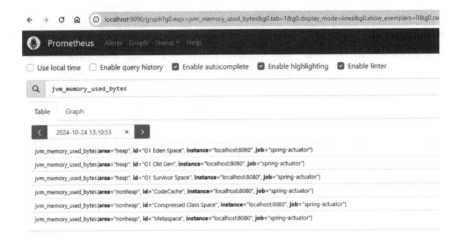

Figure 6-7. *This image shows Prometheus parameters available for* *jvm_memory_used_bytes*

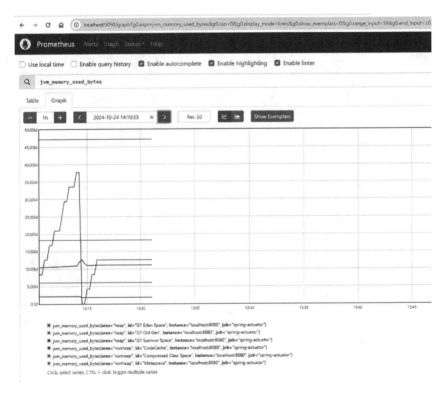

Figure 6-8. *This image shows Prometheus jvm_memory_used_bytes*

Figure 6-9. *This image shows Grafana dashboard showing input from Prometheus*

Summary

Prometheus and Grafana are a dynamic duo when it comes to metrics collection, monitoring, and visualization for Java applications and microservices. By pairing Prometheus with Java applications through Micrometer, and then using Grafana to bring those metrics to life with intuitive dashboards, teams can unlock a treasure trove of insights into performance, resource usage, and long-term trends. Embracing these tools empowers developers and ops teams alike to keep a sharp eye on their cloud-native setups, fine-tuning performance and swiftly addressing issues. This combination ensures not only that apps stay uptime and scalable, but that they respond fast in the dynamic world of production environments. The important thing is, everything gets handled as smoothly as possible—sometimes with a dash of flair!

Versioning and Backward Compatibility

Versioning microservices and ensuring backward compatibility are vital for keeping your system agile, adapting to changing business needs, and rolling out updates smoothly—without leaving your service consumers in the lurch. This guide delves into the various strategies for versioning microservices and explains how to maintain backward compatibility in Java-based environments.

One of the primary strategies is **URI Versioning**, which involves embedding the version number directly into the URI path, like /api/v1/resource. This is a clear and straightforward approach, making it obvious to consumers which version they are interacting with. It's a tried-and-true method, simple and easy to implement, but it can sometimes clutter your endpoints as versions accumulate.

Another method is **Query Parameter Versioning**, where you specify the version using query parameters, such as /api/resource?v=1. This is flexible, allowing changes without altering the URI structure, but it requires clients to be vigilant about including the right parameters.

Header Versioning adds a layer of sophistication by using custom headers to indicate the version, such as Accept: application/vnd.company. resource.v1+json. Think of it as a secret handshake between client and server—clean and effective, though it demands that clients understand how to format requests properly. Alternatively, there's **Media Type Versioning**, where the media type itself specifies the version (application/vnd.company.resource-v1+json). This approach is particularly useful when engaging in content negotiation, offering flexibility but potentially adding complexity when managing numerous versions.

Ensuring **backward compatibility** is where the real finesse comes in. It's all about evolving your services without breaking existing clients—a bit like upgrading the plumbing in your house without shutting off the water. Techniques such as **additive changes**—where you only add new features without removing or altering existing ones—help maintain stability. **Semantic Versioning** is another crucial tool, where version numbers like 1.0.0 for major updates, 1.1.0 for minor improvements, and 1.1.1 for patches clearly communicate the nature of changes. Additionally, **deprecation policies** allow you to phase out old versions gracefully, giving consumers enough time to adapt before making any disruptive changes.

By applying these versioning strategies and backward compatibility techniques, developers can ensure that their microservices architecture remains robust, adaptable, and client-friendly, even as the services grow and evolve over time.

Implementing Versioning and Backward Compatibility

Create a simple Spring Boot project with Spring Initializer and create a REST controller with URI versioning using Spring annotations:

```
@RestController
@RequestMapping("/api/v1")
public class UserControllerV1 {
    @GetMapping("/users")
    public String getUsersV1() {
        return "Version 1: List of users";
    }
}
```

Add Version 2 with Backward Compatibility

Extend the controller to add version 2 while maintaining backward compatibility:

```
@RestController
@RequestMapping("/api/v2")
public class UserControllerV2 {
    @GetMapping("/users")
```

```java
public String getUsersV2() {
    return "Version 2: List of users with additional
    fields";
}
@GetMapping(value = "/users", headers = "X-API-Version=2")
public String getUsersV2HeaderVersion() {
    return "Version 2: List of users with additional fields
    (header version)";
}
}
```

Explanation

This setup demonstrates how to implement API versioning using both URL paths and headers, providing flexibility and ensuring older clients can continue using version 1 while newer clients can take advantage of version 2.

EXERCISE CHAPTER 6-2

1. Create a new controller class (UserControllerV3) for version 3 using /api/v3 as the base path.

2. Add an endpoint /users to return "Version 3: Users with enhanced features."

3. Add backward compatibility by configuring this endpoint to also respond to version 3 requests via the header "X-API-Version=3."

4. Refactor your version 2 and version 3 controllers to use a base controller (BaseUserController) that contains common logic. Make sure that each version still works correctly and backward compatibility is maintained.

Summary

Versioning and maintaining backward compatibility in microservices are essential for handling API evolution while meeting the varied needs of clients. Implementing strategies such as URI versioning and header versioning in Java-based microservices allows developers to manage changes gracefully, enhance system flexibility, and maintain strong, reliable connections with service consumers. By understanding these approaches and applying industry best practices, teams can evolve their microservices architecture smoothly, minimizing disruptions and ensuring seamless version transitions in live environments.

Grasping these concepts and their practical application not only empowers developers to build resilient and adaptable systems but also ensures they are equipped to handle the modern complexities of secure and distributed architectures.

Conclusion

Congratulations, you've just scaled the Everest of microservices security, monitoring, and maintenance! In this chapter, we unraveled the intricate tapestry of keeping your microservices safe, efficient, and humming like a well-tuned orchestra. From the unyielding guards of authentication and authorization to the tactical ninjas of secure service-to-service communication, we've covered it all. Think of your microservices ecosystem as a fortress, with Spring Security as your gatekeeper, HTTPS your armored messenger, and JWT tokens the VIP badges for those allowed inside. Pretty neat, right?

Logging, meanwhile, became the Sherlock Holmes of our microservices mystery. With the ELK stack as our magnifying glass, even the sneakiest bugs and errors don't stand a chance. Add Prometheus and Grafana to the mix, and you've got yourself a high-tech control room with dashboards that turn raw data into stories worth telling. Whether it's CPU usage or those suspicious latency spikes, nothing escapes your watchful eye.

Of course, it's not all about what you know now but what you prepare for. Versioning and backward compatibility? They're your keys to future-proofing. As your services evolve, these strategies ensure you're building bridges, not barriers, for users and clients alike. Add the polish of Kubernetes readiness probes, and your microservices are as resilient as they are scalable.

Next up, we shift gears to dissect real-world case studies and learn from the titans of microservices architecture. "Lessons from Case Studies, Avoiding Pitfalls, and Shaping the Future" will show you not only what works but also what doesn't—because let's be honest, sometimes it's the near disasters that teach us the most. Get ready to dive into tales of triumph, stumble, and everything in between. Stay tuned!

CHAPTER 7

Lessons from Case Studies, Avoiding Pitfalls, and Shaping the Future

The move to microservices architecture has become a pivotal trend in the software world, unlocking greater scalability, flexibility, and resilience that simply outshines traditional monolithic setups. Companies from all industries have jumped on board, and their journeys offer us some pretty valuable insights—think of it as a cheat sheet of what works and what doesn't in the real world. This piece dives into case studies that reveal the nitty-gritty of the challenges faced, the creative solutions put in place, and the key lessons learned from adopting microservices in the wild.

Case Study 1: Netflix

Challenge: Netflix, once operating on a monolithic architecture, started hitting the inevitable roadblocks of scale. As their global customer base exploded and they added more service offerings, managing and scaling their monolithic system became more cumbersome than binge-watching all seasons of *Stranger Things* in one sitting.

© Sumit Bhatnagar and Roshan Mahant 2025
S. Bhatnagar and R. Mahant, *The Art of Decoding Microservices*,
https://doi.org/10.1007/979-8-8688-1267-5_7

Solution: Netflix made the leap to microservices, transforming their towering monolithic application into hundreds of independent microservices. Each of these new microservices was like a self-sufficient mini-show, encapsulating a specific business function. The payoff? They could now deploy, scale, and update these services without having to bring down the entire system or call in reinforcements. During this migration, Netflix developed several groundbreaking libraries to address specific challenges, including Hystrix, a library designed for resilience and fault tolerance, and Chaos Monkey, a tool that intentionally disrupts systems to test their robustness. Most of these libraries were released as open source, enabling other organizations to benefit from Netflix's pioneering efforts in scaling and reliability.

Best Practices

- **Decentralized Data Management:** Netflix embraced a decentralized data strategy, allowing each microservice to control its own database. This helped avoid service bottlenecks and dependency issues that could have felt like a game of *Jenga*—where one wrong move could bring down the stack.

- **Resilience Engineering:** Knowing that failure is inevitable, Netflix built in circuit breakers and fallback mechanisms. This ensured that even when one service flopped, the whole platform didn't go down with it— because, let's face it, nobody likes service interruptions during the final season of their favorite show.

- **DevOps Culture:** Netflix cultivated a DevOps culture where developers weren't just responsible for writing code, they owned their services throughout the entire lifecycle—from the joyous birth of development to the cranky maintenance days of production. This full ownership helped ensure that services remained as polished and binge-worthy as their content.

Case Study 2: Amazon

Challenge: Amazon's journey from a monolithic to a microservices architecture was motivated by the need to handle vast transaction volumes and meet dynamic scaling demands. As their customer base and product offerings expanded, their existing architecture couldn't keep pace with the growing complexity and resource needs.

Solution: Amazon broke their monolithic system into microservices that communicate via web service interfaces. By decoupling services, they achieved independent deployment and scaling, allowing them to allocate resources efficiently to services that needed more horsepower without compromising system stability.

Best Practices

- **Automation Everywhere:** Amazon emphasized automation in testing, deployment, and scaling processes to ensure efficiency and reduce human error. From CI/CD pipelines to automated scaling triggers, it was all about letting the machines do the heavy lifting.

- **Service Independence:** Each service was designed to be as autonomous as possible, minimizing the need for coordination across teams or services. Less coordination means faster development cycles and fewer bottlenecks.

- **Advanced Monitoring:** Amazon implemented sophisticated monitoring and alerting systems to keep a close eye on performance. Real-time issue detection and swift resolution became a core part of their operations, ensuring smooth sailing even under heavy load.

This approach allowed Amazon to scale dynamically, maintain system resilience, and support their ever-growing ecommerce empire.

Lessons Learned from Successful Implementations

The shift to microservices architecture marks a transformative change in how organizations design and manage their software systems. Leading tech giants have embraced this approach to boost scalability, improve resilience, and accelerate their deployment processes. Let's dive into some of the key lessons learned from successful microservices implementations, highlighting case studies from companies that have made this transition smoothly.

- **Start with a Monolith, Migrate Thoughtfully**

  One of the most important lessons is to start with a monolith and transition to microservices only when necessary. Many organizations found success by first refining their understanding of the business domain through a monolithic approach and then moving to microservices when the system became too unwieldy.

  Take *Spotify*, for instance. They started with a monolithic backend and later shifted to microservices as their scaling needs grew. By doing so, they learned the importance of defining clear domain boundaries before breaking services apart. This thoughtful approach eased their migration and helped them avoid early mistakes that could complicate the microservices transition.

- **Design for Failure**

  When everything's distributed, you're essentially
  designing for chaos. Microservices introduce a new
  level of unpredictability, with things like network
  hiccups and service downtimes popping up at the
  worst possible moments. So, you've got to build
  your system with failure in mind. **Netflix**, ever the
  trendsetter, decided not to wait for disaster to strike.
  Instead, they built the *Simian Army*, a rogue band
  of tools designed to wreak controlled havoc on
  their systems. By intentionally causing failures, they
  identified weak spots long before real issues could
  arise. The result? A system that's resilient and laughs in
  the face of minor outages.

- **Automate Everything**

  The one thing every microservices veteran will
  tell you: manual processes are your enemy.
  From testing to deployment, automation is the
  superhero of microservices. It minimizes errors,
  increases consistency, and lets you scale like there's
  no tomorrow. **Amazon**, with its colossal global
  infrastructure, deploys hundreds of times per day
  without breaking a sweat—all thanks to its internal
  automation tooling. Think about it: humans make
  mistakes, but scripts? They execute precisely what
  they're told, and they do it 24/7 without needing
  coffee breaks.

  By taking lessons from the heavyweights, it's clear that
  to make microservices work, you'll need to design like
  Netflix and automate like Amazon. Anything less, and
  you're in for a rocky ride.

- **Remain Focused on Continuous Delivery**

  When you're deploying microservices, CD is your best friend. It lets you push quickly without risk and enables new features to be rolled out much more quickly and safely. When it comes to microservices, you are dealing with a complex network of service-dependent services, and CD keeps it all moving at an appropriate speed. **Google** has been one of the most effective at delivering incremental updates through automated pipelines. This makes it easy to avoid integration snafus before they're complete disasters.

- **Spend on a DevOps Culture**

  And microservices don't end with architectural changes: they need cultural change as well. Development and operations teams should always work side by side with DevOps. **Target**, the department store giant, changed the organization of their teams toward DevOps so that they can take more ownership and responsibility to run microservices. Deploying, monitoring, and maintaining services are all much easier to manage if development and operations are in sync.

- **Keep Track and Be Watchful First**

  Once you go to microservices, your system is much more complex. In one go, you are left with dozens, hundreds of services, all of them with their own unique characteristics and dependency. Monitoring and visibility are an unassailable necessity. Just ask **LinkedIn**—they use powerful observability solutions to maintain the uptime of their microservices, identifying bugs before they devastate users.

- **Attain for API Design**

  The API is the glue holding it all together for microservices. APIs are a key to an easy service-to-service interoperability. They should be documented, versioned, and reversible. **Twitter** has perfected their API practice over the years so that version upgrades don't derail user or developer experiences. An API well designed will make a service-oriented architecture sing or snarl.

Finally, Some Final Words

And the migration to microservices isn't merely about tearing down your monolith, but changing the way you build, deploy, and administer applications. Key lessons from Google, Netflix, Amazon, and others emphasize the importance of careful planning, well-designed APIs, robust monitoring, and a strong DevOps culture. Learning from these industry leaders, organizations can adopt microservices without taking on risks or using the full potential of this powerful architectural style.

Antipatterns and Common Pitfalls

Microservices is now the favored methodology to develop highly elastic and scalable systems, but like any good trend, there's a lot of room for errors. Avoiding the pitfalls that come along can bring some harsh life lessons that take time and money to learn. For you to steer clear of these pain points, below we will go through some of the biggest antipatterns and mistakes teams make when adopting microservices—supported with real-life examples and experiences.

1. **Overindulgent Service Composition Antipattern:**
   Slicing your app into too many microservices,
   too fast. One may be easily swept away in the
   microservices fever and start siloing services left and
   right. But breaking everything down into small-sized
   services in a day can quickly combust.

   Failure: Communication overhead is a part of any
   service. If you get too much decomposition, you have
   more latency, more dependencies to handle, and a
   whole mess of services to scale and keep up with.

   Recommendation: Stick to the real-life solution. Start
   with some generic services and work your way down as
   you know your domain scope. Be open minded about
   building your architecture in its own way and not
   trying to mold it for microservices right out of the gate.

2. **Don't Pay Attention to Data Management
   Complexity:** Underestimating the distributed
   data challenges. Data ownership by every
   microservice sounds wonderful, but in the real
   world data consistency nightmares arise. Dispersed
   architecture and database integration is the Rubik's
   cube that never fits completely.

   Pitfalls: You may run into duplicate data, service
   disparity, or even distributed transactions which are
   notoriously cumbersome to handle.

   Top Tip: Implement eventual consistency where
   you can and patterns such as Saga for distributed
   transactions. Also, make sure that your service
   edges conform to your data model by domain-
   based design.

3. **Bad Interfaces—The Opposing Trend:**
   Microservices are communication based, and ill-crafted APIs are like trying to call from a tin can phone. If you expose too much internal logic, or if they aren't versioned, you're going to end up tightly coupled to services.

   Problem: If your APIs are not easily updated and modified, any slight improvement can cause ripple effects—making updating a pain and halting development.

   The Optimal Practice: Create APIs that abstract the abstraction, and write them down. Get the versioning right to keep it backward compatible and make update life less painful.

4. **Lack of Effective Monitoring and Logging:**
   Doing nothing and not recording everything. When it comes to microservices, you have more moving pieces to monitor, and you want the right monitoring and logging framework. But unfortunately, most teams fail to appreciate the significance of this and fall blind at the onset of a problem.

   Failure: Without centralized logs or high-level metrics, it's easy to miss the problem while looking for a needle in a haystack. This is the cause of slow response time and frustration when things go wrong.

Best Practice: Centrify logging and monitoring at the outset. The ELK stack (Elasticsearch, Logstash, Kibana) and Prometheus with Grafana are all very useful tools for monitoring the health of your services. So don't wait until something snaps and then spread this out.

5. **Leaving Behind DevOps Core Values:** Maintaining an era-old method of working in a microservices environment. The microservices need to be deployed and scaled continuously, and therefore operations need to be tightly coupled with development. Too often organizations don't adjust their ops tactics to avoid bottlenecks.

   Failure: The outcome is a DevOps team that's always playing catch-up, resulting in deployment lags and backlogs.

   Recommendation: Become DevOps and devo, that is, a development and operation culture. Try to be as automated as possible, from testing to deployment to scaling, so your teams can sprint without stumbling on the manual work.

6. **Compass Network Complexity (Underestimating):** Losing sight of the fact that microservices are death to the network. When the services are constantly pinging each other, be prepared for latency, bandwidth, and short-lived malfunctions.

   Problem: If network issues come up, services can go down in different ways that trigger a cascading effect.

Good Practice: Prepare for failure. Use retries, circuit breakers, and bulkheads so that your service can handle glitches without causing mass collapse.

When you have to learn microservices, there are a lot of pitfalls to avoid, but when you're aware of these most common antipatterns, you will avoid a lot of the problems that stump even experienced teams. This requires having the right mix of microservice enthusiasm, good planning, good architecture, and being flexible enough to change how you do things as your system develops. As after all, microservices should not take your life in their stride but make it easy for you.

Future of Microservices

Microservices' future is not only promising, its trailblazing innovation, and it's never going anywhere. As organizations continue to trudge along the digital revolution wave, microservices have taken center stage to bring agility, scalability, and durability to software development. But what's next? Let's glance at the horizon to see some new trends and progress in the microservices space. Spoiler alert: It's going to be fun!

Trends and Predictions

- **Increased Adoption of Serverless Architectures**

  Serverless computing is like the cool, laid-back cousin of microservices that shows up to the party, takes over, and doesn't require you to stress about infrastructure. Imagine a world where developers focus solely on business logic, while the serverless platform handles scaling, high availability, and maintenance like a pro. And the best part? You only pay for what you use.

Example: Picture an ecommerce site during a flash sale—traffic spikes, and serverless architecture ensures that the payment and order services scale up automatically to handle the sudden surge. Once the sale is over, the platform scales back down, saving resources and costs. Things such as AWS Lambda and Azure Functions are laying the foundation for this kind of architecture already.

Prediction: In the near future, we will see an alliance of serverless and microservices, where microservices automatically load into serverless environments on demand. It's like having your cake and eating it too, never thinking about the bill.

- **AI and Machine Learning Integration**

  AI and machine learning are like peanut butter and jelly—they just work better together, especially in microservices. With microservices offering flexibility and isolation, they are perfect for deploying and managing AI models across distributed systems.

  Example: Take Netflix, for instance, which uses microservices to power its recommendation engine. Each microservice handles a specific part of the data pipeline, from user preferences to content metadata, and then runs the ML models to give you the next binge-worthy show.

  Prediction: Microservices will continue to lead the charge in deploying AI and ML models, offering specialized services for every step of the AI life cycle, from data preparation to real-time inference. Imagine a future where you can scale your AI model just like you would a regular microservice—need more power for data inference? Spin up a few more instances!

- **Enhanced Focus on Service Meshes**

  Microservices and service meshes are the twins you've been missing. With the complexity of the microservices environments, it is important to make communication among them transparent. Service meshes such as Istio and Linkerd enable service discovery, load balancing, failure recovery, and monitoring—without touching your microservices code.

  Example: In a large-scale deployment like a ride-sharing platform, a service mesh ensures that the driver service, payment service, and location tracking service communicate smoothly, even when one of them hiccups (because even the best apps have bad days).

  Prediction: Service meshes will become as common as a Wi-Fi router in your house—every microservice deployment will have one to ensure secure, efficient, and reliable communication between services. After all, it's not just about building services; it's about making sure they can talk without needing couple's therapy.

- **Proliferation of Edge Computing**

  Edge computing is like the food truck of computing— it brings the service closer to where the customer is, rather than making the customer come to the service. Microservices' flexibility makes them ideal for edge deployments, whether it's for IoT devices, autonomous cars, or industrial machines in manufacturing.

Example: Imagine a network of smart security cameras distributed across a city. Instead of sending all the data to a central cloud, edge microservices process the video streams locally on edge devices, alerting authorities only when needed. This reduces latency and bandwidth while ensuring quicker response times.

Prediction: We're going to see more microservices deployed on edge devices, particularly in industries like IoT, smart cities, and even space exploration. Yes, your microservice might literally be out of this world soon!

- **Growth in Hybrid and Multi-cloud Environments**

Choosing just one cloud provider is so 2010. Today, businesses are adopting hybrid and multi-cloud strategies, and microservices are the perfect fit for this setup. Microservices can be deployed across different cloud providers, allowing companies to take advantage of cost savings, performance benefits, or compliance requirements of each provider.

Example: A global retail company might deploy its payment services on AWS for its performance, while its inventory services run on Google Cloud for its analytics capabilities. The two clouds communicate seamlessly, thanks to microservices architecture.

Prediction: Managing microservices across multiple clouds will become easier, with advanced tools enabling seamless service placement, migration, and cost optimization. The ability to switch cloud providers with the ease of changing a Netflix show? Sign us up!

- **Commitment to Sustainable Computing**

  The concept of sustainability isn't a trend anymore; it's an impetus to tech decision making. This is where microservices can play an important role in green computing as they optimize resources. With smaller-scale scaling, you only consume what you need without the resource draining burden of monolithic applications.

  Example: Let's say there is a social network that has a massive peak in traffic on big events and a decrease during the off-peak period. By provisioning microservices on or off based upon real-time demand, the platform cuts energy when traffic is low.

  Projection: Future microservices architecture will integrate sustainability by design, as we all know that resources are used efficiently and carbon footprint is minimized. You'll be designing scalable systems while you're making your little difference in the world, right?

- **Standardization and Best Practices**

  As microservices adoption grows, so does the need for standardization. Right now, every team may have its own flavor of microservices implementation, but soon we'll see more standardized protocols and best practices emerge.

  Example: Imagine a universal standard for microservices communication, making it easier to integrate different systems without writing custom connectors or workarounds. This is already happening with frameworks like gRPC and OpenAPI.

Prediction: In the near future, expect more formalized design patterns, deployment strategies, and tools that make building microservices architectures as straightforward as following a recipe. You'll have fewer "how do we integrate this?" moments and more time to focus on building what matters.

The future of microservices is as exciting as it is dynamic. From serverless architectures to AI integration, edge computing, and service meshes, microservices are set to redefine how we build and scale applications. The key takeaway? Stay flexible, stay informed, and embrace the changes as they come. The journey is just getting started, and it's one worth taking! And who knows, your next microservice could be running on the edge of space or saving the planet—all in a day's work.

Microservices in AI and IoT

Adding microservices with AI and IoT is truly a paradigm shift. Suppose that real-time data from billions of connected devices flows directly into smart systems, predicts, makes automated decisions, and keeps things working in a seamless way. Microservices are ideal for this type of dynamic ecosystem—modular, scalable, and ready to tackle distributed systems like a champ. But let's dive deep into how microservices are being applied to AI and IoT and the promising (and challenging) possibilities.

What Are the Advantages of Microservices for AI and IoT?

Scalability is one of the obvious benefits. As IoT devices spread and AI asks for more and more processing power, microservices allow systems to easily scale. If it is tracking the data from an autopilot or processing data for a machine-learning algorithm, microservices let you build only what you need. Want more data ingestion power? It's fine. Have a need to reduce analytics at night? Simple.

Microservices are self-flexible. IoT products are insanely diverse—from microsensors in oil wells to big house hubs. With microservices you can create services for different devices and tasks without making it the same as another application. Whether it is a device beaming data out to the edge of the network or a central data center hosting a complex AI model, microservices are keeping it all in check.

Resilience is the unsung hero of AI/IoT microservices, where once a single component failed, it could be all your services failing. Microservices run your other services. So, if one smart thermostat crashes, or an AI fails mid-teaching, the rest of the system can persevere.

Also, microservices support faster implementations. AI and IoT are moving targets, and microservices allow you to make a deployment or release feature immediately without stopping the entire system. Are you looking to optimize your AI prediction engine or add new capabilities to your IoT appliances? Microservices let you apply changes, test, iterate, and roll out without much disruption.

Some Challenges

And yes, all this looks awesome in theory, but what about the hassles? Oh, data administration is one of them. AI/IoT algorithms generate a tremendous amount of information which has to be handled at a very fast pace. This is the massive amount of throughput, and the microservices have to be robust enough to support low latency.

Solution: Use a messaging or streaming service such as Apache Kafka, so data is moving seamlessly from one service to another and gets processed in a consistent way.

And then there's the elephant in the room: safety. And if microservices are distributed across locations (just like IoT sensors are distributed across networks), there's always the potential for unauthorized use and leakage. The more components you have, the more gateways to hacking.

Solution: Implement security mechanisms on all layers, from device authentication to secure API calls. Data protection entails features such as mutual authentication and secure gateways.

Service coordination, no less. Multiple services, especially with multiple workloads such as AI computation or IoT collection, can be messy. You've got to make sure these services run in concert without interfering with each other.

Solution: Service meshes are an excellent solution to control service-to-service messaging. They perform the hard-to-quantify service discovery, load balancing, and failover—so you don't have to worry about how all your microservices are talking to each other.

Microservices architecture is driving AI/IoT transformation with more responsive, flexible, and resilient systems. The future will bring us the microservices, and while AI keeps pushing boundaries and IoT keeps expanding by the second, we are all here to ensure that everything is on a tin roof, can scale effortlessly, and be able to handle whatever the future brings. Whether it's automation of homes, factories, or healthcare, microservices, AI, and IoT are a force multiplier that will continue to expand.

Conclusion

Crafting resilient and fault-tolerant Java applications is like building a system with a built-in superhero cape—ready to swoop in and save the day when things go wrong (which they inevitably will). In distributed environments, where services can fail or slow down, these principles become the glue that holds everything together. Implementing patterns like the trusty Circuit Breaker (microservices.io) or adding retry mechanisms is like giving your app a second chance to succeed. These techniques help minimize disruptions and keep things running smoothly, even when the unexpected strikes.

And here's where frameworks like Resilience4j and Spring Retry come in, turning these strategies into easy-to-apply solutions for boosting reliability. By weaving resilience into the fabric of your Java applications, you're not just preventing total system meltdowns—you're also ensuring that when things go south, your app knows how to bounce back with style and grace. High availability? Check. Calm in the storm? Double-check.

CHAPTER 8

Conclusion and Quick Recap

In "The Art of Decoding Microservices", we've taken a deep dive into the exciting world of microservices architecture and how this strategy has transformed the construction, deployment, and management of today's software systems. By splitting an application into discrete services that can be delivered by themselves, the microservices architecture provides agility, scale, and resilience that could not exist with traditional monoliths. Below are some of the main takeaways and how they will influence software development in the future.

Basic Principles and Ideas

The philosophy of autonomy and modularity is central to the concept of microservices. As microservices follow the Single Responsibility Principle and centralized data management, they set the framework to make systems more manageable, scaling, and updateable. All services focus on one business activity, and the separation ensures that services grow autonomously. This not only accelerates development but reduces the chance of a distributed crash by disaggregating issues within services.

Development and Distinctions from Classical Architectures

Microservices have come as a response to monolithic architectures which we all know fall like a house of cards if one piece breaks. Microservices, by contrast, share responsibility, making the applications robust and scalable. Although there are similarities between SOA and microservices, modularity and autonomy are enhanced with microservices, resulting in faster deployments and fault isolation. It's an evolution of necessity in the zeitgeisty, Internet-first age.

Design and Development

Designing for a good microservices architecture starts with the best designs—this is where DDD comes into play. With DDD, you can set service limits in line with business features to make it manageable and scalable. And don't forget about the design patterns solving everyday microservices issues. Whether it's an API Gateway for handling service calls, Circuit Breaker to break cascades, or Sidecar to handle operations, these patterns are fundamental to the creation of successful architectures.

On the development side, technology stack is key. Java, Spring Boot, Docker, and Kubernetes are now the de facto tools for creating, deploying, and orchestrating microservices. Whether you're building RESTful services, synchronous or asynchronous communications, or even security, tools and best practices will lead you toward the win.

Deployment and Security

The deployment of microservices is also challenging—mainly the service discovery, load balancing, and security. In dynamic service discovery, services discover each other without human intervention. Load balancing guarantees that traffic is evenly balanced, thereby preventing bottlenecks and efficiently utilizing resources. As for security, methods such as mutual TLS and OAuth2 secure interservice communications, a vital part of the day's burgeoning data breaches.

Testing and Monitoring

Testing microservices can be a bit like shepherding sheep, but it is necessary to keep the system stable. Unit tests, integration tests, and contract tests are your companions when it comes to testing the functionality and interactivity of each service. As your architecture scales, centralized logging and monitoring becomes an absolute must. ELK and other tools such as Prometheus/Grafana can give you real-time data about the health and performance of your system, and you catch problems before they grow bigger.

Practices and Practical Case Studies

Our guide to best practices throughout the book is: embrace continuous delivery and DevOps to be on par with new releases, polyglot programming to choose the tool appropriate to the task at hand, and resilience engineering to make your system fault-tolerant. Netflix, Amazon, and Uber have all shown how microservices can make a difference, how these principles translate into actual benefits in the form of faster time to market, higher scalability, and continuous innovation.

Next Future Trends

Microservices is on an upward trajectory. As AI and IoT become commonplace, microservices will be the architecture that companies use to crunch vast amounts of real-time data. Things such as serverless computing and event-driven architectures are also set to make scaling and administration easier, which will help make microservices even more desirable for flexible and efficient organizations. For insights into the convergence of microservices, AI, IoT, serverless computing, and event-driven architectures, consider the following Springer publications:

- *Practical Event-Driven Microservices Architecture* by Hugo Filipe Oliveira Rocha

- *Artificial Intelligence, Internet of Things, and Society 5.0* edited by Hamzeh Aljawawdeh, Mohammad Sabri, and Louai Maghrabi

- *IOT with Smart Systems* edited by Tushar Champaneria, Sunil Jardosh, and Ashwin Makwana

Other books on microservices which can be referred to along with this

- *Microservices: Science and Engineering*

- *Cloud-Based Microservices: Techniques, Challenges, and Solutions*

- *Microservices for the Enterprise: Designing, Developing, and Deploying*

- *Practical Microservices Architectural Patterns*

One Last Thing to Say

Microservices architecture has endless possibilities but isn't a cure-all. And, for the companies that invest time and resources into learning what it is and how to do it right, the payoffs are huge—scalable, robust, and flexible software systems that adapt to change. Follow the suggestions in this book, and you will find yourself doing a great job on how to learn microservices and develop a system that can meet the current needs and provide support for future needs.

In short, the journey to decode microservices is ongoing. With the right mindset, tools, and practices, you're equipped to design, develop, and maintain architectures that drive innovation and success in the ever-evolving world of software.

APPENDIX A

Glossary

API Gateway: A server/API frontend that receives API requests, handles security and throttling, forwards the request to the right service, and aggregates the results.

Autonomous Services: Microservices that can run independently and are not dependent on other services for execution, which makes them more isolated and resilient.

Bounded Context: In DDD, it defines the scope where a domain model is defined and valid. Each microservice typically defines a bound context.

Circuit Breaker Pattern: An approach that avoids a network or service downtime spreading to other areas of the application. It picks up when things go wrong and offers backups.

Continuous Delivery (CD): A solution that automates testing and deploying code changes to production so you can provide new features and upgrades rapidly and reliably.

Continuous Integration (CI): The automated rollup of code updates into a common repository and testing them regularly to catch the bugs before they happen.

Containerization: Packing apps and dependencies into containers (e.g., Docker) that can be run across multiple environments.

Decentralized Data Management: A concept where each microservice is in control of its own database and therefore has more agility and autonomy.

© Sumit Bhatnagar and Roshan Mahant 2025
S. Bhatnagar and R. Mahant, *The Art of Decoding Microservices*,
https://doi.org/10.1007/979-8-8688-1267-5

Deployment Pipeline: An automated process of application deployment—usually building, testing, and pushing code across environments.

Domain-Driven Design (DDD): A software design paradigm where complicated software systems are modeled according to the business domain they cover—concepts such as entities, value objects, and bounded contexts.

Event-Driven Architecture: Asynchronous services that emit and consume events, for decoupled and responsive interactions.

Horizontal Scaling: Growing an application by deploying more instances (or replicas) of a service to accommodate increased load, typically through container orchestration like Kubernetes.

Inversion of Control (IoC): An inverse control flow principle where objects do not generate dependencies but are supplied (dependency injection).

Kubernetes: An open source platform to automate container application deployment, scaling, and management.

Load Balancer: An equipment or software that reroutes network or application traffic between multiple servers to guarantee reliability and performance.

Microservices: Software architecture that model the application as a set of loosely integrated, independent, business capabilities.

Monolithic Architecture: Traditional Software Architecture: The entire application codebase—the whole application becomes a single codebase that can be more difficult to scale and evolve.

Polyglot Persistence: The adoption of multiple types of data stores (SQL, NoSQL, in-memory) within a system, each of which has been chosen to support different kinds of services.

Prometheus: An open source monitoring and alerting framework to collect and visualize service and application metrics with Grafana.

Resilience Pattern: Patterns (e.g., retries, timeouts, circuit breakers) that will keep the service running even if dependencies break.

Service Discovery: Automatic discovery of services on a microservices model so that services can discover one another automatically.

Sidecar Pattern: Microservices design with an auxiliary service running alongside the main service to do logging, monitoring, and messaging.

Single Responsibility Principle (SRP): A design standard that says a class or service only needs one reason to be updated and allows for modularity and maintainability.

Spring Boot: A framework to make developing Java apps easy by providing ready-made components and pairing it with microservices architecture tools.

Testing Pyramid: A concept that is focused on testing with multiple test levels (unit, integration, end-to-end) in the desired proportion to be effective and complete.

Token-Based Authentication: Authentication mechanism in which the token, usually JWT (JSON Web Token), authenticates the requests from clients and services.

Vertical Scaling: Scaling a single instance or node with more resources (CPU, RAM) instead of launching additional instances.

Zero Downtime Deployment: Application persistence and upgradability strategy where applications are maintained and functional in the event of an update—usually by means of blue-green or rolling updates.

@Autowired

- An annotation used in Spring to automatically inject dependencies. It marks a constructor, field, or method to be autowired by Spring's dependency injection facilities.

@Bean

- This annotation indicates that a method produces a bean that should be managed by the Spring container. It is often used in configuration classes to define beans manually.

@Configuration

- Used to mark a class as a source of bean definitions. It indicates that the class contains methods annotated with @Bean, which will be managed by the Spring container.

@Controller

- This annotation is used to define a controller class that handles HTTP requests in a Spring MVC application. It is often combined with @RequestMapping to map requests to methods.

@EnableDiscoveryClient/@EnableEurekaClient

- Annotations used to register a service with a discovery server (like Eureka). They enable service registration and discovery for Spring Boot microservices.

@EnableFeignClients

- Enables Feign clients in a Spring application. It allows for creating declarative REST clients and simplifies HTTP communication between microservices.

@EnableWebSecurity

- Marks a class as the configuration for web security in Spring Security. It is used to customize security settings and manage authentication and authorization.

@GetMapping

- A shortcut annotation for @RequestMapping that maps HTTP GET requests to specific handler methods. It simplifies the creation of RESTful endpoints.

@PathVariable

- Used to bind a method parameter to a URI template variable. It captures values from the URL and makes them available as parameters in controller methods.

@PostMapping

- Similar to @GetMapping, but for HTTP POST requests. It maps POST requests to specific methods in a controller, often used to create new resources.

@PutMapping

- This annotation maps HTTP PUT requests to a specific method, typically used to update existing resources in a RESTful application.

@DeleteMapping

- An annotation for mapping HTTP DELETE requests to specific handler methods. It is commonly used to delete resources.

@RequestBody

- Used to bind the HTTP request body to a method parameter, allowing a controller to accept JSON or XML payloads and map them to Java objects.

@RequestMapping

- A versatile annotation for mapping HTTP requests to controller methods. It supports various request methods (GET, POST, etc.) and can map paths, parameters, headers, and more.

@RestController

- Combines @Controller and @ResponseBody, making the class serve RESTful endpoints where the return values of methods are automatically serialized to JSON or XML.

@Service

- Indicates that a class is a service component in the Spring framework. It is used to denote business logic layers and helps with Spring's component scanning.

@SpringBootApplication

- A combination of three annotations: @Configuration, @EnableAutoConfiguration, and @ComponentScan. It marks a class as the main configuration class and entry point for a Spring Boot application.

@Transactional

- An annotation used to manage transactions in Spring. It can be applied at the method or class level to ensure that all operations within the scope are executed within a transaction context.

@Valid

- This annotation is used to validate objects, such as request bodies, based on constraints defined in the object's fields. It works with validation annotations like @NotNull or @Size.

@Value

- Used to inject values from properties files or environment variables into Spring beans. It allows for dynamic configuration based on externalized settings.

@Component

- Marks a class as a Spring component, making it eligible for component scanning and dependency injection. It is a generic stereotype that is often used for repository or service classes.

@FeignClient

- An annotation used to declare a Feign client, which enables creating REST clients in Spring Boot applications with minimal code. It simplifies communication between microservices.

@Scope

- Defines the scope of a bean (singleton, prototype, etc.). It allows for configuring whether a bean should be created once or multiple times when requested.

@Scheduled

- An annotation used for scheduling tasks in Spring applications. It allows methods to be executed periodically based on a specified schedule.

@Profile

- Used to define beans that should be activated for specific Spring profiles. It allows conditional loading of beans based on the active profile, such as development or production.

@EnableCircuitBreaker

- Enables circuit breaker functionality in a Spring application using Spring Cloud Netflix Hystrix or other implementations. It is used to handle and manage failures in microservices.

@EnableHystrixDashboard

- Activates the Hystrix Dashboard in a Spring application, providing a real-time view of the circuit breakers and the state of service interactions.

@EnableScheduling

- Enables scheduling in a Spring application, allowing the use of @Scheduled annotations for task execution.

@LoadBalanced

- Used with a RestTemplate bean to indicate that it should use a load-balanced client, enabling communication with services registered in the service discovery.

@ResponseBody

- Indicates that the return value of a method will be written directly to the HTTP response body, typically used in REST controllers.

@ExceptionHandler

- An annotation that specifies a method should handle specific exceptions thrown by controller methods. It is used to manage error handling in a consistent manner.

APPENDIX B

Closure and Final Thoughts

With the end of "The Art of Decoding Microservices", let's pause and look back at the journey we've taken together, as well as give you some final gems of wisdom as you begin your journey of microservices architecture mastery. These are your survival guide when you're wading through the exciting (and sometimes turbulent) waters of designing scalable, robust, and agile systems.

Embrace the Fundamentals

So, before you go off into the advanced stuff, you always want to make sure you know what's going on. These fundamentals such as Single Responsibility Principle, service independency, and decentralized data management make up the core foundation of any good microservices implementation. Each service must be focused, discrete, and cater to a business requirement. From there, start off with these basics.

© Sumit Bhatnagar and Roshan Mahant 2025
S. Bhatnagar and R. Mahant, *The Art of Decoding Microservices*,
https://doi.org/10.1007/979-8-8688-1267-5

Start Small and Iterate

Microservices are the holy grail, but seriously—migrating a giant monolith to microservices can be like fighting a dragon. So, start small. Choose a couple of easy services to decouple and grow on their own. Make it small, and make it big, from every little step you take and keep learning. So, you'll be at less risk and with more experience, and the transition won't be an eye-opening nightmare.

Invest in Automation

Automation is a microservices best friend. It's your weapon against the complexity of running thousands of services. Save money by investing in good CI/CD pipelines that build, test, and deploy the code. Automated testing, monitoring, and scaling are your insurance policies for ensuring your microservices are not just up and running, but growing.

Prioritize Security

For security, you don't just fuck around. Security is not an option, but a must in microservices. Use strong authentication and authorization, lock down your service-to-service communications, and patch things as needed. Then imagine enforcing a castle: a well-planned defense against the intruders (hackers) will keep them out.

Foster a DevOps Culture

Microservices aren't only a technical shift, but a cultural change as well. By utilizing DevOps principles, development and operations teams can work together, share accountability, and continue to be better. A DevOps culture is the grease that keeps the microservices engine oiled, increasing agility, quality, and speeding up delivery.

Monitor and Observe

As services exist across multiple environments and networks, monitoring and observability are not extras but essentials. Set up real-time monitoring and logging to see how your services are performing. Visualize data and metrics with Prometheus, Grafana, and the ELK stack to spot problems before they are nightmares.

Plan for Failure

The worst can happen—and not just with distributed applications such as microservices. But don't fear them; make arrangements for them. Resilience: Structure your services with circuit breakers, retries, bulkheads, and more. Test your system's robustness by doing daily chaos engineering activities, just like a gym stress test on your architecture. The result? A stronger, more fault-tolerant system.

Embrace Polyglot Programming

One of the best parts about microservices is that you have complete control over which tools to deploy. Accept polyglot programming, where various services can choose the right languages and technologies to work with. But as with all great power, there is also responsibility, so be sure to take care of dependencies and interoperability to keep your ecosystem cohesive and not chaotic.

Keep Learning and Adapting

Microservices are not an exception to this tempo of the tech world. Don't just be curious but stay on top of the newest trends, technologies, and best practices. Dig into community boards, conferences, and industry publications to stay in front of the game. Not only for beginners but also for experts: There's always something new to learn.

Balance Innovation with Stability

You can chase any new tool or technology, but you have to keep things in check. Innovation is essential, but stability is what keeps your machine ticking over. Strike a balance between going crazy and keeping your services up and running. Try before you buy and validate new technologies are really worthwhile to invest in before you leap.

Closing Words

Learning microservices is never a one-time solution; it's a continuous process of improvement, learning, and adjusting. Those rules, patterns, and best practices that we've gone through together in this book build on top of it, but then magic occurs when you implement them out there in the real world, with the challenge of actually trying things out.

Remember, microservices' endpoint is to create systems that are not only scalable and robust but that can change with business requirements. With the tips and tricks here, you'll have everything you need to be able to manage the microservices world and create beautiful, effective applications.

Thanks for joining us on this journey of "The Art of Decoding Microservices". We hope the book helped equip you with all the resources you need to be a master of the ever-changing world of software architecture. Now go out and create something awesome—happy coding!

Index

© Sumit Bhatnagar and Roshan Mahant 2025
S. Bhatnagar and R. Mahant, *The Art of Decoding Microservices*,
https://doi.org/10.1007/979-8-8688-1267-5

TLS, *see* Transport Layer
Security (TLS)
Transport Layer Security (TLS), 130
Two-tier architecture, 13

U

Unit testing
benefits, 236
code structure, 238, 239
definition, 236
JUnit and Mockito, 236–238
setup() method, 239

V, W, X, Y, Z

Versioning/backward
compatibility, 294–297
code explanation, 296
header/media type, 294
implementation, 295
query parameter, 294
semantic process, 295
URI path, 294
Virtual Private
Networks (VPNs), 131
VPNs, *see* Virtual Private
Networks (VPNs)

Printed in the United States
by Baker & Taylor Publisher Services